BASEBALL IN BALTIMORE

JAMES H. BREADY

BASEBALL
IN BALTIMORE

The Johns Hopkins University Press   Baltimore and London

Published in Association with the Babe Ruth Birthplace and Baseball Center

The Johns Hopkins University Press

2715 North Charles Street

Baltimore, Maryland 21218-4363

www.press.jhu.edu

Library of Congress Cataloging-in-Publication Data
will be found at the end of this book.

A catalog record for this book is available from the British Library.

ISBN 0-8018-5833-X

CONTENTS

PREFACE

What matters, in baseball, is of course tonight's game, tomorrow's standings, the season's outcome. Sometimes, though, there is no game all week, or all month. Sometimes there is a game but—ugh, what a disaster. In such situations, baseball doesn't shut down; it steps back into its past. Play it again, Sam, or Frank and Brooks, or Howie, or Rube, or Jack, or Hughey and Joe and Wizard, or John and Wilbert. Play it again and again, Willie. There haven't been very many Sams, come to think of it, in Baltimore box scores, but the long-ago Oriole rosters do include an Alva, Boris, Cadwallader, Delphia, Elzie, Fay, George (Ruth? yes), Hormides, Italo, June, Maurice, Nigel, Orell, Perce, Royal, Sylvester, Tyrus (Cobb? no), Vernal, Wade—first names, these, often mercifully obscured by nicknames.

The past, in Baltimore baseball, goes back to 1859. With so many thousands of games behind us, for anything today that's great or that's awful, there is forever some past moment that was correspondingly great or, consolingly, more awful. And the anniversaries, properly selected, never cease.

An earlier Jim Bready—my father—took my brother Gerry and me to watch real major league games at Shibe Park, Philadelphia, on press passes. Forever, I can say I saw Babe Ruth play; Lefty Grove, too. Much later, the first Oriole game I remember attending had Baltimore playing a team from Springfield, Massachusetts. "The Ints," I muttered (to myself, so as not to offend my wife, Mary, whose idea it was to be there). *Infra* the *dignitatem* of a modern metropolis. Fifty years later, the International League is long behind us and Baltimore lacks not for dignity, just a dependable 20-game winner.

Once, we had a 46-game winner. And a 63-homer hitter. And a team that scored a thousand runs, in a season of only 128 games. Three times, we had the best team in the Negro Leagues. It was sublime, being on hand at Memorial Stadium for World Series games; but the game I boast of having been present for—by virtue of a family expedition—is one at Westport Stadium.

What follows is an attempt to keep such memories "jangling," to borrow a term from Satchel Paige (who in 1930 wore a Baltimore uniform). For the details of seasons long gone, for indications of factors not always played up in sports pages, I have turned not only to venerated former participants and reel after reel of microfilmed newspapers but also to the encyclopedias, books, and articles produced in the last few years by baseball historians. Long live the Society for American Baseball Research.

The story of baseball in Baltimore—the game begun by gentleman amateurs but taken over by well-callused pros—is followed here from the beginnings to 1954, the moment when interminable exile ended and Baltimore was finally restored to the major leagues. The innings since then are for someone else to make sense of. Me, I'm at Oriole Park in Camden Yards, waiting for somebody during a game to hit one that reaches the warehouse on the fly, somebody on the home team.

It was Bob Brugger who first suggested that the earlier parts of *The Home Team*, published in 1958 and thrice revised, could be redone, in greater detail. To Martha Farlow all honor and glory for book design and layout. For help along the way, I am in great debt to Dave Howell, Burt Solomon, Bob Brown, Mike Gibbons, Greg Schwalenberg, Barbara Lamb, Jack Goellner, Miriam Tillman, Carol Zimmerman, Jack Holmes, Tom Roche, Richard Powell, Robert Leffler, Al Kermisch, John Dean, John Steadman, Bob Davids, Bob McConnell, Joe

Katz, Jack Neustadt, Peg Randol, Ed Young, A. D. Emmart, Bill Klender, Henry Kimbro, Dick Hall, Fritz and Bob Maisel, Jim McKay, Chuck Hoffberger, Hal Williams, Hal Piper, Mike Lane, Jim Burger, Charles Camp, Ric Cottom, Jacques Kelly, Gwinn Owens, Dee Lyon, Jean Packard, Paul McCardell, Deborah Golumbek, Mark Rucker, Mike Bowler, John Stubel, Charles Devaud, Carleton Jones, Ted Patterson, Carol Warner, Eugene Balk, and Ron Menchine. I am grateful beyond words to the patient, resourceful librarians of the *Baltimore Sun*, Enoch Pratt Free Library, and Maryland Historical Society. Long live the Oriole Advocates.

Most of all, I thank the family—Mary Hortop Bready, Richard and Karin, Chris and Anne, Steve, Laurie, Alex.

BASEBALL IN BALTIMORE

Baltimore's oldest base-
ball. This relic from
the Madison Avenue
Grounds era, shel-
lacked and gilded
(its cover, a single
piece of leather), was
preserved by descendants
of the early Baltimore player
Wally Goldsmith. The lettering
seems to identify it as the ball used
in the Pastimes's 1867 victory over
Mutual of New York. Now in a
Babe Ruth museum vault.

At the grounds of the Pastime club, on Madison
Avenue yesterday afternoon, the pleasant weather
and stirring breeze enabled the Pastime and Maryland clubs
to play with spirit and vigor . . . . The result was one unlooked for
by the knowing, and at the announcement that the Maryland's
score was 47 and Pastime's 15, the friends of the former club gave
vent to hearty cheers. The Pastime club, as base ball connoisseurs
are aware, has heretofore held the championship of the State.

Baltimore Sun, WEDNESDAY, AUGUST 21, 1867

At the Madison Avenue Grounds yesterday afternoon there was a
gathering of about 4,000 ladies and gentlemen, larger, perhaps,
than ever heretofore attended a base ball game in this city. It ended
in a result totally unlooked for by base ball-ists, a victory for the
Pastime club over the Mutual of New York by a majority of 16 runs,
the score of the Pastimes being 47 runs to the Mutual's 31.

Baltimore Sun, WEDNESDAY, AUGUST 28, 1867

CHAPTER ONE

THE BEGINNINGS

Most things sprout unseen—but not serious baseball in Baltimore. Its start can be dated, placed, and named. The very man who started it can be identified, and his picture, whiskers and all, can be printed. He was Henry B. Polhemus, the Brooklyn, New York, representative for Baltimore's Woodberry Mills. Leaving the office of an afternoon, he liked to join other South Brooklyn businessmen who were afever to play the new competitive team sport, baseball. Polhemus was indeed the biggest man on the Brooklyn Excelsiors, a big name in baseball back in 1858.

Polhemus was an outfielder. Captain and catcher for the Excelsiors was Joseph B. Leggett, a wholesale grocer, and one afternoon that summer Leggett invited a Baltimore business acquaintance, George F. Beam, to watch a game. Beam was converted on the spot. Back home, he set about organizing a Baltimore club, and its first meeting is recorded as having been in a building on Commerce Street near East Lombard. Beam, also a grocer, was chosen captain. Admiringly, the members christened themselves Excelsiors, too.

In standard mythologies, baseball was invented by Abner Doubleday in 1839. In fact, informal baseball (rounders and the like) had been going on for generations; formal, team baseball is now traced to mid-Manhattan and fraternal clubs, especially the New Yorks and the

Flat Rocks, the scene of Baltimore's first formal baseball, as recalled years afterward by William Ridgely Griffith. *Top:* the original, 1859 Excelsior Base Ball Club diamond; *bottom:* the 1861 diamond of the Continental Base Ball Club, an early rival. The setting is now part of Druid Hill Park reservoir.

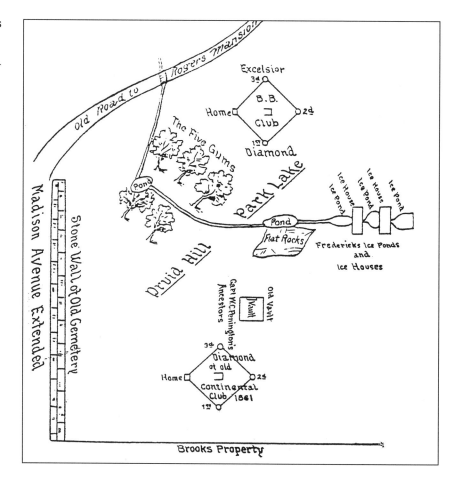

Knickerbockers, toward 1840. The Knickerbockers were the first into uniform and into print. Their 1845 code of rules and then their appearance in a Currier & Ives print (showing their rented diamond, in Hoboken, N.J.) added up to everlasting fame. Brooklyn's Excelsiors dated from 1854. So many clubs were forming that in 1857 a National Association of Base Ball Players was established, linking some 60 New York–area teams. Early in 1860, the association elected its first non–New York officer, Vice President Hervey Shriver, of Baltimore, who was also second baseman and secretary of *its* Excelsiors.

In that era, organized athletic events were few and largely for the well-to-do: prizefights (illegal), horse races, rowing, yachting—and cricket, on the English model. (More popular in the East in 1850, cricket had lost out to baseball by 1860.) The common man worked up to 12 hours a day for six days a week. His employer, though, could nip out of the office Wednesday and Saturday afternoons and ride a club-chartered, horse-drawn omnibus up Madison Avenue. Reaching the ball grounds, the eager Baltimore Excelsior could limber up, toss the ball about, and practice his swing at the direction of a tall, mutton-chopped player from the famous Brooklyn Excelsiors.

Baltimore's original ball diamond, where Polhemus coached Beam's friends, is under water now. The west end of Druid Lake, in Druid Hill Park (to which the city had just taken title), covers Flat Rocks, the area where the first bases were laid out. Evidently no one thought to photograph the site nor is there evidence that the Baltimore Excelsiors ever had a team picture taken. But in the 1890s, William Ridgely Griffith, a surviving president of Pastime Base Ball Club, wrote a published memoir of the early days and included with it a map showing the lay of what used to be land.

Before long, the Excelsiors broke into print. A wordy paragraph about them near the bottom of page one of the *American and Commercial Advertiser* for Tuesday, July 12, 1859, constitutes (until somebody finds something older) the first local-baseball write-up to appear in a Baltimore newspaper. To wit:

THE EXCELSIOR BASE BALL CLUB.—Within a few days past, a number of young men residing mostly in the Western section of the city have formed an association known as the Excelsior Base Ball Club, principally with the view of promoting physical exercise and healthful recreation. The following officers have been elected:—W. D. Shurtz, President; George W. Tinges, Vice President; Henry (sic) Shriver, Secretary. Committee of Inquiry:—A. K. Foard, George F. Beam and M. N. Howe. The name was selected in honor of the Excelsior Base Ball Club of Brooklyn, N.Y., and the membership consisting almost entirely of young merchants, have selected their playground at a spot known as "Flat Rock," near the Madison street avenue.

Typically, sides were formed within the membership (Fats vs. Slims, Benedicts vs. Bachelors). But greater glory was in store. That fall, Washington's first clubs, the Potomacs and the Nationals, began play. (Secretary and second baseman for the Nationals was 21-year-old Arthur Pue Gorman of Laurel, Maryland, former Senate page and future Maryland Democratic senator.) The Potomacs kept winning, and the following spring, the pride of Washington challenged the pride of Baltimore to a game.

It took place Wednesday, June 6, 1860, on the "White Lot" behind the White House (on what is now called the Ellipse). J.W.F. Hank of the Excelsiors was the day's batting star. An audience of several thousand, including almost 400 women, enjoyed a cloudless sky and a tight game—until the Excelsiors dented home plate 13 times in the sixth inning. The final score was 40-24, in Baltimore's favor.

That game, which Baltimoreans read about next day in the *Baltimore Sun*, is important. Outside greater New York, it was the first intercity baseball game in U.S. history. It also originated the tradition that Baltimore plays winning baseball. The *Washington Evening Star*'s account of "the friendly match" on this cow pasture "south of the President's Mansion" noted that the opposing nines accepted the outcome "with perfect equanimity" and "partook of rich entertainment" that night at the Potomacs' expense.

Here is the Excelsior batting order as noted (minus some first names) in the newspapers of the day, for the enjoyment of all those able to trace their genealogy to the FBFB (first baseball families of Baltimore):

George F. Beam, p	Williams, lf
David Woods, 2b	Dr. J.W.F. Hank, 3b
Hervey Shriver, c	Hazlitt, 1b
Alexander P. Woods, rf	Thomas J. Mitchell, lf
Edward G. Pittman, ss	

If baseball historians have scanted that splendid clash, one reason is its eclipse later that summer by the Brooklyn Excelsiors' tour, the first of all team tours. The Polhemus-Leggett nine started off playing upstate teams; then they journeyed south to Philadelphia and Baltimore. They beat everybody.

The first intercity game played in Baltimore (Excelsiors vs. Excelsiors, September 22, 1860) has been neglected in histories of Baltimore—which is understandable, given the final score of 51-6. And yet, from the visitors' arrival at President Street railroad station to the game itself at the new Madison Avenue Grounds (just below what is now North Avenue) to the postgame banquet at Guy's Monument House on North Calvert Street, excitement ran high all over town. The home nine was a composite of the best players from other local teams. Brooklyn's lineup included 19-year-old Jim Creighton, baseball's first superstar; in Baltimore Creighton, playing outfield, started what is now considered baseball's first triple play. Asa Brainard, pitching, toyed with Baltimore's batters. And in that intrepid time before masks and gloves, Captain Leggett amazed the 5,000 onlookers by moving up after two strikes and catching from directly behind home plate. Next day, Baltimore's first published box score—a far cry from today's compound arithmetic—appeared in the *Baltimore American*.

A year later, the Association of Base Ball Clubs of Baltimore was formed: from Alpha to Zephyr, by way of Deluge, Freethinking, and Quicksteps, 38 teams in all. (*Baseball* was spelled as two words until about 1890.) The Excelsiors, outclassed, faded fast; in 1861 the team merged with Waverly, the club that had built the Madison Avenue Grounds. The new, joint name was the Pastimes. A rival Baltimore powerhouse was the Marylands, captained by Mike Hooper. By then, Washington was traveling to Baltimore—Marylands 17, Nationals 10.

Throughout the Civil War, baseball was prominent among the recreations of soldiers in camp. Civilians went on playing; every summer, intercity Baltimore-Washington games were recorded. Partisans of North and South were sometimes on the same team, neutralized by passion for the game. On the Fourth of July 1863, Baltimoreans were on edge awaiting news from the great battle at Gettysburg; nonetheless, a considerable crowd gathered at the Madison Avenue Grounds to watch a game between two groups of Pastimes.

With peace, baseball activity flamed nationally and on many a vacant Baltimore lot. The Pastimes put up Baltimore's first grandstand and fence and charged 15 cents admission; often they rented out the grounds to other local teams. The Excelsiors were probably the first Baltimore team to be uniformed. The Pastimes were decked out

Madison Avenue Grounds, Baltimore's first enclosed ballpark, with spectator seating and player clubhouses. The focus of Baltimore baseball from 1860 to the 1870s, it was the home grounds for both Pastimes and Marylands. *Top:* Excerpt from the 1869 Sachse *Bird's Eye View of Baltimore* shows Madison Avenue (*left diagonal*) and Boundary Avenue (later North Avenue; *center horizontal*). Note bleachers, flagpole (*left*), separate entrances for men and women. *Bottom:* diamond layout, as later traced by William Ridgely Griffith.

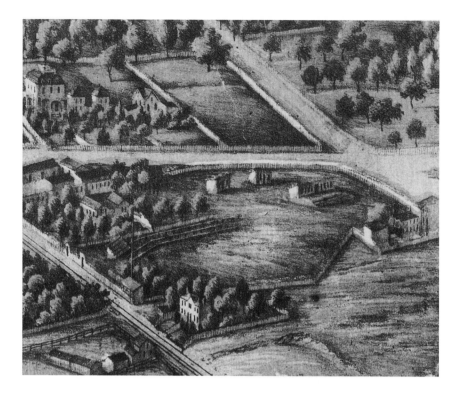

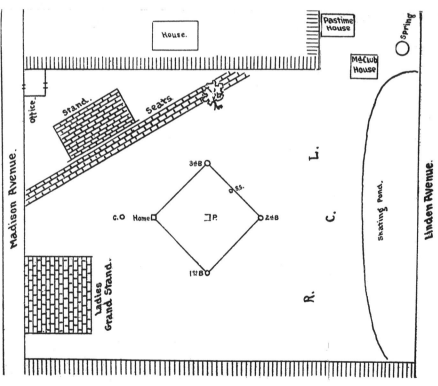

in the first uniforms of which description remains: blue cap with white visor, white shirt with large *P* sewn on it, blue full-length trousers—and neckties. Play continued far into November (elsewhere, games on ice skates were attempted). Baltimore's first baseball column started up, in the *Sunday Telegram*. In 1866 a New Yorker, George Gratton, opened the Base Ball Emporium, a sporting-goods store on Baltimore Street east of Calvert.

Smoothly, the sport became a business, run by entrepreneurs who split the gate receipts. By August 1865, a Philadelphia team had arrived and proved insuperable. In 1867, on the other hand, the Pastimes took on New York's Mutuals, the self-styled national champions, and—balm in Gilead!—won, 47-31. But the Marylands had already risen up and beaten the Pastimes (and reigned alone locally through 1870—the score in an 1869 showdown broken off after seven innings: Marylands 55, Pastimes 19). In 1867, delegates from 33 teams around the state convened in Baltimore and founded the Base Ball Association of Maryland. Clubs contended for an annual Silver Ball Championship.

And that summer, Arthur P. Gorman, age 28, took his Washington Nationals on the first-ever team trip across the Appalachians, as far as Illinois. The barnstormers won every game but one, and Gorman served a term as president of the National Association. Still another event that year, so soon after the Civil War, was a policy establishment regarding African-American teams: the National Association refused them membership.

Two years after the Washington club's tour, the Middle West retaliated stunningly as Cincinnati's improved Red Stockings swept through the East, in what is still the only undefeated season by a top-level team. Their tour included a Madison Avenue Grounds stop-off (Red Stockings 47, Marylands 7).

Those 69 consecutive victories and one dubious tie, by players wear-

Baltimore's oldest known baseball photo: the Pastimes, about 1867. Now the problem is to match 9 faces with 11 names: Shannon, rf; Sellman, 1b; Mitchell, p; McDonald, 2b; J. Popplein, c; Gregg, ss; Buck, cf; McKim, 3b; Mallinckrodt, lf; G. Popplein, ss; Sears, 1b.

ing new-fangled knee pants, were possible because the Red Stocking management of 1869 had singled out the highest-rated player anywhere, position by position, and had openly hired him. Only at first base was there a player from Cincinnati. Such change, in merely 10 years. The energetic young businessman-ballplayer had become obsolete; replacing him in many lineups was a superior working-class athlete. The latter, on quitting mill or farm, needed income. Brooklyn's partisans are nowadays thought to have been quietly subsidizing Jim Creighton. Arthur P. Gorman, in his alternate role as politician, could inscribe his players' names on the federal job rolls.

The dispute over payment split the National Association—and individual clubs. In Baltimore in 1870 the proud (and increasingly ineffectual) Pastimes remained "strictly amateur"; the Marylands had a payroll. That summer, the Brooklyn Atlantics (unlike the Excelsiors, composed of working men) finally broke Cincinnati's streak in 11 innings in Brooklyn. In Baltimore soon after, the Red Stockings consoled themselves by trouncing the Marylands *and* the Pastimes. For their part, each Baltimore team then essayed a road trip.

The Pastimes, "a club of gentlemen," could afford return tickets from New York state; the Marylands, gone off to Ohio and Indiana, drew so poorly the trip was cut short, leaving the players to get home as best they could. But they played well enough to impress businessmen in Fort Wayne, Indiana, whose local-player team, the Kekiongas, had incautiously brought in the famous Cincinnati team and been thrashed, 41-7. Conversations with the Baltimore players ensued; half a dozen Maryland B.B.C. stalwarts agreed to become Kekiongas the following spring.

With no sorting of teams into leagues, mismatches did happen. "The largest score on record," newspapers called it in 1869 when two Buffalo clubs did battle of a sort: Niagara 209, Columbia 10. Since

---

STATE CONVENTIONS IN 1867.

This year is the first of the official recognition of State Associations, and in accordance with the Constitution of the National Association, the Maryland State Base-Ball Association was organized, and on February 20th, 1867, this Association held their first Convention, the locale being Sanderson's Opera House, Baltimore. Thirty-three clubs were represented, the following being the names of the clubs and delegates:

Active—Baltimore, M. W. Holmes, S. C. Weaver.
Alert—Cumberland, J. C. Simms, R. Shriver.
Allegany—Cumberland, E. P. Rupert.
Antietam—Hagerstown, H. H. Keedy.
Annapolis—Annapolis, A. D. Ruan, J. W. Randall
Associate—Baltimore, P. Walton, Wm. Rudolst.
Arctic—Baltimore, J. McCleery, E. Lawson.
Avalanche—Cecil, A. J. Pennington.
Calvert—Baltimore, J. P. Reul, F. A. Cochran.
Continental and Church Hill—Carroll, C. N. Newcomer, L. Dunbracco.
Carroll—Uniontown, G. E. Franklin, C. B. Meredith.
Chesapeake—West River, J. H. Hopkins, F. Owens.
Chesterfield—Queen Ann's, J. H. Thompson.
Dorcester—Milton, B. H. Woodgood, J. O. Skinner.
Enterprise—Baltimore, L. A. Carl, T. R. Bayley.
Excelsior—Frederick, J. C. Killingsworth, P. H. Birly.
Excelsior—Sudlersville, 3. S. Goodband, E. B. Peirce.
Friendship—Anne Arundel, O. M. Wells, F. D. Griffith.
Independent—West River, C. Sheppard, B. Tongue.
Maryland—Baltimore, C. Young, Wm. P. Vaughen.
Mechanic's—Frederick, A. Freely, J. A. Simpson.
Mountain City—Frederick, J. W. Brubacker, C. Albaugh.
Mount Washington—Baltimore county T. E. Sollers, J. W Webb.
Monumental—Baltimore, H. McK. Herring, W. A. Munson.
Mutual—Baltimore, J. A. Goode, J. Funk.
Nameless—Frederick, L. V. Baughman.
Olympian—West River, H. E. Fiddis, L. B. Byers.
Patasco—Westminster, J W. Perkins.
Pastime—Baltimore, W. R. Griffith, W. R. Prestman.
Recreation—Millersville, A. Freeland, C. H. Brown.

Cincinnati had already edged Niagara 42-6, a Buffalo paper calculated, had the Red Stockings played Columbia, the score would have been "1,463 to 1 or 2." Huge-score games, be it noted, took three hours or more.

By this time, batting averages were being calculated, and published; baseball was hailed as "the national game"—and professionals dominated the play. Finally, in 1871, common sense took over and the first league was formed, its teams holding franchises and bearing city names.

But first, the narrative art in that age of "base-ballists" is worth a parting glance, to savor not only its quaintness but also its spirit: "During the fourth inning, Frank Popplein [of the Pastimes] made a beautiful catch. . . . He was on a full run, and when the ball lodged in his hands, his body was so far overbalanced that it was with the greatest difficulty that he could recover." From two years later (an 1869 game, the Marylands versus the Brooklyn Eckfords): "Martin, the famous slow pitcher, bewildered the Baltimore players by his peculiar style; it appeared as if the ball, when it quitted his hand, would fall to the ground before reaching the bat, but it went to the catcher very fast; [when hit, the ball] assumed an upright position and was easily taken by the Eckford players."

By now, authentic baseball artifacts from 1870 or earlier are of extreme rarity. Then, when a single baseball sufficed for all nine innings, it was customary to present it to the game winners, who if in funds would have it shellacked and lettered with team names, date, and score. Such a baseball, sewn from a single piece of leather, descended in the family of Wally Goldsmith of the Marylands; it was then presented to the Babe Ruth museum (at his birthplace, 216 Emory Street) by Lloyd Kirkley. The ball commemorates a victory over the New York Mutuals, on a date no longer legible. The Maryland Historical Society is custodian of an elaborate eight-foot red silk banner that proclaims, "Presented by the Ladies of Baltimore to the Maryland B. B. Club." And the Popplein family preserved Pastime B.B.C. material, including an 1869 team photo recording that long-gone component of the formal baseball uniform—a necktie. Indoors at a photographic studio, hatless, their dark trousers full length, their collared white shirts sporting the monogram letter *P,* the Pastime players hold three of antiquity's long, thin bats. (Another oddity, to modern eyes, is the shirt pocket. At the end of the century, the uniforms of Baltimore's major league Orioles still had shirt pockets—indeed, the team's identifying block letter *B* was sewn onto them.)

Finally, there is the small paperback written and published by William Ridgely Griffith in 1897 (Baltimore's first pennants having aroused interest in the game's origins locally): *The Early History of Amateur Base Ball in the State of Maryland.* Griffith, the reminiscer, was an early president of Pastime B.B.C. His testimony is the sole and entire source for the story of Polhemus in Baltimore. Only two copies of Griffith's 93-page monograph are known to have survived, each in a public library; portions of it were reprinted in the summer 1992 issue of *Maryland Historical Magazine.*

Banner presented in the 1860s to the Maryland Base Ball Club. At eight feet long (photo is shortened), of red silk with gilt lettering and well preserved, it is a glorious relic.

There is no statistical way to compare popular enthusiasm for baseball then (shortly after the Civil War) and now (when any regular-season game is transmitted to millions of TV screens). Admittedly, there are more women fans now than formerly. But not more boys. In olden time, baseball sometimes outdid even party politics as a peacetime release for mass emotion. Baseball led the way with its new order of heroes, its new theme of intercity antipathy, and its brilliant new careers for a few agile members of the unprivileged young. No wonder one member of New York's original Knickerbockers asked, in his will, "that I be buried in my base ball suit."

Financial diary kept by unknown businessman during Lord Baltimores' first year in the National Association. Note that gate receipts at Newington Park outstripped those in Brooklyn, Philadelphia, and Washington that week.

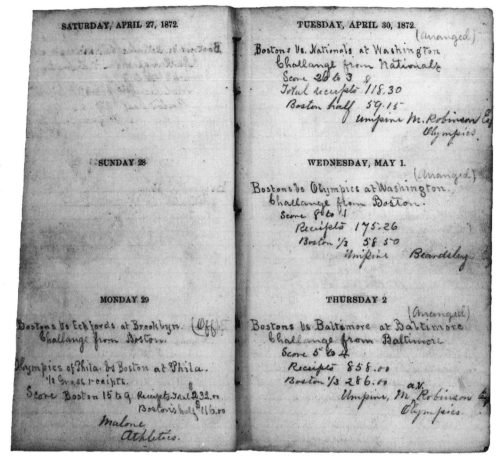

Anyone who searches through the old records and pieces together information on how the game was played in the 1860s and 1870s will find that there is a lot less new in baseball than is often thought. Much that we generally consider modern was old hat to the early pros.

HAROLD SEYMOUR, THE DEAN OF
BASEBALL HISTORIANS, IN *Baseball: The Early Years*

CHAPTER TWO

THE LORD BALTIMORES

The more baseball teams there were, the harder it was to agree on a national champion. On March 17, 1871, representatives from 10 of the leading city teams met at a hotel facing New York's Union Square. After forming a National Association of Professional Base Ball Players (thereby cocking their snooks at the amateurs), they agreed that every member team would play every other team a best-three-of-five series, that the winner of the most total games would be champion, and that a franchise in this new group (for convenience, the NA) would be available to all who applied, for $10.

NA play began in May among nine teams: Boston Red Stockings, Chicago White Stockings, Cleveland Forest Citys, Fort Wayne (Ind.) Kekiongas, New York Mutuals, Philadelphia Athletics, Rockford (Ill.) Forest Citys, Troy (N.Y.) Haymakers, and Washington Olympics. Why was Baltimore, a stronghold of the game, not on the list? Because its best players were wearing the uniform of a small city in Indiana and answering to an indigenous tribal name.

For the National Association's grand opener, Boston (which had hired most of the famous but disbanded 1869–70 Cincinnati Red Stockings) was to play Washington in Washington. But it rained heavily. And the honor of playing and winning the first of all major league games went instead to the disguised Baltimoreans.

Baltimore's first league-franchise team, the 1872 Lord Baltimores, as pictured in the *Clipper*, a New York sports weekly. *From left, top:* Everett Mills, 1b; George Hall, of; John Radcliff, ss; Bobby Mathews, p; Tom Carey, 2b; *bottom row:* Lipman Pike, of; Tom York, of; Richard Higham, c; Cherokee Fisher, 3b, p; Bill Craver, c.

On May 4 at Fort Wayne the home team played Cleveland and won, 2-0. The Kekionga roster included Samuel Armstrong and Edward J. Mincher, outfielders; Wallace Goldsmith, Frank C. Selman, and Thomas J. Carey, infielders; and the battery: Robert T. Mathews, pitcher, and William F. Lennon, catcher. All were from the Maryland B.B.C. On Opening Day, Lennon scored the first run, but Mathews was the star. Only 19 years old, standing 5 feet 5½ inches and a right-hander, Bobby Mathews of 1337 North Woodyear Street was to become in time the outstanding native Baltimorean in 19th-century baseball. His five-hit shutout (before some 200 spectators) turned out to be the NA's only shutout all year.

Before long, the powerhouses took over. Chicago (most of whose players came from New York) was on track to win that first of all pennants when the Great Fire of 1871 wiped out its ballpark and club-

house. Thereafter playing on the road with borrowed equipment, the White Stockings lost to the Athletics.

By then, the slumping Kekiongas were no longer around. The team broke up in late August, after two or more of the players proved to be rummies and two others jumped the team. But back on the Fourth of July, after a game in Washington, Fort Wayne had come to Baltimore to play the Pastimes. Far from resenting their fellow-townsmen's desertion to Indiana, Baltimoreans turned out in force. After rain interrupted the first game, they came back the next day and watched the pros beat the amateurs, 14-6. Impressed by Baltimore's ardor, Fort Wayne and Washington's Olympics decided to resituate their July 8 game. The two teams (the Olympic lineup including the rest of the Cincinnati Red Stockings) came instead to Baltimore, to the Madison Avenue Grounds. After six innings, the score was 7-7; but then Mathews tired. The cheers of a thousand hometown fans not availing, the scoring ended at 15-7 for the Olympics in this first major league game ever to be played in Baltimore.

As 1872 began in Baltimore, the clamor for an NA team was rewarded. Funding came, at least in part, from Alphonso T. Houck, a billboard magnate. His firm also built or rented a whole new venue, Newington Park, at Baker, Carey, and Gold Streets and "Pennsylvania Avenue Extended." This open lot two miles north and west of Baltimore's solidly built-up center city was only three blocks from the Madison Avenue Grounds. From downtown, horse-cars (the Citizens' Passenger Railway and "the White and Green Line") ran up Fremont and then Pennsylvania Avenues, right past the ballpark, en route to their terminus at Retreat Street. (Why "Newington"? No answer today, except that a housing development some blocks away used that name.)

For a decade, Newington Park was important to Baltimore, serving also as the site of cricket matches, track and field meets, and Barnum & Bailey Circus performances. Yet if anyone ever made a sketch or photo of Newington Park, the 20th century has been unable to find it. The stands were built of lumber, but it is not known if there was a roof, whether the seats had backrests, or who advertised what on the outfield fence. Newspapers did mention a clubhouse for the home

Robert C. Hall, club president as 1872 began, was a leading Baltimore coal dealer. The number of shares issued, at $25 each, is unknown.

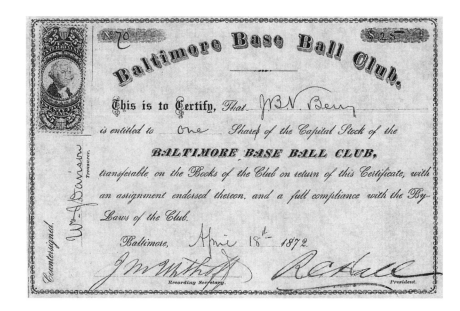

team. Newington's advertised seating capacity was 3,000; often the attendance was less than that. Admission was 50 cents; added to carfare, it was beyond working-class reach. The payroll was high: top-of-the-order players made about $1,200 (a farm's hired man, working a comparable season, might be paid board and $75).

The team name, the Lord Baltimores, was equally new. The fans or (in the word of those times) kranks shortened it to the Lords. To other players, however, the new team—whose yellow uniform shirts were made of silk instead of the usual flannel—was frequently, insultingly, the Canaries.

Help in player recruitment came from Nicholas E. Young, a Treasury Department auditor and an NA founder, even though he was also business manager of the Washington Olympics. Stock-share sales provided enough money to hire 10 veterans; all (in the absence of a reserve clause) had played in 1871 for at least one of the league's other teams. An innovation was the presence of *two* pitchers: Baltimore's own Bobby Mathews and William (Cherokee) Fisher of the late Rockford team. (On rosters that totaled 12 at most, the pitcher who was between starts usually played outfield.) William H. Craver, catcher, was captain—the equivalent of today's field manager. Albert H. Henderson, whose title was manager, was responsible for the business operation.

The Lords, their shirts emblazoned with the baronial Calvert arms, set out to earn their keep. The first major league appearance by a Baltimore team was in a road game, April 18, 1872: it drubbed the Olympics 16-0. (Washington had two NA teams that year; by midsummer, both had disbanded.) Then came Baltimore's first-ever home opener, on Monday, April 22, against the New York Mutuals. The foe was known to be strong and shifty. Baltimore crackled with excitement. Spectators, overflowing the park, clung to nearby trees, poles, and rooftops. Cherokee Fisher was in good form that afternoon; Bill Craver hit a home run, and New York took a licking, 14-8.

But Boston followed, led by Albert Goodwill Spalding. At age 21, a six-footer from Illinois (to which he returned for his subsequent career in sporting goods), Spalding was the league's foremost pitcher: across the NA's five years, he averaged 41 wins. Early baseball, too, had its Wright brothers—Harry and George, both cricketers to begin

The 1872 Lord Baltimores, the city's first major league team. *Top row:* Lipman Pike, Cherokee Fisher, Tom Carey (a Baltimorean); *middle row:* George W. Hall, John J. Radcliff, Tom York, Bobby Mathews; *front row:* Dick Higham, Bill Craver, Everett Mills. Note broad white belts and yellow argyle stockings.

with, both long since in baseball's Hall of Fame; and both in Boston's lineup. (From 1872 on, Boston always finished first in the National Association.) Eleven teams started that year; Baltimore's 35-19 won-lost total was good for third place, behind only Boston (38-8) and defending champion Philadelphia (which, with Adrian Anson at first and Al Reach at short, finished 31-15).

Lord Baltimore fans had many favorites: outfielder Lipman Emanuel Pike, for instance, the first Jewish major leaguer, who in the 1860s had hit six home runs in one game. Along with Bill Craver and fellow-outfielder Thomas J. York, he had spent 1871 with the Troy Haymakers. The third outfielder was English-born George W. Hall, who for a while was the team's leading hitter at .300. Then, in midsummer 1872, Troy collapsed and its third baseman, David W. Force (at 5 feet 4 inches, 130 pounds, sometimes called Tom Thumb), took the train to Baltimore, where he batted .409. Tom Carey, the second baseman, had played for the Marylands and then the Kekiongas. The shortstop was John J. Radcliff, from the champion Athletics. At first base, Everett Mills was from Nick Young's Olympics. Richard Higham, utility man and another native Briton, batted .339. Several players were veterans also in the military sense (Craver, for example, had fought for the Union).

In hits and in runs, the Lords led the league. As to individual honors, Pike was tops in homers and runs batted in; Hall in triples; Mathews (25-19 for the year) in strikeouts. One October day, the Lords, scoring in every inning, beat the Brooklyn Atlantics 39-14— still the highest run total by a Baltimore team. Scott Hastings, part-season catcher, had seven runs and six hits.

That year, six was enough to win home-run honors for the left-handed Lipman Pike, dubbed the Iron Batsman. Of the six (no record having been kept), all or none may have been over the fence; Pike's speed on the base paths would have mattered when he was trying for an inside-the-park homer. To a 19th-century fan, the homer was an occasional pleasure, not yet a heroic deed. Again in 1873, Pike's pokes (four altogether) led the NA. Pike, from New York, became a year-round Baltimorean, living at what is now 310 West Saratoga Street and opening a cigar store on Holliday Street just below Fayette.

Base Ball,
NEWINGTON PARK, PENNSYLVANIA AVENUE.
THIS (MONDAY) AFTERNOON, April 22d, at 3.30.
Inauguration of the New Grounds.

GRAND CHAMPION MATCH
FOR WHIP PENANT.
Baltimore's Pride vs. New York's Boast.
THE NEW CLUB vs. THE MUTUALS.
Accommodations for Five Thousand Spectators.
A Special Reserve Made for Ladies.

Base Ball.
HAYMAKERS, OF TROY,
vs.
BALTIMORE, OF BALTIMORE.

The Haymakers are the largest Salaried Nine in the United States, which amounts to over $20,000 per year.
SATURDAY, MAY 11TH.
3.30 P. M.,
NEWINGTON PARK.

Tickets for sale at MAUL'S, Baltimore and Calvert streets.

LORD BALTIMORE'S NINE

(sung to the tune of *Down in a Coal Mine*, lyricist unknown)

We are a jovial Base Ball Club,
   Our hearts are light and free,
And though we meet with some
   defeats,
   Oft gain the victory.
Give us fair play, and win or lose,
   We'll never make a muss,
But be content and act like men,
   Yes, that's the style for us.

Chorus:
Out at the Newington Park
   On the Base Ball Ground
When in earnest contest
   Our gallant Nine are found,

Struggling with their rivals,
   For victory and renown,
Out at the Newington Park,
   On the Base Ball ground.

Of all the manly games in vogue,
   Enumerate them all,
There's none you'll find that can
   compare
   With that known as Base Ball.
'Tis jolly fun when on the run,
   Or when with eagle eye
You watch your adversary's ball
   And take it on the fly.

We make no boasts but stand
   resolved
   To win ourselves a name,
And we will do the best we can
   To merit all we claim.
We're not afraid of rival clubs,
   We'll meet them anywhere,
And when they choose to meet us
   here,
   We'll act upon the square.

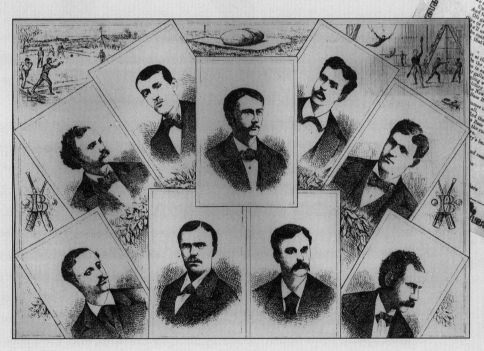

The 1873 Lords of Baltimore. Figure at *top center* is William (Candy) Cummings, the star pitcher.

BASE BALL.

PHILADELPHIA vs. BALTIMORE | July 4th AT 4 O'Clock.

Reserved Seats can be secured at Brown's, 12 West Fayette street, or at E. A. Maul's, corner of Baltimore and Calvert streets, up to 1 o'clock of the day of game. Admission 50 cents.

jy2-3t†

DON'T FAIL TO SEE

THE

Only Grand Display

OF

FIRE WORKS

In the city on the FOURTH OF JULY, commencing at 8½ o'clock P. M., at NEWINGTON BASE BALL GROUNDS, Pennsylvania Ave. Extended.

A fine Band in attendance. Room for all, seating capacity 3,000. Admission 25 cents. Children 15 cents.

Prof. BOND will superintend. Citizens' Line and White and Green Line Cars pass entrance.

jy8-2t†

fielder was gone. In the 1870s, as the historian William J. Ryczek explains, baseball entrepreneurship took either of two forms: the joint-stock corporation or the cooperative. The former, with its venture capital, offered contracts; the latter was merely an arrangement for splitting the gate receipts. Co-op baseball resembled the semipro system of later times. The loosely operated NA was indifferent to its members' method of financing. In general, players who had been re-jected by the joint-stock teams constituted the co-op lineups.

The 1873 Marylands had been only a co-op; sadly, 1874's Lord Bal-timores were on the same feeble footing. This time their manager-captain was Warren White, the third basemen; their new pitcher was the same Asa Brainard who had opposed them back in 1860 when he was a Brooklyn Excelsior (later, he had pitched for the undefeated 1869 Cincinnati Red Stockings). But Brainard, a late-nighter known as the Count, had been pitching since 1857; at age 33, he could no longer be depended on. Brainard's 5-24 record that year comple-mented the team's batting average, which fell from .301 to .228. Still another 1869 Red Stocking, Charles H. Gould, was at first base; he hit only .225. By September, ranking eighth and last (9-38) and for-saken by a public so recently adoring, the Lord Baltimores had quietly ceased play. (To end it with a smile, perhaps the 1874 team was in the wrong sport. On August 6 at Newington they took on the Baltimore Cricket Club for a spot of oh-well-played-sir. Won, too, 94-70. But the Lords never had a chance to demonstrate their skill at Lord's, the famous London cricket club.)

As 1875 arrived, Baltimore was what it had been in 1871, when major league play began: an outsider. An NA game was played in Bal-timore on June 9, in which Philadelphia drubbed Washington, 17-5, at the Madison Avenue Grounds. How Baltimoreans responded to this sprinkle of salt in the wound is unclear, for lack of an attendance figure.

To Bass (sic) Ball Players
Just received a large lot of
CANVAS shoes,
suitable for the above sport.
GEORGE S. CLOGG
No. 2 S. Calvert Street

Baltimore Sun,
SATURDAY, SEPTEMBER 9, 1865

CHAPTER THREE

EARLY-TIMES BASEBALL

Baseball, as played in the 1860s, 1870s, and well into the 1880s at early Baltimore "base ball grounds," differed from the game played nowadays at Oriole Park at Camden Yards. The pitcher threw underhand, from a lined, rectangular "box," which was level with the playing field and closer to home plate than today's mound. The catcher's first protection was a mouthpiece. Not until 1875 did anyone wear a glove; the catcher's mask did not come into vogue until 1877. Raw speed in a pitcher was a doubtful asset; slower, trickier stuff led to fewer injured catchers. (Bobby Mathews, the Baltimore phenom, is now thought to have pioneered the spitball.) No matter how lopsided the score, there were ordinarily no substitutions. How physically tough were the players? One of the Old Oriole myths was that a catcher jammed on a finger by a foul tip would simply stab his finger into the dirt to make the bleeding stop. In actuality, the regulars of 1894–96 lost many games to injury or illness (the toughest of them, John McGraw, spent the most days out sick). There was no team physician, then; not even a trainer in the modern sense. On July 26, 1887, when Bill Greenwood, the Baltimores' second baseman, slid home, he tore a finger on one corner of home plate and had to leave the game.

It was an offense-minded era; but even when the score soared, a game usually took less than two hours. One factor was the infre-

quency of pitcher changes and another, of course, was the absence of broadcast advertising between innings. Every game was at the sun's (and the umpire's) mercy: in the course of a season teams could expect several of their games "called on account of darkness" to end in a tie.

Until 1877, there was no league schedule; teams worked out their own arrangements for a season's set total of games to be played. They were thereby free to play many additional games with nonleague teams, or even with those across the border. In the heat of July and August, when members of the NA tended to go about other business, the 1873 Lord Baltimores went to Ontario to play the likes of London's Tecumseh and Guelph's Maple Leaf nines. Canadian baseball had started out with rules of its own—5 bases, 11 fielders—but by this time the players had U.S.-style skills and insights. Guelph held the title of national champion. Since Canada's players still claimed amateur status, it was embarrassing back home when Guelph beat the Lord Baltimores. Similarly, in midsummer 1874 the Boston Red Stockings and the Philadelphia Athletics sailed off to England in the misguided hope of converting cricketers to baseball. Once summer heat waned, stateside play resumed, running on far into October. Published attendance figures were estimates at best.

On the whole the players, mostly northern town- or city-bred,

OLD BASEBALL SLANG

When a base hit was a "stroke," a batter was a "striker." Today, a fan; yesterday, a "rooter"; back when, a "krank." The *Sun* couldn't decide whether fans were "base ball-ists" or "base ball-ites." The opposite of a ground ball was, naturally, an "air ball." The pitcher had no mound to stand on; he could take two running steps forward inside a marked-off rectangle instead of being limited to a rubber or slab (the phrase "knocked out of the box" survives from that era). He and his catcher "occupied the points." To be "skunked" was to go down one, two, three; to be "Chicagoed" was to be shut out for nine innings.

The front office hectored its errant player for "drunkenness and bummerism." The "championship game" was one that counted in the pennant standings; a season's many others were "exhibition games." The first box scores (in the American Association) printed a column of team names individually matched with two columns of numbers: O (outs) and R (runs). Beneath, by team, were supporting data (here, from an 1867 game): "Passed balls 3, called balls 13; missed flys 1, flys caught 6; home runs 2." A game account usually named the umpire and made clear his credentials.

New York Gothams	Brooklyn Grays, Gladiators,
Worcester Ruby Legs*	Bridegrooms, and Superbas
Washington Statesmen	Cleveland Blues
St. Louis Perfectos	Columbus Solons*
Philadelphia Pearls	Toledo Blue Stockings*

*major league

were a rough lot. Evenings, which were free except during travel, all too often became an avenue to alcoholism. Many a player had little or no paid work during the winter layoff. After card games on the long, slow train rides, many ended up deeply in debt; others bet on horses. Since player trades in the modern sense were unknown, players were at liberty in the NA to dicker anew after every season. Some players, known as "revolvers," signed with a different team every year.

The spectators (mostly grown men, suited and hatted) sometimes exhibited a kindred rapacity. Betting and its blood brother, the fix, stood out in the postwar letdown of standards. Professional gamblers sat in the stands holding satchels full of money. In the 1860s, William M. Tweed, Tammany Hall's boss of bosses, controlled the New York Mutuals; sometimes, while spectators called out their bets, the Mutuals would square off against a clearly inferior team and manage not to win. (*Hippodroming* was the players' word for it—not playing as well as they were able.) The fixers' furtive instructions could be confusing. The historian William J. Ryczek describes one 1875 game, Philadelphia versus Chicago, in which it became apparent that players on *both* sides were trying to lose. Until the 1890s, there was but one umpire; what with cheating players and cheated bettors, his was a frequent, nay urgent, need for police protection. Meanwhile, nothing prevented an investor from holding shares in more than one franchise.

Baseball's rules were years in evolving. The form and number of strikes and balls for an at-bat permutated, sometimes annually. For a strikeout, at one point, four were necessary; for a base on balls, the requirement shrank gradually from nine in 1876 to four in 1888. A

"MODEL" REGULATION BASE BALL BATS.

Our assortment of the above is the largest in the country. Clubs, in ordering selected Bats from the following styles, can depend on getting the best in the market. In ordering, order by numbers. Also, state what lengths are required. Men's, or Regulation Bats, are 36, 38, or 40 inches long. Boys' Bats are from 26 to 34 inches long.

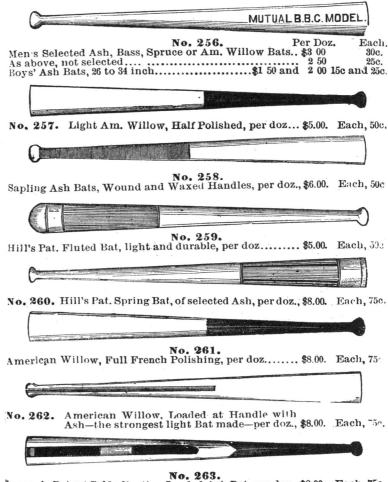

MUTUAL B.B.C. MODEL.

No. 256.	Per Doz.	Each.
Men's Selected Ash, Bass, Spruce or Am. Willow Bats..$3 00		30c.
As above, not selected....	2 50	25c.
Boys' Ash Bats, 26 to 34 inch......................$1 50 and	2 00	15c and 25c.

No. 257.   Light Am. Willow, Half Polished, per doz... $5.00.   Each, 50c.

No. 258.
Sapling Ash Bats, Wound and Waxed Handles, per doz., $6.00.   Each, 50c

No. 259.
Hill's Pat. Fluted Bat, light and durable, per doz.......... $5.00.   Each, 59c

No. 260. Hill's Pat. Spring Bat, of selected Ash, per doz., $8.00.   Each, 75c.

No. 261.
American Willow, Full French Polishing, per doz........ $8.00.   Each, 75c

No. 262.   American Willow, Loaded at Handle with Ash—the strongest light Bat made—per doz., $8.00.   Each, 75c.

No. 263.
Lyman's Patent Self-adjusting Loaded Ash Bat, per doz , $8.00.   Each, 75c.
☞ Clubs or Dealers ordering one doz. assorted Bats at one time are entitled to our doz. prices. Bats by express, C. O. D., or on receipt of price.

"batsman" could call for the pitch to be above (or below) his waist. At first, pitching was required to be underhand; not until mid-1885 was overhand pitching universally accepted (and in its wake came an outbreak of sore arms). To counteract the growing freedom in a pitcher's arm movements, the distance between him and home plate changed from 45 feet to 50 feet to (in 1893) the present 60 feet, 6 inches. For some years, the hit landing in fair ground but crossing the foul line before first or third base was a "fair-foul" and in play. Fouls didn't count as strikes; no pinch hitters; no infield fly rule; no take-your-base for the batter hit by a pitch; only gradually was the substitution of players sanctioned (early teams carried as few as 10 men).

The manager at first was the club's business agent; out on the diamond, a team answered to its captain, who was one of the players. No dugouts; "the bench" sat on a bench. No screen to shield the grandstand spectator from a straight-back foul. The visiting team provided the game ball; if it came apart or got lost (five minutes' limit on searching), the home team produced a replacement. The numerous manufacturers' baseballs differed as to characteristics. There was an advantage in batting first, before the ball became dirty and hard to see. The lone umpire took his position well behind the catcher, but moved out behind the pitcher once runner or runners was on base.

In midsummer 1875, four of Boston's best players, led by Al Spalding, signed to play the following season for Chicago— an unpunished rule violation. A Chicago stockholder, William A. Hulbert, had resolved not only to field a first-place team but to exclude other teams displaying easy morals or representing cities too small for profitable operations. That winter, in a second and larger coup, Hulbert and associates formed the National League of Professional Base Ball Clubs (not Players). Businessmen were now in control. The franchise fee rose; an applicant could be blackballed. Sunday games, gambling, the sale of liquor? Flat-out no. (In an 1877 test case in Louisville the NL outlawed four players for life for taking bribes; the franchise then collapsed.) In the face of such determination and rectitude, the loosely assembled NA simply dissolved, its best teams joining the new, eight-club NL. As the celebration of a hundred years of nationhood began, Baltimore, lacking in baseball organizers and investors, remained, wan and distant, on the outside.

Latterly, some baseball historians would deny the NA the status of major league. This thinking overlooks the prime importance of having been the nation's first annual intercity competition in any sport.

Metropolitan.	1	2	3	4	5	6	7	8	9	10	R	B H	S B	P O	A	E
Radford, R. F.																
Orr or Donohue, 1 B.																
Jones, C. F.																
Hankinson, 3 B.																
O'Brien, L. F.																
Knowles, 2 B.																
Cross, S. S.																
Kinslow, C.																
Lynch, P.																
Total.	0	0	0	0	0	0	0	0								

BALTIMORE.	1	2	3	4	5	6	7	8	9	10	R	B H	S B	P O	A	E
Greenwood, 2 B.																
Burns, 3 B.																
Purcell, R. F.																
Tucker, 1 B.																
Sommer, L. F.																
Davis, S. S.																
Trott, C.																
Daniels, C. F.																
Kilroy, P.																
Total.	0	1	0	6	0	2	1	1								

Umpire John Kelly defeated the Baltimore Base Ball Club yesterday afternoon at Oriole Park in the presence of a large concourse of people by a score of 11 to 3. The Cincinnati club assisted Kelly.

Baltimore Herald, JUNE 16, 1883

Without a doubt the finest and most interesting game of ball ever played on the Oriole grounds was that between the Baltimores and the Alleghanys yesterday afternoon, in which the home team defeated 10 men, including the umpire, by a score of 8 to 6.

Baltimore Herald, AUGUST 23, 1884

CHAPTER FOUR

A SECOND MAJOR, EVEN A THIRD

Seven years—what a long time to be without a major league franchise. So it seemed to the baseball fans of 19th-century Baltimore, represented in no league from the end of 1874 through the end of 1881. This is not to say, however, that Baltimore had no professional baseball.

On the contrary, during several summers a team of Baltimores was collecting admissions at Newington Park or was on tour for games with counterpart city clubs (and sometimes with teams from the National League, the one existing major). The NL instituted several improvements in this period, to its credit: turnstiles, protective wire screens behind home plate, and a longer (50-foot) pitching distance. However, expulsion and discord shrank the early NL, with its 84-game schedule, to six clubs. New York, Philadelphia, and Washington were among the cities that, lacking NL franchises, supported independent teams.

In 1880, three members of the unaffiliated Baltimores were box-office draws: Levi Meyerle, Dennis Brouthers, and Hugh Ignatius Daily. Long Levi, at third, had played for Philadelphia's 1871 original pennant-winners; in that 28-game season, he hit .492, still the majors' highest batting average. But he was also a sloppy fielder. Big Dan, at

Brickyard Kennedy
Buttermilk Tommy
  Dowd
Orator Jim and Voice-
  less Tim O'Rourke
Noodles Hahn
Angel Sleeves Jones
Germany Schaefer

The Only Nolan
The Smiths
  Broadway, Egyptian,
  Phenomenal, and
  Klondike
Fido Baldwin
Dandelion Pfeffer
Trick McSorley

first base, was another six-footer, a 22-year-old left-hander from New York state and one of the first true distance hitters. And in the box for Baltimore was a native son, One-Arm Daily. "He is certainly the most remarkable pitcher that ever sent a ball to the bat," the *Baltimore American* wrote. "He has no left hand at all, that member having been shot off in an accident [in boyhood, at the Front Street Theater], but with his strong right hand he makes a magnificent delivery of the ball, and even employs the stump in catching." A pad was attached to his left wrist. Daily went on to pitch half a dozen years in the majors. He threw a no-hitter; in 1884, at age 27, he rang up a then-record 483 strikeouts and in one game fanned 19. One year Daily *batted* .214. Unhappily, among his eight teams in the majors (he had a bad temper), Baltimore was not one.

With no pennant chase, however, how was excitement to build? On a good day, the 1880 Baltimores could beat Providence (second in the NL that year), but soon after would come a bad day—against Worcester, 15 errors. Summer lasted longer than the Baltimores.

By 1882, a formal challenge to the NL was under way. Four western clubs, with Philadelphia business connections, decreed a rival American Association. A sixth and final franchise (in a last-minute substitution for Brooklyn) was issued to Baltimore for $50. That summer, the search for a local owner led successfully to Henry R. Von der Horst. His father, John H., of Swedish-German descent, was the builder and owner of Eagle Brewery and Malt Works on Belair Road just above North Avenue. Among Baltimore's two dozen breweries at the time, Eagle was one of the largest.

The AA (unrelated to the 20th-century's minor league of the same name) authorized Sunday games where there were no blue laws (Baltimore: very blue), countenanced liquor sales, and charged 25 cents instead of 50. The so-called Beer and Whiskey League recruited various NL players. A year of this and the NL (spoken of at the time as "the League") came to terms: recognition of the AA ("the Association") as a second major; in return, acceptance of the NL's reserve clause, which, binding a player to whatever club he signed with, forestalled jumping by players and raiding by managements.

The Baseball Agreement of 1883 was a boon to the sport. The AA expanded to eight teams; AA and NL schedules lengthened to 134 games; Ladies' Day began; umpiring was professionalized; soon there was a postseason series of sorts between the respective pennant-winners. Fielding gloves became universal; before long, overhand pitching was okay; some of the fanciest-ever uniforms appeared. The public was lyrical (e.g., *Casey at the Bat*, published in California, and *Slide, Kelly, Slide*, celebrating Mike [King] Kelly, catcher for Chicago and then Boston). To be sure, a rising undertone bespoke trouble: profits were mounting, and the owners saw no need to cut in the play-

WHOSE IDEA WAS THE ORIOLE NAME?

When did Baltimore start calling its baseball team the *Orioles?* There is no single, documented answer. In the National Association, the name was Lord Baltimores (Lords, Yellow Stockings, etc.). In 1882, entering the American Association, the team was simply the Baltimores (sometimes, the Baltimore). Two years later, newspapers occasionally called the team the *Orioles*.

The transition is shadowy. In 1883, AA home games were moved from Newington Park to Oriole Park (Greenmount and 25th), earlier the site for phases of a late-summer festival called The Oriole.

Then in 1884 when Baltimore had two teams, the name Orioles distinguished the AA team from the Baltimore Unions. Nationally, most 1870s sports writing had been done in the sober manner of news writing. Chicago newspapers, livening up the baseball prose of the 1880s, soon had imitators. The name Orioles was part of the exuberant style that by 1884 was in vogue at the *Baltimore American, Herald,* and *News*.

Not until the 1890s did the *Sun* begin referring to them as *Orioles*.

ers. The color line became a burning issue. Nonetheless, some latter-day baseball researchers now rank the 1880s overall as something of a golden age.

The matter of race arose with the American Association. Its Toledo club's lineup included the brothers Fleetwood and Welday Walker as catcher and outfielder. The Walkers, from Oberlin College, were the first African Americans to break baseball's color line. Meanwhile, 6 of the 10 teams in the high-minor International League put at least one black player into uniform, whereupon white players, led by Adrian C. Anson of the Chicago NL, set out to exclude blacks from Organized Baseball. All too easily, the bigots succeeded. Two generations had to go by before the color bar finally came down. (In Baltimore, blacks had been among the players almost as soon as baseball began. More than once in later years it seems likely that an African-American team was Baltimore's best.)

The adventures of the early black teams can be reconstructed now only sketchily. White newspapers often ignored them; black newspapers, not being dailies, sometimes left gaps. Some of the Negro leagues that formed in the 20th century gave low priority to records preservation. Finally, their members' finances often precarious, the Negro leagues were a variable quantity; Baltimore, ultimately winning three championships, did so each time in a different league.

As early as August 16, 1870, the Madison Avenue Grounds, Baltimore's best ballpark, was the scene of an intercity game between black teams. "Some of the most terrific batting ever seen on the grounds," in the words of the *Baltimore American*, ended in defeat for the hometown Enterprise club, victory for the Washington Mutuals, 51-26. Baltimore's Enterprise learned one of the game's sternest lessons: a 10-run first inning may not be enough. (Did Frederick Douglass, living then in Washington, D.C., travel over to watch? His son Charles R. Douglass was the Mutuals' catcher.)

In 1874, two South Baltimore teams, the Lord Hannibals and the Orientals, were playing each other at Newington Park, ordinarily the site of Baltimore's home games in the all-white major league. More than half the 800 spectators were white, the *Sun* reported of a game played June 4; Howard pitched and Simms caught for the victorious Orientals.

By 1887, black baseball was popular enough nationally to warrant an attempt to create an eight-team league. To this end, answering the call of a black businessman, Walter S. Brown of Pittsburgh, the founders assembled in Baltimore at the Frederick Douglass Institute, 210 East Lexington Street. Franchises in this National League of Colored Base Ball Clubs went to Boston, New York, Philadelphia, Baltimore (which revived the team name Lord Baltimores), Washington, Pittsburgh, Cincinnati, and Louisville. Jesse J. Callis, a waiter, was Baltimore's manager and was elected league vice president.

Play began in May, the Lords renting Baltimore's AA park. Some wild, wonderful ball followed: Baltimore committing 20 errors while losing to Philadelphia, 26-6; Baltimore beating Pittsburgh 22-10 thanks to a 15-run ninth inning. Cummings, the captain, and Stewart pitched for the Lord Baltimores, who appear to have been in first place, with a 6-3 record, when in June the league folded. The economics of it was grim: few African Americans could take the time off from work to watch or, if not working, could afford to buy a ticket.

The 1880s, however interesting in retrospect, were less enjoyable to Baltimoreans white or black than to baseball fans elsewhere. In 6 of the 10 AA years the Baltimores finished below .500, in 4 they finished last. Still and all, this was the time when Kilroy was here, the incomparable Matt Kilroy.

The 1882 season was played at mouldering Newington Park by a team stocked in haste from Philadelphia, young players with no major league past or future. One, an English-born outfielder and base-stealer named Tom Brown (but not from a school named Rugby), did go on to a respectable career. Another, Charlie Waitt, batted .156, allegedly the lowest ever by a full-season major league outfielder. Henry Myers, 24, from Philadelphia, was shortstop, leadoff man, and manager. Winning 19 times and losing 54, Baltimore finished last, 14½ games behind the seventh-place team. After a typical game, the *Sun* remarked: "The feebleness of the home club's play . . . caused much dissatisfaction, which was rather warmly expressed."

Bill Barnie, competent baseball man and Oriole manager in the 1880s. He had no hair on top; ordinarily, a hat shielded him from notice. But nothing could hide his other problem—no pennants.

During the final week of the American Association's 1884 schedule, with Indianapolis in town, Baltimore's management, trying to rise from sixth place), played two games on one October afternoon. There was no pennant-season precedent, here or elsewhere.

The Orioles did beat the Indians twice, 7-3 and 6-2, with Bob Emslie and Hardie Henderson pitching. A single 25-cent ticket was good for both games.

The following has been compressed from the *American*'s account:

The aforesaid multitude took in five hours of ball. Some had their lunch with them. Others went behind the scenes and gnawed the terra cotta sandwiches which were to be had. The heavy batting of the Orioles won the first game. Dan Stearns encompassed all four bases on the longest drive that has yet been made on the grounds. It was simply a "corker."

The second game was by far the more exciting. Base hits were few throughout the six innings played, and errors were scarce and excusable up to the sixth innning, when the Indianapolis boys went to pieces like an old flour barrel.

Griffin, the Association umpire, got sick, and his place was filled by Sullivan, a Union umpire.

Disgusted, Harry Von der Horst arranged for not only a whole new team but a whole new park. Some of 1883's players were from the nonleague Brooklyn Atlantics, complete with their manager, William H. (Bald Billy) Barnie, a retired catcher; and the location was now due north of downtown, at York Road (later called Greenmount Avenue) and Fifth Street (later Huntingdon Avenue, later still 25th Street). Early christened Oriole Park, the new field was outside the city limits until the expansion of 1888 moved the boundary many blocks north. The AA now had eight teams. One thing was not new — Baltimore in last place, at the close of a 28-68 season.

In the off-season, Barnie lived on Robert Street, operated the Apollo roller skating rink at Carrollton Avenue and West Mulberry Street — and searched the hinterland for hot prospects. His 1884 team finished 63-43, thanks especially to his new, hard-working right-handers, Bob Emslie (32-17), a Canadian, who was later a long-service umpire, and James Harding (Hardie) Henderson (27-23), from Philadelphia. In this first year of plus-100-game schedules, Baltimore was the scene of the first recorded doubleheader (to make up for a rainout). Five hundred people, each paying a single 25-cent "entrance fee," watched the Baltimores beat Indianapolis, 7-3 and then 6-2; the early darkness of October 4 limited the second game to six innings.

Also playing for Baltimore for part of the season was outfielder Lewis P. Dickerson, native of Tyaskin and first among the many Eastern Shoremen who have made it to the big show. Dickerson is further memorable from that time of nifty nicknames: standing 5 feet 6 inches, he was Buttercup Dickerson.

Entrepreneurship outdid itself in 1884: 3 majors and 34 franchises. The AA had 13 teams, as here and there a franchise fizzled and moved (Baltimore's 63-43 was good enough only for sixth place). Meanwhile, a rival Union Association took the field, and one of the less shaky of *its* 13 teams was the Baltimore Unions, who played home games at the Belair Lot at Forrest and Gay Streets in Old Town. Much of the Unions' capital investment came from Albert H. Henderson—the same Argyle Avenue "clerk" who had been a leader of the amateur Marylands and then business manager of the Lord Baltimores; by 1884, he was a downtown mattress manufacturer. Henderson also bankrolled the Chicago Unions. Yet to the modern fan, he is an utter unknown.

The UA, largely the creation of Henry V. Lucas, a self-indulgent St. Louis millionaire, barely finished one season; but Baltimoreans

Joe Sommer (*left*), outfielder, and Chris Fulmer, catcher, spent seven and four years, respectively, in the service of the 1880s Orioles. Neither ever batted .300; but, after posing in a photographer's studio, they joined the cigarette-card lineup of many an admiring young collector.

were pleased to have had a fourth-place team (58-47) and the battery of Sweeney and Sweeney: respectively, Bill (40-21), from Philadelphia, and John, from New York. William J. Sweeney worked 538 innings and was the UA's most proficient pitcher, only to go back afterward, in a tighter job market, to the minors.

The total number of Baltimore teams that overloaded year was actually three. The Eastern League (which today, as the International League, is the oldest continuously operating minor) started play in 1884. Thanks to George W. Massamore, a Eutaw Street dentist, Baltimore was a founding member. Its Monumentals used a baseball grounds at Druid Hill Avenue and Whitelock Lane (now Whitelock Street), with seating for some 3,300 spectators. (Larry Zuckerman, a historian of the nation's baseball parks and the modern discoverer of this forgotten sports temple, notes that the major league Unions, attracted by the greater spaciousness of Monumental Park, moved there in August, only to find its turf lumpy and bumpy. After one game, they returned to the Belair Lot. Nevertheless, that lone game adds Monumental Park to the list of Baltimore's major league parks. The current total, down through Oriole Park at Camden Yards, is 10.)

But the Monumentals lacked something, perhaps patronage. Unpaid, after 3 games won and 10 lost, the team dissolved, then reassembled under another name in Lancaster, Pennsylvania. (The next

Actual signed contracts from the 19th century are rare documents. This one descended in the family of Dennis Patrick Casey (*above*), a two-season Baltimore outfielder and slugger (.288, 6 home runs). Somehow, the line specifying dollars per month (probably about $350, until season's end) is blank.

→❊ CONTRACT ❊←

UNDER THE RULES OF

The American Association of Base Ball Clubs.

THIS AGREEMENT, made the 20 day of *August* eighteen hundred and *Eighty four*, between *The Baltimore Base Ball Club* of the City of *Baltimore* and State of *Maryland* a corporation created by, and existing under the laws of said State, being a member of the AMERICAN ASSOCIATION OF BASE BALL CLUBS, party of the first part, and *Dennis P Casey* of *Binghamton NY*

time the Eastern League put a franchise in Baltimore, in 1903, the club stayed longer.)

Another Oriole of distinction, an outfielder for Billy Barnie in 1884 and 1885, was Dennis Patrick Casey. He batted left (.273), threw right, and before and since Ernest L. Thayer's epic 1888 ballad, was the only major league Casey to have been a slugger. Dennis Casey came from Binghamton, New York, and had a longer-lived brother Dan who, in his later years, masqueraded as the great Casey; but Dan was a pitcher. Dennis Casey was Baltimore's sturdiest batter, and Dennis Casey hit home runs.

One day, however, Barnie took the team to Westminster to play the local nine. When his major leaguers, frisking around, lost the game, Barnie went into a rage and hired the amateurs' star outfielder, Ed Greer. At this, the pros rebelled, capering now in AA games. So Barnie fired Emslie—and Casey (who went home, never returning to the majors). It is possible to make a case for Dennis as the model for Mudville's mighty hero, but the story doesn't play well beyond Baltimore's city limits.

The last-place 1885 Orioles. Alas, snazzy uniforms did not a successful season make. *From left*, *back row:* Tom York, of; Bob Emslie, p; Dan Stearns, 1b; Mike Muldoon, 2b; Sam Trott, c; Dennis Casey, of; Jake Evans, of; Joe Sommer, of; *middle row:* Manager Bill Barnie; Tim Manning, 2b; Jimmy Macullar, ss; *front row:* Vincent (Sandy) Nava, c; Tom (Oyster) Burns, 3b; Bill Traffley, c; Hardie Henderson, p.

Few scorecards have survived from the Union Association, which lasted one year (1884, the most recent year in which Baltimore was home to two major league baseball teams). Here, the Washington Nationals take on the Baltimore Unions, in Washington, on August 7. Baltimore breaks it open in the seventh, winning 8-6.

Bill Sweeney of Baltimore was on his way to a remarkable 40w-21L season, in which his 538 innings pitched led the league; they included 58 complete games—and a 2.59 earned-run average. After the Union Association broke up, Sweeney went to California, never to pitch in the majors again.

Another 1885 figure—a young outfielder dumped after but one game—was John K. Tener. Born in Ireland, Tener (pronounced "Tenner") is acclaimed for having done better *after* baseball than anyone else from the 19th century. Tener served as governor of Pennsylvania and as president of the National League. (Late in life Al Spalding ran as the Republican candidate in California for U.S. senator, but on that occasion he lost.)

In 1885, not only did Baltimore finish eighth and last again (41-68, 36½ games behind), but the St. Louis Browns came in first. This turned into a habit, as St. Louis dominated the AA four years in a row. To a 20th-century observer, however, a simultaneous failure in the NL had more chilling overtones. At the end of 1885 Providence, not just a member but a power (two pennants in eight years, two second places, never lower than fourth), was dropped. Too small and too close to a larger city, Providence still hasn't returned to the majors.

What saved n'er-do-well Baltimore from a similar stringency, or at least gave it an interesting team, was that in 1886 Barnie finally got lucky. From the Southern League minors he brought up a teenage left-hander who humbled St. Louis. His name was Matthew Aloysius Kilroy; he came from Philadelphia; and he threw bullets. Matt didn't turn 20 until June that first year. He had four good years, all with Baltimore, and then his arm went dead. The first two of them, he pitched 583 and 589 innings, respectively (people exclaim when a modern pitcher goes 300). The offense, that first year, was pitiable; among full-season team batting averages, 1886 Baltimore's .204 remains the lowest ever. (The home-run total was eight—for the whole team—which finished again in last place, 48-83.) The defense not being much better, the one dependable way to put a batter out was with three fastballs, so Kilroy pitched 513 strikeouts—still the all-time major league record.

In 1886, Kilroy went 29-34; in 1887, 46-19 (the rest of 1887's staff went 31-39). There were hitters, in 1887; three of the Baltimores batted .300 or better, notably Thomas P. (Oyster) Burns, a 22-year-old shortstop from Philadelphia who hit nine homers, a mark unsurpassed by major league Baltimore until 1955. (Baltimore's 1887 totals: 77-58, third place.) Kilroy's 46 victories in one season are still the majors' unapproached tops for a left-hander. (Bill Sweeney in 1884, Matt Kil-

MARKETING IN THE GOOD OLD DAYS

The ballclub went in for marketing, the historian David Nemec points out, as on holidays, "Von der Horst would present each fan with a picnic lunch, a schooner of his Eagle Beer and an invitation to linger after the game and dance under the stars on a platform set up in Oriole Park."

The inscribed gold watch presented to Matt Kilroy by his Baltimore admirers still exists. An oddity, that Baltimore's best pitcher was from Philadelphia; Philadelphia's (Bob Mathews), from Baltimore.

One prominent baseball fan was August Mencken Sr., the West Lexington Street cigar manufacturer and dealer, and part-owner of the Washington Nationals (also in the American Association). Occasionally, to the delight of Mencken's small son Harry (H. L.), one or another player was invited to the Menckens' home at 1524 Hollins Street.

Presumably the Kilroy cigar sold for 5 cents. This late-1880s lithograph, in faded color, survives from having been pasted into one of young Mencken's scrapbooks. It is the only copy known—also, the only known time when Aug. Mencken & Bro. did such honor to a ballplayer.

roy in 1887; Baltimore hasn't had a 40-game winner since.) And Kilroy's combined 75 victories are still the most ever by a pitcher in his first two years—each year, 66 complete games. How many pitches did Kilroy throw in a game? No one kept count then. His walk totals were low, 182 and 157, but his 70 wild pitches in 1886 would have pushed many a batter back. When on October 6, 1886, Kilroy set down the Pittsburgh Alleghenies 6-0, it was the first time Baltimore had ever had a no-hitter to glory in. The following year, Kilroy pitched and won a doubleheader against Cleveland: the first game was a shutout; in the second, his own wild throw allowed the only opposing run.

The fans gave him a gold watch. When Kilroy brought his sweetheart Fanny Denny from Philadelphia and married her in Baltimore, the fans gave them a silver service. (The Kilroys settled at 449 East Lanvale Street.) In his honor, Aug. Mencken & Bro., cigar makers, created a five-cent stogie, the Kilroy. (Later, the proprietor's teenage son, Henry L. Mencken, was for a while high on baseball. He sketched from 1890s photos a series of Oriole heroes; scrapbook examples suggest that Mencken could have made a living as a commercial artist.)

Might there be another one like Matt back in Philadelphia on the semipro Kilroy family team? One day in 1888 against Louisville Mike Kilroy was the Baltimores' starter: a right-hander. But a 9-3 loss ended the tryout—plus the *Sun*'s verdict that "his delivery was hardly speedy or steady enough." Mike Kilroy does have a place in the books, however: his age, misstated as 18, was 15 years and not quite 10 months, making him the majors' second-youngest player ever.

For latter-day pursuers of trivia, the 1886 season also offered a pitcher named Zay, supposedly from Pittsburgh. His major league career consisted of two ineffective innings with Baltimore. Then Zay vanished. The Society for American Baseball Research, which maintains a file on every man ever to appear in a major league box score, still seeks Zay's height, weight, place and date of birth and death, and —egad—first name.

One more footnote, quietly: On June 24, 1886, an away game's final score was Brooklyn 25, Baltimore 1—for the latter, apparently its worst-ever performance. (If the topic be embarrassment, there was also that 22-5 game in Louisville. For the Eclipse, as the foe was known in 1886, Guy Hecker hit three home runs and three singles and drew a walk. All seven times, he scored—the one-man record then and still for a nine-inning game. What should have especially depressed the opposing Baltimores was that Hecker was Louisville's pitcher.)

Mike Griffin, Oriole centerfielder, indoors and gloveless, makes as if to catch a ball that is hanging on a string. As far back as the 1880s, posing for the photographer (and then gracing the front of a small cigarette card) constituted part of a major league player's income.

Photography goes outdoors: the 1888 Orioles. *1.* Joe Sommer, of; *2.* Jack Farrell, ss; *3.* Matt Kilroy, p; *4.* Bill Shindle, 3b; *5.* Chris Fullmer, c; *6.* Tommy Tucker, 1b; *7.* Mike Griffin, of; *8.* Bill Greenwood, 2b; *9.* Bart Cantz, c; *10.* Bert Cunningham, p; *11.* Walt Goldsby, of; *12.* Jack O'Brien, c.

The following year, 1887, was to be Baltimore's best in the AA. The whole season was dramatic, thanks to a series of rules experiments: four strikes instead of three, five balls instead of four, and a walk counting as a hit. Behold, a year of .400 batting averages. Along with it came Kilroy's best year ever and a rookie outfielder from New York state, Mike Griffin, 22, who homered on his first at-bat. By June, the doormats were in second place—and challenging the champion, the first-place St. Louis Browns.

The Browns came to town for four high-tension games. Baltimore went wild. The foe's right-handed batters were led by Charles A. (Commy) Comiskey, manager and first baseman, and James E. (Tip) O'Neill, outfielder, who batted .435 that year; their pitchers, by David L. Foutz, successively a Carroll County, Marylander, a Colorado gold miner, and as 1886 ballplayer, a 41-game winner. (His 147-66, .690 lifetime winning percentage has never been bettered. In the mid-'90s, Foutz managed the Brooklyn Bridegrooms.) For that series opener—Kilroy pitching—the governor, the mayor, and 15,000 fans squeezed into the park: Baltimore's biggest baseball crowd up to that point. Game one went to Baltimore: pandemonium. Game two was a tie and a near-riot. Games three and four—it is better not to ask. And as summer went by, the team drifted down to third place.

In 1888 and 1889, Baltimore resumed its second-division habit. The team forever lacked hitters, although in 1889, Thomas J. (Tommy) Tucker, its first baseman and one of baseball's first switch-hitters, batted .372 and led the AA. Frank Foreman, from Baltimore's Hampden, was effective as second pitcher, finishing 23-21. (In his 11 years as a major leaguer, Foreman was to pitch four different times for Baltimore in three different leagues.) One difference was the scene of these labors. In 1889, a new park with more seats was built farther out Greenmount Avenue (called York Road then), again on the west side, between Barnum and Homewood Avenues, now 28th and 29th Streets. But nothing was new in the results from many a road game. In mid-July, the *Sun* lost its customary cool. "At Last! At Last!!

Frank Foreman, the pride of Hampden. A rare 6-footer, Foreman pitched 20-some years for his living. A graduate of four separate major leagues and seven teams (four separate times, he was an Oriole), Foreman came out ahead, 96w-93L. Here he is an Oriole in 1889, having his only 20-game season, 23w-21L. Frank's younger brother Brownie was a pitcher; he, too, briefly made it to the majors.

At Last!!!" its baseball headline read; with Frank Foreman pitching, "Baltimore Wins a Game from St. Louis."

Two diversions further illuminated this period. In October 1887, the respective champions (AA, St. Louis; NL, Detroit) decreed a World Series. Chartering a train, they scheduled no fewer than 15 games in 11 cities, of which Baltimore was the ninth. In the morning they played in Washington, that afternoon in Baltimore. Detroit won, 13-3, for the eighth and deciding time; Maryland's Dave Foutz was the losing pitcher. The *Sun* was meek: "Seldom in late years has Baltimore had the good luck to be the city in which a national event was decided; but she struck in finally when, yesterday afternoon, the world's baseball championship was decided at the Huntington Avenue Grounds." Regardless, the two teams got back on their train and elsewhere played out their series.

On April 10, 1889, the World Tour teams arrived in Baltimore for preseason games. The previous autumn, missionary impulse had led Al Spalding to embark his Chicago NL team and 10 opposing all-stars headed by John Montgomery Ward, shortstop for the New York

The 1899 Orioles. *Top right:* Frank Foreman; *seated, third from left:* Matt Kilroy.

Giants, on a cruise across the Pacific, Indian, and Atlantic Oceans, with game stops at principal cities. The few natives who watched did not convert. But when the travelers reached Baltimore, a figure of triumph in his Chicago uniform was John Tener, by this time a pitcher; a more interesting figure to modern eyes—and a star in both these Baltimore stop-off games—was the Detroit centerfielder, Edward H. (Ned) Hanlon.

But below these pleasant surfaces was a pot ready to boil over. On most teams, player-owner relations had been worsening. No antitrust or federal labor relations laws then; for the wronged player, no court redress. So in 1885, National Leaguers formed the Brotherhood of Professional Base Ball Players; its goal was bargaining recognition, as a step toward modification of the reserve clause and an end to uncompensated player sales. The owners' answer was a burst of hostility: they proposed a salary cap—at a time when the money was no better (and sometimes worse) than in the early 1870s. Matt Kilroy, 46-game winner, was paid only $2,400.

In June 1889, Louisville arrived in Baltimore for a four-game series. The club president, having declared himself also the manager, was traveling with the team. It was having a dismal losing streak; he was so short of funds that the club was for sale (asking price: $9,000, according to a Louisville newspaper cited by the researcher Dean A. Sullivan). Imaginatively, the owner-manager had begun fining his players not only so much per individual error, but so much per losing game. The historian Bob Bailey finds a clear purpose: to cut the payroll, heedless of the president's own signature on player contracts. A written, signed player protest was rejected. Thereupon, half the team's 12 players refused to suit up; they included the team's two superstars, Guy Hecker and Pete Browning. Agog, Baltimoreans clustered outside Pepper's Hotel, where the Colonels were staying, across Holliday Street from City Hall. To field a team that afternoon, Louisville hired a new outfield consisting of three Baltimore semipros: Charles Fisher, Michael J. Gaule, and John Traffley. In two at-bats, Fisher and Traffley got a hit, and accordingly each has a lifetime batting average of .500 in the baseball encyclopedias, where the names of

Why was the name *Union* Park? The answer may lie in streetcar history. For more than 30 years, the city's baseball fans had ridden to the park in cars pulled by horses. Speedier alternatives having failed — steam, cable, third rail, battery — the overhead-wire electrical method was introduced early in the 1890s. Specifically, as the streetcar historian Michael T. Farrell relates, by June 1, 1891, three passenger railway companies (the Baltimore, Peabody Heights & Waverly; the North Baltimore; and the Baltimore & Yorktown Turnpike) had been consolidated into the Baltimore Union Passenger Railway. As a business promotion, Union Passenger may have paid some of the new ballpark's construction costs. Earlier, the York Road route had stood out as Baltimore's only transit line with double-decker cars.

An impetus for SPCA

En route to and from baseball games, it was the sight of prolonged lashings by streetcar drivers, as the horses strained uphill to pull cars overloaded with fans, that inspired other Baltimoreans to form the SPCA, for the prevention (i.e., the outlawing) of cruelty to animals.

these three one-gamers rate type of the same size as is used for Babe Ruth, Ty Cobb, and Walter Johnson.

Then, counseled by Oriole manager Billy Barnie, the holdouts went back to work. Most of the fines were canceled and nobody's name went to the AA blacklist. The losing streak, reaching 26, ended. In July, new and more temperate owners took over Louisville's franchise. But in retrospect, the episode enlarges: that dramatic weekend in Baltimore constituted Organized Baseball's first player strike.

Meanwhile, the Brotherhood of Professional Base Ball players, led by Monte Ward of the New York Giants (in later life, a lawyer), undertook action on a larger scale. In 1890, it begat a new, third league. Seven of the Players' League's eight franchises were in NL cities; the rival New York ballparks physically abutted.

In Baltimore, Harry Von der Horst was heading in a different direction. Persuaded that St. Louis's grip on the AA was unbreakable, he and Barnie bade Matt Kilroy and others who had been offered long-term PL contracts good-bye. (Kilroy, his arm worn out, never had another good year. In retirement, he became a Philadelphia saloon-keeper, across the street from Shibe Park.) Wanly, Baltimore's management dropped out of the majors, filing for membership instead in a minor league, the Atlantic Association. There, Baltimore (77-23) was dominant, only to drop out. In August, with St. Louis beaten and another American Association team folding—namely Brooklyn, home that year to franchises in all three leagues—Baltimore meekly returned to the majors, playing out AA Brooklyn's schedule, 15-19. Nationally, the outcome of this tumultuous, red-ink year was victory for the Players' League in attendance and in play; but also defeat and collapse, as the PL's businessmen backers got cold feet and walked out on it. Acrimony remained alive and well: the Players' League personnel were taken back without penalty, but the NL set about signing the best of them. The peace treaty of 1883 thereby reduced to a scrap of paper, the AA renounced it, futilely. At the end of the schedule, 1891's AA emulated 1890's PL: it caved in.

For Baltimore, a founding AA father but still never a reigning champion, the timing was a last straw. The Von der Horsts were at odds—John H., the father, finding baseball a poor investment; his son Harry sinking ever more money into it. Not only did Harry spend on players from other teams; he sprang for a new ballpark, supposedly the American Association's largest—and the first in Baltimore to have a double-decked grandstand—back on today's 25th Street but one block west, at Barclay. It was christened Union Park and at the first game there on May 11, 1891, Baltimore bested St. Louis 8-4. (Most appropriately, the umpire that day was Bobby Mathews himself, native Baltimorean and retired pitcher whose feats included three straight 30-win seasons with the 1880s Athletics.) Tension over the team's failure to produce (72-63 and fourth place, that year; 22 games behind, this time Boston) came into the open. Von der Horst fired his manager, Barnie, who had been around longer than any other in the AA. Farewell, late in the season, to Blue-eyed Billy, the Bald

The *battery* (a 19th-century term still in use) of McMahon and Robinson. Bill Barnie pried them away from Philadelphia late in 1890. At once, Mac (later, Sadie) became the number one pitcher; in time, Robbie was named team captain. Their Oriole service totaled, respectively, 7 and 12 years. John J. McMahon won 130 games as an Oriole; five times Wilbert Robinson was a .300 hitter.

Opposite page: In the later 1800s, telegraphy was the king of speed. One or more downtown print shops stood by at afternoon's end to report ballgame results from other cities, hot off the wire, to people on their way home from work. Newsboys on street corners hawked these official baseball scorecards; in particular, saloons posted them.

Eagle of Chesapeake Bay, as the *Sporting News* called him, the newsman's friend with his ready supply of quotable remarks. And make way for a playing manager, the 26-year-old Oriole outfielder George Van Haltren.

Manager Van Haltren, from Missouri and the Players' League, was a left-hander and a .300 hitter. His nine home runs for 1891's Orioles had tied the team's existing record. He was to hold office, however, only a few months. And the fans learned to favor instead a new battery, obtained late in 1890 from the collapsing A's: John J. McMahon and Wilbert Robinson. Of Massachusetts' Robbie, more later. McMahon, a Delawarean, promptly won 36, lost 21. He was the winning pitcher in Union Park's first game, and the best in the AA for wins, innings pitched, and strikeouts when, at the end of 1891, that league crashed.

What next, for a club with no franchise, uncertain backing, and not much self-confidence? Salvation came from an unlikely source. Standing there alone on the battlefield, as 1892 began, the NL rechristened itself the National League and American Association of Professional Base Ball Clubs; but everyone went on speaking of it as the League. And it expanded. Hoping to preclude the formation of any more rival leagues, the NL took in four AA cities: St. Louis, Louisville, Washington, and Baltimore. The only one of them ever to finish higher than fifth in this unwieldy, 12-team league of the 1890s was Baltimore.

Official Base Ball Score Card

KAMES & BURGAUER, Publishers, N. W. Cor. Baltimore & North Sts.   J. CHASE PHILIPS, Manager.

VOL. 9   BALTIMORE, AUGUST 10, 1891   NO. 118

AMERICAN ASSOCIATION.

At St. Louis	1	2	3	4	5	6	7	8	9	10	11	12	Rns	BH	Err
ST. LOUIS	1	0	0	0	0	2	0	0	0				3	5	4
BALTIMORE	0	1	3	2	0	7	0	2	0				15	11	5

Stivetts & Munyan, Home Bat'y   Kerins, Umpire   Healy & Robinson, Opp't Bat'y

At Cincinnati	1	2	3	4	5	6	7	8	9	10	11	12	Rns	BH	Err
CINCINNATI	4	1	0	1	0	0	2	0	0				8	9	4
ATHLETIC	2	2	1	5	1	2	0	3	0				16	17	5

Crane & Kelly, Home Bat'y   Davis Umpire   Sanders & Milligan, Opp't Bat'y

At Columbus	1	2	3	4	5	6	7	8	9	10	11	12	Rns	BH	Err
COLUMBUS	0	0	3	0	0	1	1	0	0				5	10	4
BOSTON	0	1	0	0	0	0	4	1	0				6	4	3

Knell & Dowse Home Bat'y   Mahoney, Umpire.   Griffith, & Murphy, Opp't Bat'y

At Louisville	1	2	3	4	5	6	7	8	9	10	11	12	Rns	BH	Err
LOUISVILLE	0	0	3	0	1	0	3	0	2				9	8	4
WASHINGTON	1	0	2	0	0	1	1	0	0				5	9	4

Meekin & Cahill, Home Bat'y   Ferguson, Umpire   Eitlejorg & McGuire, Opp't Bat'y

SUNDAY GAMES, { BALTIMORE 14   ATHLETIC   6   LOUISVILLE   11   BOSTON   10
{ ST. LOUIS   2   CINCINNATI   5   WASHINGTON   4   COLUMBUS   0

NATIONAL LEAGUE.

At Brooklyn	1	2	3	4	5	6	7	8	9	10	11	12	Rns	BH	Err
BROOKLYN	0	2	0	0	2	0	0	2	0				6	10	3
CINCINNATI	2	4	0	0	0	0	0	2	0				8	9	5

Terry & Kinslow Home Batt'y   Lynch, Umpires.   Rhines & Keenan, Opp't Bat'y

At New York	1	2	3	4	5	6	7	8	9	10	11	12	Rns	BH	Err
NEW YORK	0	0	0	2	0	0	0	0	1				3	11	4
CHICAGO	2	0	0	0	0	0	0	0	2				4	8	3

Rusie & Buckley, Home Batt'y   Powers, Umpire   Hutchinson & Kittridge, Opp't Bat'y

At Boston	1	2	3	4	5	6	7	8	9	10	11	12	Rns	BH	Err
BOSTON	0	0	0	2	1	4	2	0	0				9	6	3
PITTSBURG	1	0	1	1	0	2	0	0	0				5	9	10

Nichols & Bennett, Home Bat'y   Battin & McQuade, Umpir   Baldwin & Miller Opp't Bat'y

At Philadelph'a	1	2	3	4	5	6	7	8	9	10	11	12	Rns	BH	E.
PHILADELPHIA	1	0	0	0	1	0	0	1	0				3	7	4
CLEVELAND	0	2	0	1	4	0	0	0	0				7	8	3

Thornton & Clements, Home Bat'y   Hirst. Umpire   Viau & Zimmer, Opp't Bat'y

American	Won	Lost	Per C.	American	Won	Lost	Per Ct.	National	Won	Lost	Per Ct.	National	Won	Lost	Per Ct
Boston	64	30	685	Columbus	46	50	479	New York	47	35	573	Philada.	44	44	500
St. Louis	61	37	623	Cincinnati	42	53	442	Chicago	54	36	600	Brooklyn	42	45	481
Baltimore	54	37	594	Louisville	33	66	333	Boston	50	37	575	Pittsburg	35	53	397
Athletic	48	45	516	Washing'n	30	60	333	Cleveland	43	48	472	Cincinnati	37	54	406

Does history have it backward? It was the American Association that was known as "the Beer and Whiskey League" down to its demise in 1891; so why does this official scorecard (in noble colors) from the sober, earnest National League, speak over and over to a fan's thirst?

Boston would give Bunker Hill Monument, New York the Statue of Liberty, and Philadelphia the old Liberty Bell to be in Baltimore's shoes just now.

Baltimore Herald, SEPTEMBER 26, 1894, THE DAY AFTER BALTIMORE CLINCHED ITS FIRST PENNANT

CHAPTER FIVE

THREE PENNANTS IN A ROW

For some while afterward, the final years of the 19th century were spoken of as the Gay Nineties. By now, however, the phrase has little meaning—songs? night life?—and another term, suggesting decadence, coexists: *fin-de-siècle*. The decade's shadows included a long, harsh economic depression, a spirit (following war with Spain) of overseas land-grabbing, and at home a surge of robber-baron exploitation. Jim Crow thrived. In baseball, monopoly thrived: "the big league." For a while, the magnates of the 1890s fancied themselves a baseball trust, like the steel or oil trusts; smoothly they imposed a salary cap. (And for the ill or injured player, no pay at all.) Once the Panic of 1893 had subsided and the economy improved, nothing obstructed the National League in its 12-team grandeur, nothing except monotony. Three cities won all the pennants; in nine other cities, the fans came, watched, yawned, left, and didn't come back.

This is not to suggest that the game stagnated. In 1892, the NL owners reduced squads to 15 men, then 13, and salaries were cut 30 to 40 percent in midseason, ignoring the players' contracts—much is possible in a collusive monopoly. The squads were later enlarged but, the historian Harold Seymour notes, "$2,400 was the unofficial [salary] limit through the 1890s"—below the level, he adds, reached by the better players of the 1880s.

Also in 1892 the league introduced a split season. The two halves did produce different winners, but the postseason series between them proved a box-office flop, and the scheme lapsed. In 1893, to upgrade the hitting, the distance between pitcher and batter, then nominally 50 feet, was lengthened to 60½ (the pitcher had been required to plant one foot against the back line of a 4-by-5½-foot box until ball release, making the true distance about 55½ feet). Batters and catchers, given more time to track the pitch, rejoiced. This was the final adjustment in the diamond's dimensions, and it is why historians tend to mark 1893 as the start of the modern age in baseball.

Also, the (automatic out) infield-fly rule was adopted. And from 1894 through 1897, there was a best-four-of-seven series between first- and second-place teams, for a $600 trophy called the Temple Cup; but this artificial conflict was uneven, a pennant-winner having no primacy to gain, the runner-up no respect to lose. So the league returned the cup to its donor, a Pittsburgh businessman (and instead lengthened its pennant season from 132 to 154 games, without pay increase). Finally, as the 1890s wore on, the NL opened its door to syndicates, a corporate device whereby an owner could simultaneously hold shares in a second city's team. Trades between the two teams could become shams, as an interlocking management deployed star players from the weaker to the stronger of its two markets.

To much of this, Bostonians and Baltimoreans were oblivious. For them, the 1890s were magnificent up to a point. The first three years and again in 1897 and 1898, Boston (the Beaneaters by then, instead of Red Stockings) added to its list of pennants. In Baltimore, the middle-years winner, joy rose higher still. Where Baltimore's 1870s National Association team had started strong but fizzled, where its 1880s team had been the only founding member of the American Association never to win a pennant, now for the first time its champion Orioles seized the throne and sat down, the undisputed monarchs of baseball creation. In 1894, 1895, and 1896, Baltimore won and won and won.

The 12-team NL story begins in 1892, as Baltimore, one of 4 newcomers, felt its way around in the league it had been accustomed to detest. By this time, *Orioles*, as a team name was in universal use. And 15 was the standard quotient of uniformed players. In addition to 8 position regulars, a major league team usually had 5 pitchers, an exchange ('change) catcher for use in doubleheaders, and a utility man. Trades, or discharges and callups, could be made throughout the season. The bench on which the middle row sits in the photo below is the literal bench on which nonparticipating players sat during games, in that pre-dugout era. The player bench was movable. Even so, the proximity of bench to stands, of heroes to admirers, arrests a modern eye; but that was also the pre-autograph era. Double-decked Union Park appears to have been Baltimore baseball's introduction to lettered rows and numbered seats, not just sit wherever you please or there's space.

The Von der Horsts could have imposed a different bird—as brewers, their brand name, after all, was Eagle. Enough, however, that fans bought their beer: when not at Union Park, then downtown at the saloon at 9 South Street run by a relative of the brewery head, J. Herman Von der Horst. It adjoined the Orioles' headquarters (the business office and the downtown ticket window for grandstand seats), which was inside the *Baltimore American* building. The *Ameri-*

1892's pre-Hanlon Orioles: *top row, from left:* Curt Welch, of (a famous player, but past his prime); John Pickett, 2b; Bill Johnson, of; John McGraw, 2b; Billy Shindle, ss; Pete Gilbert, 3b; *middle row:* Lew Whistler, 1b; John (Egyptian) Healy, p; George Washington Cobb, p; John J. Waltz, mgr; Harry Von der Horst, owner; George E. M. Van Haltren, of; John McMahon, p; Charley Buffington, p; *bottom row:* Harry Stovey, of; Wilbert Robin-son, c; Les German, p.

Edward H. Hanlon

Union Park. In use for major league games for only nine years, yet so heroic were the exploits there by the Orioles and also some of their foes that the name Union Park is an enduring echo in books on old-time baseball.

Built of beams and boards, Baltimore's first double-decker grandstand wasn't expected to last indefinitely. Note the two press boxes, *center*, separating Baltimore sportswriters from out-of-towners.

can and the *Sun*, bitter morning-paper rivals, were both on the south side of East Baltimore Street, two sizable corner buildings separated from each other by South Street. In news columns the *Sun* omitted— and the *American* proclaimed—the location of Baltimore Baseball & Exhibition Co. headquarters.

The new manager, George Van Haltren, quickly proved himself better as player (and then was traded). The Von der Horsts installed a brewery official pro tem and launched a talent search. In June, at the Tremont Hotel in Chicago, it ended in the scratching of a pen. The signature on their contract read, Edward H. Hanlon.

The new man was originally from small-town Connecticut. A 34-year-old centerfielder, a .260 batter but a great ballhawk, the captain of 1887's world champion Detroit Wolverines, he had been playing manager in Pittsburgh for its NL team, its PL, and its NL again. But Pittsburgh had done badly, and a knee injury had benched Hanlon for good. Down on his luck, Ned Hanlon was ready for a fresh start, even

with a last-place team. The terms he struck included total field responsibility plus stock and, in 1893, the club presidency. He moved his growing family into the large corner house at 2403 North Calvert, a block from work.

Victorious in but one of their first 15 games, the new NL Orioles had far to go. By the end of the split schedule's first half, they were last. At season's end, they were still last, 48-105; but in the second-half standings, with Hanlon in charge, Baltimore rose to 10th. A California pitcher named George Cobb, of whom little is known—1892 was his only season in the majors—won 10 games and (still a Baltimore record) lost 37. Even so, there was a feat to boast about: on a spring day in 1892, at still-new Union Park, during a 25-4 conquest of St. Louis, Wilbert Robinson went seven for seven (a double and six singles), a majors record not even tied until 1979.

As 1893 began, Baltimore fans had something else to talk about— Hanlon's taking his Orioles late in March to Georgia for Baltimore's

Willie Keeler

Dan Brouthers

first warm-weather spring training. The added momentum told: in 1893, with the NL back down to a 128-game schedule, the Orioles' 60-70 performance was good for eighth place. And personnel changes were going on.

While in Pittsburgh, Hanlon had been impressed by his leftfielder, Joseph J. Kelley, young, handsome, muscular, from Massachusetts; Hanlon sent them Van Haltren in exchange for Joe. From St. Louis, in '93, Hanlon extracted centerfielder Walter Scott Brodie, of Roanoke, Virginia. Named for the famous Scottish novelist and nicknamed, of course, Sir Walter, Brodie was more often called Steve, after the New York Brodie who was alleged to have leaped off Brooklyn Bridge and lived. Completing his 1894 outfield, Hanlon obtained from Brooklyn 22-year-old William H. Keeler (originally O'Kelleher; in his teens, a scorekeeper shortened it, and Willie wasn't one to argue). Both the Giants (his first team) and the Bridegrooms felt that a 140-pound fellow standing 5 feet 4½ inches, who in 1893 had broken an ankle, would never make the grade.

Hanlon's infield was equally new: at third, John J. McGraw, 21, promoted from utility man; at short, obtained from Louisville, Hugh A. Jennings, a Pennsylvania coalminer's son; at second, a Chicagoan, Henry P. Reitz, from the Pacific Coast League; and at first base, Hanlon's old Detroit teammate, the redoubtable (though, in 1894, 36 years old) Dennis J. Brouthers, pronounced "Broŏthers," the same Big Dan who had played for Baltimore in 1880. For catcher, Hanlon inherited Wilbert Robinson (and added William J. Clarke, of New York, also brought up from high-minors California); for pitchers, besides young William V. Hawke, he had the mainstay, John J. McMahon (at first nicknamed Matches, later Sadie). In '93, Hanlon brought in an old-timer, Anthony J. Mullane, who could not just bat but throw either-handed; Tony was as much of a celebrity as Dan Brouthers. Sports writers spoke of the new manager as Foxy Ned.

Hanlon bought or traded for at least as many additional players, veterans and rookies. The important thing was, he could sense which ones had promise. The ones that didn't fit, the ones whose direction was down, he had the fortitude to get rid of. The risk with Brouthers (6 feet 2 inches, 205 pounds—impressive then) was justified; with

Mullane, age 35, born in Ireland and known to his fans as the Count, the risk was not. Elsewhere Mullane had won more than 260 games, but in 1894 he proved to be worn out and was let go. In contrast, Dick (sometimes Bill) Hawke, from Wilmington, Delaware, pitched the Orioles to a 5–0, away game win over Washington in August 1893 that stands out in the record books: the NL's first no-hitter at the new, longer pitching distance. Not until 1897 did anyone (Cy Young, then with Cleveland) match it. Hawke's no-hitter also proved to be the entire Oriole pitching staff's only shutout all year. At Union Park other hurlers came, others went. Pitching remained the single area in which Hanlon, short on luck or on judgment, never quite filled out his roster with what it needed for full invincibility.

Then came 1894. A sweet year—nay, as it turned out, an epochal year—in Baltimore history. Down south, that spring, the Orioles beat everyone in sight. On Opening Day, 15,000 fans streamed into a park seating 9,000. The foe was New York—it had not gone south, but its lineup included Monte Ward, manager and second baseman, famous as the Players' League prime mover; a young Indiana farmer and

The 1894 champions, Baltimore's first ever. When a professional studio scheduled this photo shoot, word got out and almost as many civilians as Orioles crowded onto the set. The ensuing picture then had an adventurous existence, as somebody set about painting out the non-Orioles. With no civilians showing, or three, is often seen. This version—all 13 nonplayers basking in the glow—is rare.

Celluloid lapel badges (in color) are
slightly smaller than shown here.

John McGraw (with mustache) and
Joe Kelley. In the spring of '96,
McGraw caught typhoid fever and
almost died. He grew the mustache
during convalescence, shaving it off
when finally able to rejoin the
team.

pitcher, Amos Rusie, who threw cannonballs—and in center field the
spurned Van Haltren. Seated in the out-of-town press box were 13
New York reporters, who telegraphed, presently, the details of Baltimore's 8-3 victory. Next, their news was of a home-team series sweep.

Then Boston arrived, proposing to walk off with a fourth straight
championship. Its famous pitcher—in an average year, he won 33
games—was Charles A. (Kid) Nichols. (In those days, the nickname
"Kid" usually denoted not a youth but a kidder.) The home team
treated Nichols to the biggest ninth-inning outburst in major league
history. Batting first (the custom then) and trailing 3-1, the Orioles
scored 14 more runs.

Baltimore was developing that unplannable asset, team spirit. The
players got on with one another. A *New York Clipper* story found by
the writer Burt Solomon followed the Orioles to their billet, the
Oxford House, on Greenmount Avenue a block or so north of the

ballpark. Ten Orioles put up there, readers learned, in separate rooms. On its "spacious lawn . . . every morning the players exercise and breathe the pure air of Waverly. . . . On the porch at night, the players may be heard singing favorite songs, with Mullane's profundo basso in the lead, while [Bert] Inks plays a piano accompaniment in the sitting room." On the back porch was a hammock; who grabbed it, morning after morning, to read the baseball news in comfort? That small, 21-year-old human firecracker, McGraw.

Baltimore did lose games soon enough, but contrary to all predictions it stayed among the three leaders. ("Setting the league on fire" would be an inadvisable metaphor, that year when the all-wood grandstands burned in Boston and then Philadelphia, each time with the Orioles present.) McMahon, 25-8; Hawke, 16-9; and an Indiana left-hander, Bert Inks, 9-4 (originally Inkstein; from Notre Dame, he was one of the majors' first collegians), kept the team in contention.

Wilbert Robinson (with decker, the old-time word for mitt) and Henny Reitz. Shirt collars are a carryover from the 1860s, when ballplayers posing for a studio camera sometimes put on a necktie. As for shoes, heels are now out and metal cleats in. Why (see pp. 68 and 70) do major league baseball uniforms in the 1890s still come with a shirt pocket?

Left: Steve Brodie (after Hanlon traded him away, the Orioles ceased winning pennants) and *right:* Hugh Jennings (Oriole fielding is seldom spoken of nowadays, but Hughey was that infield's best glove man).

But they needed help, especially after a sore arm sidelined McMahon. Hanlon in midseason substituted three other established starting pitchers, Charles (Duke) Esper, a left-hander from South Jersey, who went 10-2; George E. Hemming, from Ohio, 4-0; and William (Kid) Gleason, 15-5. Gleason, also from South Jersey, was small, skilled, and adaptable. His arm weakening after 1894, he then had an even longer, five-city tour as infielder (his career culminated, unhappily, as the manager of Chicago's 1919 Black Sox). These newcomers did what was asked of them—so much so that the 1894 Orioles are still the only pennant-winner to have begun and ended the year with wholly different sets of starting pitchers. For a contrary quirk: throughout Baltimore's 129 games, it fielded the same, unchanged outfield of (left to right) Kelley, Brodie, and Keeler.

It was an astonishing season, 1894. The new, longer distance discombobulated the pitchers. A Boston outfielder batted .440; Philadelphia's outfield averaged .401; Baltimore's whole team averaged

.343. In those 129 games, Willie Keeler, batting second, hit safely 219 times and, so fast was he afoot, 55 of his hits went for extra bases. He scored 165 runs; so did the Adonis Joe Kelley, while posting a new record for on-base percentage, .502. Henny Reitz (pronounced "Reetz") hit 31 triples, a feat surpassed only once since. Reitz did it playing in only 108 games. One day against Cleveland, he and his mates smote 9 triples; their 1894 season total of 151 was the record, is the record, will go on being the major league record. Big Dan Brouthers, his batting average above .300 for the 14th straight year (ultimately, his slugging average was the 19th century's highest), drove in 123 runs. John McGraw, the leadoff man, worked the pitchers for 91 walks; he worked the catchers for 78 stolen bases. Red-headed Hughey Jennings became adept at the hit-by-pitch method of getting on base (as many as three times in one game and 286 times in his big league career, which is still the record; he wore padding). Pitchers excepted, the lowest number of runs driven in, up and down Baltimore's batting order, was 92. In 129 games, Baltimore batters (pitchers included) struck out only 200 times, the league's fewest. They made 1,171 runs (in the 20th century, no set of major league Orioles has scored as many as 900 runs). Hanlon's team also made the NL's fewest errors.

Along with the rat-a-tat-tat of Baltimore's base hits went the cagey teamwork of sacrifices, single and double base-stealing, the hit-and-run, cutoff plays (when a hit sends a base-runner home, the infielder stops the throw from the outfield and fires it to second to catch the advancing batter), and the now seldom-credited Baltimore Chop (the hit that slants down onto fair ground near home plate, then bounces so high that by the time the ball comes down again, the batter is crossing first). "Inside Baseball," all this has been called; but it was also a big-inning strategy, profiting from pitcher fatigue in that era of small staffs and complete, no relief pitcher games. The 1890s style, it should be evident, differed from the deadball, run-at-a-time baseball of 1900–1920.

In July, Baltimore slumped, falling five games back. But these Orioles had spirit. In a game in Pittsburgh, they came roaring back to win from nine runs behind. As Boston slipped, Baltimore and New York

Tydings, the ballpark sandwich man. The 1894 caricature book, *Pennant Souvenir*, gave a page to every Oriole—and one to Tydings. H. L. Mencken recalled him later in the Sun: "A big fellow, with a fine baritone voice. He would travel about the bleachers singing, 'Are you hon-gree-ee?' and sell hundreds of the most vile sandwiches at every game."

The Temple Cup is now on display at the National Baseball Hall of Fame and Museum in Cooperstown, N.Y. *Below:* the often reprinted Henry Sandham print, *Playing for the Temple Cup at the Polo Grounds, 1894.*

closed out their schedules with long western tours. The Giants' manager, Monte Ward, relied on his Hoosier Thunderbolts, Amos Rusie (36-13) and Jouett Meekin (33-9). In reply, the Orioles simply won 18 straight and 28 of their final 31 games. Day after day, Baltimoreans crowded into Ford's Opera House to follow the telegraphed play-by-play. The clincher, 14-9, came in Cleveland with a week to go. That gave the home folks time to plan a proper reception.

Eastward, via the Baltimore & Ohio, the train paused at every population center from Grafton, West Virginia, on for local celebrations. In Washington, an advance committee climbed aboard with tuxedos for the players to wear. In fine weather, an immense throng hailed the heroes on their arrival at Camden Station. Dismounting, the champion Orioles climbed into open carriages for a parade east to City Hall and then north to the Fifth Regiment Armory, a procession estimated by the *Sun* to be nearly five miles long. One highlight: the actual 1894 pennant, red, white, and blue and 25 feet long by 5 feet high, designed and stitched in haste and cut in the form of a burgee (two tails at the whip end), was floating from a pole atop the *Baltimore American* building. Following the armory reception, there was a banquet at the new Rennert Hotel, at Saratoga and Liberty Streets. "Members of the Oriole team!" cried their captain, Wilbert Robin-

son. "Glasses up—and glasses down!" Abstain, the idea was, and be in fit condition for postseason play. In political jamborees, there are always nonparticipants—the losers. That wonderful night, all Baltimore was a winner. To many, it was the hottest time ever in the old hometown.

Two days later, the Temple Cup series began at Union Park amid sharp dissent as to how the receipts should be split. Another question: had Baltimore's insistence on lionizing the players left them tired and unready? New York (Rusie and Meekin) took the first two games, and then at the Polo Grounds, New York (Rusie and Meekin) swept the series. Baltimore shrugged it off. The scores, if you want them: 4-1, 9-6, 4-1, 16-3.

The 1894 playoffs were long-lived, however, because a New York publisher had commissioned the noted 52-year-old Canadian painter-illustrator Henry Sandham to portray the action. As a print, Sandham's "Playing for the Temple Cup at the Polo Grounds" became one of the 19th century's outstanding examples of sport in art. The white knight Giants are at bat; the unlabeled Orioles, their dark road uniforms casting them negatively, are in the field. So that all nine will show within his frame, Sandham pulls the rightfielder into the infield.

A pause, along the way: on July 4, 1894, John H. Von der Horst, age 69, died of cancer at his home on 1204 North Caroline Street, leaving two sons, Henry R. (Harry) and John H. Jr., and a daughter. His obituary rated page one, this German-born, well-to-do brewer who had undertaken to give Baltimore membership in the American Association. Von der Horst did not live to see and enjoy the finally triumphant Orioles; rather, in old age he had soured on baseball. The historian Burt Solomon notes that Von der Horst's ballclub agent, son Harry, as Oriole secretary-treasurer, was disbursing so many dollars in futile pennant chases that ultimately father went to court seeking to restrain son.

For 1895, the champions added two young men from the minors. Brouthers, starting his 17th season, could still hit, but in the field his moves were slow and few. Hanlon brought in George Carey, called

The *Sporting News*, a national weekly published in St. Louis, hails the Baltimores (and shows what a National League pennant looked like, then). *From left:* Captain Wilbert Robinson, c; Hugh Jennings, ss; John McGraw, 3b; Joe Kelley, lf; Willie Keeler, rf; Bill Clarke, c; Sadie McMahon, p; Henry Reitz, 2b; Duke Esper, p.

Bill Hoffer on the pitching slab (no mound, then) at Union Park.

Scoops—good glove, lackluster bat. The big addition was an inconspicuous Iowan with a tricky curveball, William L. Hoffer. Before long, his arm wore out, but from 1895 through 1897, Wizard Hoffer gave the Orioles 300-plus innings a year and 78 victories against 24 defeats. For once, Hanlon had a pitcher.

On Opening Day, against Philadelphia, the crowd went home disappointed. By June, the Orioles were only in third place. A sick list formed: Reitz (broken collarbone), McGraw (malaria), Robinson (split finger). Worse, new rivals were gaining momentum: first Pittsburgh, then the Cleveland Spiders. Formidable was the word for Cleveland's pitching: big Denton True (Cy, as in cyclone) Young, having the finest season of his incomparable career (36-10), and small George Cuppy (born Koppe, 26-14). No less menacing were such Spider batters as leftfielder Jesse Burkett (.409). A local connection: their second baseman, Clarence Algernon (Cupid, also Paca) Childs, was from Calvert County, Maryland.

The Giants, meanwhile, nose-dived: a new and cantankerous owner had wrecked morale. For Baltimore, George Hemming won 20 games and Sadie McMahon, recovered, won 10 vital games. As summer wore on, the Orioles took command once more; they won 41 of their final 51 games. The season's finale and planned climax was an Oriole-Giant series in New York; wiping out their dispirited foe, the Orioles gained vengeance and a second pennant.

This time, the Temple Cup series opened in Cleveland. Coming east afterward, although down three games to none, the Orioles had been giving it their best; and Baltimore's fans showed their faith in a gesture apparently without historical equal: in early October, they more or less filled 50-plus vehicles in a downtown streetcar parade.

Baltimore vs. Brooklyn at Eastern Park, Brooklyn in 1895. Batteries: Hoffer and Robinson; Stein and Grim. Orioles 11 runs, 19 hits, 1 error; Brooklyn 0 runs, 5 hits, 2 errors. The symbols used by this thorough scorer differ materially from today's. Note the *M* (middlefielder). *C* for centerfielder is unavailable—it means catcher.

Above: Jack Doyle; *right:* Bill Clarke. When not in that day's starting lineup, Clarke was often a base coach; and, doubling as cheerleader, would stir up the spectators.

Regardless, even at home the Orioles won but once. The winning pitcher, three times: Cy Young. For the record: 5-4, 5-2, 7-1, 0-5, 5-2; McMahon and Hoffer each lost two; the Oriole winner, Esper.

Starting 1896, the Baltimore Orioles had respect and deference. The team radiated energy: its stolen-base total, 441, was far beyond any other team's that year (stolen-base scoring requirements differed slightly then). Whether at home or on the road—the team traveled by chartered Pullman—the fans expected Baltimore to win. The Orioles, too, felt that way. And for once, the opposition disputed them less fiercely. Amos Rusie, New York City's first athlete-hero, sat out the year, having been offered an insulting contract. The season-series sweep was a rarity, then; Baltimore took all 12 games with Philadelphia. Did it portend ill that Cleveland won its season series against Baltimore? No matter: the Orioles, winning 90 games for the first time and losing but 39, clinched this pennant at home. At season's end, Baltimore was nine and a half games in front, compared to three games in both 1894 and 1895. Save for a relaxed finish, the team would have had a .700 season.

A factor in the 1896 onrush was Trader Hanlon's latest response to the first-base problem. In return for Kid Gleason, reduced by now to utility infielder, New York sent him Jack Doyle, its Ireland-born playing manager. Other clubs howled in protest, especially as Doyle then gave Baltimore two of his best years. Another factor was Erasmus Arlington Pond, pitcher (16-8). At the University of Vermont, Arlie Pond had beaten Harvard; now, a wintertime medical school student, he was of course Doc Pond. Meanwhile, Hughey Jennings had blossomed as a batter (.401, 209 hits). This is not to overlook Wilbert Robinson, portly and 34, yet .354 with bat in hand. Finally, Willie Keeler was turning into a legend. He could be depended on for 200-plus hits: his lowest total, in five years as an Oriole, was 210 (Keeler's simple formula, "Hit 'em where they ain't," was put on record by a

Batteries for today's game: Hoffer and Robinson, Cuppy and Zimmer. And Baltimore beats Cleveland, 6-2, each pitcher going the route. As for the beer ads, with their four-digit phone numbers, two national firms already dispute Baltimore's claims to brewing excellence.

The Big Four, as an expression, may have been borrowed from the financial pages and railroad writers. Other Orioles don't seem to have minded that the power center wasn't called a Big Five (Robinson) or Big Six (Brodie). The elegant attire of Keeler, Kelley, McGraw, and Jennings was beyond the means of an average fan.

sports writer in post-Baltimore years). In those 128-game seasons, Keeler averaged more than 50 stolen bases. He averaged three homers a year (McGraw, one). A downtown tailor named John M. Keeler took out big ads in the home-game programs, hoping fans would think he was related.

The Temple Cup? No letdown this time. The Orioles crushed the Spiders in four straight: 7-1, 7-2, 6-2, and 5-0. Twice, Bill Hoffer outpitched Cy Young; twice, Joe Corbett (a California newcomer and younger brother of the former heavyweight champion Jim Corbett) won also. Afterward, Willie Keeler reported, the Orioles discovered the cup held seven quarts; to make sure, they repeated the test, in all filling it with champagne three times. The following week, the cup went on display in a jeweler's window back home, in the jewelry-store district in the first two blocks of East Baltimore Street.

After the celebrating subsided, the Big Four plus Arlie Pond, bachelors all, went down to the harbor and embarked for Europe. (McGraw had not played until August that year, after nearly dying from typhoid fever; Jim Donely, ultimately an 11-team man, filled in capably. McGraw's recovery was slow but full.) Ordinary sightseers, these, but interested in foreign athletics as well as the standard monuments and entertainment. In succession, they had a look at Liverpool, London, Brussels, Paris, London again, Dublin, and the Irish countryside. Returning in December, four Orioles posed for a remarkable studio photo—baseball players attired in British formal wear, complete to top hats and at least one furled umbrella. Willie Keeler kept a diary (discovered by the modern historian Burt Solomon), the entries generally brief and matter-of-fact. (But in Dublin, Keeler wrote, "we had more fun in an hour today than we had in a week in Paris.")

That small book, the scrapbook of telegrams and newspaper clippings kept by Mrs. Wilbert Robinson, a scrapbook kept by Mrs. Walter Brodie, and the McGraw-Jennings material at St. Bonaventure University in New York state appear to be about all that remain by way of personal documents from the Orioles of the Golden Age. One treasure, coming to light a century afterward, is the so-called Popplein Hoard, presented to the Babe Ruth museum by Helen Hall. A Baltimore paint salesman and a relative of the Poppleins prominent in 1860s amateur baseball, George A. Popplein saved lithographed program-scorecards of one or more home games from 1894 through 1904. For their respective years, several seem to be unique surviving examples.

Manufactured keepsakes were, however, a different matter. Baltimore's pride in its baseball team is manifest in the variety of souvenir material put on sale, when collectors were still ingenues. Quality was high in these pamphlets, badges, ribbons, and photos, which command giddy prices in modern auctions. In his *Baseball: The Early Years*, the historian Harold Seymour put it pragmatically: "Baltimore businessmen acknowledged that nothing had ever advertised the city as much as its ball club."

Over the generations, assessments of and salutes to the Orioles of the mid-1890s have been even more expansive. The Cooperstown historian Lee Allen properly hails their zest: for breakfast, they favored "gunpowder and warm blood"; then at lunch, "having feasted on scrap iron," the Orioles "nailed the umpires to trees." They were "a team whose stars peaked together, whose best years came at the same time," Robert W. Creamer points out in *The Ultimate Baseball Book*; this was "the greatest team of all time until the 1927 Yankees came along." The Old Orioles, in Creamer's apt summary, "were not a dynasty at all but a nova, a sudden manifestation in the baseball skies that flared brilliantly," but then disappeared.

As for the actual 1894–96 Orioles, when in 1954 Baltimore's long night ended, a fair number of them were still alive to rejoice at the news. John J. McMahon, who in his seven Oriole years had won 130 games and lost 92, died shortly before Opening Day that year. John J. Doyle, long a major league scout, died on the last day of 1958. The battery-mates Bill Hoffer and Bill Clarke died within eight days of each other in July 1959; aged 88 and 89, they were the last of the Old Orioles.

At least three of the out-of-towners married Baltimore girls. The first was Clarke. After the wedding, he moved into the home of his wife, the former Isabelle T. Thomas, at 120 West 22d Street. His brother J. Stanton Clarke operated a saloon and bowling alleys at 317

John J. McMahon (*left*) and Walter S. Brodie, pitcher and centerfielder, were alike in that neither was ever addressed by his given name. Holler "Sadie!" and "Steve!" and they'd look up.

Bill Hoffer was born in Cedar Rapids, Iowa, grew up there, lived and died there. In 1895, his freshman year as an Oriole, at 24 years old Hoffer was 31w-6l, with 32 complete games. Since then, no one pitching for the major league Orioles has won as many as 30 games.

ERA for the 7 seasons of his majors career was 3.75. Dropped by Hanlon when his arm weakened, Hoffer nonetheless was with Cleveland in 1901. He was a starting pitcher in the first of all American League games.

On a team of roughnecks, Hoffer (5 feet 9, 155 pounds) was modest and quiet. Afterward, he was for years a motorman on an Iowa interurban transit line. Unlike most old-time players, he preserved his baseball souvenirs.

West Fayette Street, across from Ford's Opera House. Clarke was one of many whose last major league service was with the New York Giants, hired by that sentimentalist, John McGraw. Then for decades Clarke coached the baseball team at Princeton University (Jack Dunn III was one of his players). In retirement, the Clarkes (married 64 years) operated an antiques store across Nassau Street from the campus. As for McGraw, he was married twice, each time to a young Baltimore woman. Minnie Doyle McGraw died in 1899; Blanche Sindall McGraw, by then a New Yorker, was formally honored by the new AL Orioles and survived until 1962.

The Orioles brought Clarke to Baltimore for 1954's grand Opening Day. Also present were Jack Doyle, from Holyoke, Massachusetts, and Charlie Harris, from Gainesville, Florida (who during the 1899 season had filled in at third for the injured McGraw).

The senior member of these elderly warriors was Francis Isaiah Foreman, pitcher and Baltimore native, who lived on, at 218 Union Avenue in Hampden, through the 1957 season; he attained age 94. A 6-foot left-hander, Frank Foreman pitched for Baltimore in three different leagues (AA, NL, and AL). He broke in with Chicago, in the Union Association. He won 23 games for Billy Barnie in 1889, and he was 12 and 6 with the original 1901 American League Orioles. Foreman had a way of grimacing; disconcerted batters nicknamed him Monkey. H. L. Mencken, however, in his classic *Happy Days*, recalled Frank Foreman's "immortal name" for "incomparable virtuosity." Frank Foreman had "the widest and wickedest curves I've ever seen."

Ralph D. Miller rates mention, too. From Cincinnati and a pitcher, Miller had a two-year stay in the majors: with Brooklyn in 1898, then (for five games) with the 1899 Orioles. What finally lifted Miller out of obscurity was his feat of becoming, a few months before his death in 1973, Organized Baseball's first centenarian. Another centenarian was Riley M. Davis, who reached 100 in 1994. During World War I, Davis had been a pitcher for the Baltimore Black Sox.

The first two men got on and then the next batter just stood there, arms folded, bat against his chest. Each pitch I threw, he spit at it. That rattled me, all right. It was in Pittsburgh — my first road game as one of the Orioles. Yeah, I walked him.

BILL HOFFER, NED HANLON'S ONLY 30-GAME WINNER,
IN 1957 INTERVIEW

CHAPTER SIX

HEROES OF LEGEND

Across the years, when people spoke of the Old Orioles, what they had in mind was peerless play by a band of brothers—or gang of toughs. Much of this was summed up in the most famous player, John J. McGraw. Growing up poor in upstate New York, he also grew up small and determined and agile. Manager Billy Barnie brought him into the majors in 1891, with the American Association Orioles. McGraw, standing 5 feet 7 inches and weighing 121 pounds, was 18 —and a shortstop.

Ned Hanlon, the new manager of the new National League Orioles, cleared house of all but three players: the battery of McMahon and Robinson, and the aggressive youngster whom he had moved to third base—and leadoff batter. Mac (sometimes Little Mac) stayed there one semisolid decade. Now ill, now injured, he missed time in five scattered years. But once in the day's lineup, he got on base, and then he kept on going until he had scored. A sample 1899 box score read: McGraw, 3b AB 1 R 4 H 0. By 1902, he and Wilbert Robinson had set a length-of-stay record, and, Ned Hanlon at that point being identified with Brooklyn, John McGraw was manager and part-owner of the Orioles and a Baltimore personage.

Early in 1897, he married a Baltimorean, Minnie R. Doyle. The wedding, at St. Vincent's Church on North Front Street, was a big

Today, the site of the Diamond Cafe is a large flat parking lot. But a century ago, the 500 block of North Howard Street was an after-hours bright lights belt. On the west side of Howard were the Academy of Music and the Auditorium theaters; around the corner on West Franklin was the Maryland Theater.

Many an old picture postcard shows that west side; never, the east. For 50 years or more baseball collectors have been seeking a photo of the Diamond Cafe, exterior or interior, in vain.

local event; groom and bride then moved in with her father, at 1815 Guilford Avenue. Shortly afterward, McGraw went into business with Wilbert Robinson, buying and renovating a saloon at 519 North Howard Street, across from the Academy of Music. Renamed the Diamond Cafe, it was an instant success—year-round, *the* hangout for players and fans. It had bowling alleys in the back; duckpins, that Baltimore variation on tenpins, is thought to have originated there. Later, the Robinsons and the McGraws settled into expensive, adjoining nine-room houses at 2738 and 2740 St. Paul Street. Within two years the Diamond, McGraw said aloud, earned him more income than all his years of ballplaying had done.

McGraw didn't laugh much or seek friends. In his "harsh view of the baseball field," the historian Benton Stark comments, it was "a jungle where survival depended upon a lethally aggressive approach at all times." "The main idea," McGraw said, "is to win." (His lifetime batting average was .333; in his 11 Baltimore years, he scored more than a thousand runs; his lifetime on-base percentage, .466, is baseball's third highest, behind Ted Williams's and Babe Ruth's.) The taunt, "Hey, Muggsy!" from the enemy bench as McGraw stood there guarding third, would seldom break his concentration. After the pitch, McGraw would respond in coarser epithets; and his turn came when the taunter, as base-runner, next arrived at third base. (Growing sentimental later in life, McGraw put several Old Orioles on his NL New York payroll.)

The attitude had its reverse image: McGraw and others needled the fellow-Oriole whose effort that day struck them as having been insufficient. Protective alliances seem to have been present as well: McGraw's buddy was Jennings; make light of Keeler and you had to answer, supposedly, to Kelley. Another aspect of Kelley, aware of his good looks and his young women admirers, came out during a game in Cincinnati. An object was seen falling on the grass: it was the small mirror normally out of sight inside Joe's cap. Teammates, however, did not join in on the derision. The most famous internal fight broke out one day in 1897, in the team clubhouse, when McGraw slanged Keeler for having missed a game or two and Keeler charged his tormentor, fists swinging. Wilbert Robinson broke it up.

Cheating and corner-cutting were, of course, at variance with the National League's stated intent to clean up the game. But other teams, particularly Cleveland, had a corresponding notoriety. No one appears to have asked individual umpires to rate the rowdies. Honus Wagner, later with Pittsburgh but in 1897 a Louisville rookie, offered a famous description of his first game against the Orioles: "On my first time up, I got a single. The next time, I might have had a triple but Jack Doyle gave me the hip at first, Hughey Jennings chased me wide around second, and John McGraw blocked me off at third, then jammed the ball into my belly, knocking the wind out of me." In another version, "when I finally limped into third John McGraw was waiting for me with a shotgun." (Speaking of Louisville, it was the opposing team in September 1896 when, to make up for rainouts, a doubleheader was scheduled at Union Park, and then a tripleheader. It seems to be the most concentrated winning any major league team has ever done—five Oriole victories in two days.)

There were too many individual heroics for valid comparison in that age of rudimentary statistics. On Labor Day 1894, for instance, in a jam-packed home doubleheader against Cleveland, Joe Kelley went nine for nine, a feat still unduplicated, and scored seven runs; in

Left: Joe Kelley (with his curly hair) came to Baltimore, married a Baltimorean, stayed the rest of his long and happy life. *Right:* Joe Corbett came to Baltimore, but then went back to California. Wherever he was, Corbett was overshadowed by his older brother Jim, the former heavyweight boxing champion. In retirement, Jim even played baseball, with barnstorming teams.

No smiles: these Orioles thought about the next pennant. *From left, top row:* Joe Quinn, utility; Sadie McMahon, p; George Hemming, p; Duke Esper, p; Frank Bowerman, c; Bill Clarke, c; Jimmy Donely, utility; *middle row:* Walter Brodie, cf; Bill Hoffer, p; Joe Kelley, rf; Edward H. Hanlon, manager; Wilbert Robinson, c; Hugh Jennings, ss; Henry Reitz, 2b; *bottom row:* Jack Doyle, 1b; John McGraw, 3b; Willie Keeler, rf; Doc Pond, p. *Inset:* Joe Corbett, p.

the afternoon game, he doubled four straight times—off Cy Young. Also, Kelley stayed healthy, averaging more than 500 at-bats as an Oriole. According to the historian Robert L. Tiemann, the highest-paid Oriole, at $2,700 a year, was Joe Kelley. Or think of Hugh Jennings (later in life the Detroit manager and a lawyer): in 1895, he rang up 425 putouts, still the maximum for a shortstop. Cal Ripken, playing modernity's 162 games, averaged about 300.

For several years, McGraw, Jennings, Pond, and others lived during the season in a boarding house at 12 West 24th Street (still standing, like the houses at 2738 and 2740 St. Paul Street, and Robinson's earlier house, at 2620 St. Paul). Two blocks away was the Woman's College of Baltimore (later, Goucher College). These young men parted their hair in the middle and (mostly) disdained the 1880s' mustaches; evenings, instead of heading for downtown and its bright

lights, the Orioles sat around at home analyzing the game just past, devising strategy for the one tomorrow, and testing one another on the rule book. Proper Baltimore may have found them uncouth; it overlooked their intelligence.

Who first thought up the hit-and-run play, which some writers have associated with Baltimore? (It calls for a runner on first base to take off for second with the pitch, in an apparent steal; this pulls the second baseman over to take the catcher's throw; instead, the batter drives the ball through the hole in the defense.) The honor has nine times nine claimants. Who invented the Baltimore Chop? For decades, it bore the name *Baltimore*, even though proof of its origin was lacking. When a later generation's broadcaster has occasionally failed to preface "chop" or "chopper" with "Baltimore," resentment has risen in the home-town fan.

Here are a few more occasional devices associated with baseball at Union Park in the good or bad old days:

- The diamond underwent "special" preparation. The Orioles were good bunters, so the grounds crew discreetly built up the foul lines to keep a batted ball from rolling foul. Another trick was soap chips in the dirt surrounding the pitcher's rubber to make the ball slippery. When rubbing up the ball, the Oriole pitcher would use the clean dirt in his hip pocket.
- Back when the same ball was in use inning after inning, its surface grew naturally scuffed, and a pitcher hardly needed to alter it further. Nonetheless, the impulse was common. One day in 1893, an umpire caught Henny Reitz grinding the ball into the ground before tossing it back to his pitcher; he was fined $5.
- An occasional tactic was throwing objects at the feet of a runner coming in to score. Players not in the lineup sat on team benches and were closer to the playing field then they are in today's dugouts. The Orioles were on the third base side. To make the runner stumble, tossing a bat or catcher's mask was pretty obvious, but also effective.
- Some of these ploys sound like sandlot stuff. But the volume of accusations suggests that base-runners in the majors also employed

Matchsafe given to John J. McMahon (Mac) by old hometown friends from Wilmington, Delaware.

The single greatest baseball photo surviving from nineteenth-century Baltimore [photographer unknown]. Union Park was on the south side of 25th Street, where Barclay now cuts through. The brick dwelling at rear was still there until the 1960s. Note elevated police hats and sign-painter artistry.

tricks. For example, while en route from first to third they were sometimes wont to shorten the trip by cutting inside an untagged second base. A lone umpire was on duty; he couldn't be looking all ways at once. (Seldom was the umpire's lot a happy one. In 1894 the *Baltimore American* reported, straight-faced, that "[John] Hartley escaped from the New York Asylum for the Blind, and became an umpire.")

• One form of intimidation has been repeatedly attested to. On the sidelines, waiting for the game to begin, the Orioles brought out hand files with which they noisily sharpened their metal shoe cleats.

• The 1899 sports writers had fun with this one. An Oriole base-runner is on third; Brickyard Kennedy is pitching for Brooklyn. "Let me see that ball, son," comes the order from Manager McGraw, who is coaching at third. So Kennedy lofts the ball in his direction; before it has stopped rolling, an Oriole run has scored.

Few of the exact spoken words of those times have survived. Sports reporters ordinarily interviewed only the team manager (and in print, his words were somehow models of correct speech); the press didn't go onto the field before games or into the clubhouse afterward. Newspaper accounts were fairly basic—the run-scoring plays, the errors, the umpiring—to satisfy readers for most of whom this detail was fresh information. The (or a) war cry of the 1890s Orioles on taking the field is recorded as, "Get at 'em!" Conversational humor, too, eludes the researcher. But gentlemanly Bill Clarke, the change (i.e., alternate) catcher, who lived longest of the Old Orioles, in a 1950s interview recalled the teasing when he essayed to grow a mustache. In a nice metaphor, teammates dubbed him "Nine on a Side."

Uniforms then were of baggy flannel, with wide leather belt, metal shoe-cleats, caps mostly of a solid color (the first bird appeared on them in 1897), and gloves, tiny by today's standards. The standard-issue garment for cold weather was a wool coat-sweater. Ordinarily, a player was issued two uniforms: a white one for home games, a gray one for the road. Usually the former bore a large *B*; the latter, the word *Baltimore*. (The 1901 Orioles are Baltimore's only team so far to sport instead an *O*, in large gothic type.) No names or numbers on the back: the fans were close enough to recognize faces. One year's hard use, and new uniforms were needed; changes in the *B*'s font and

FIELD DAY COMPETITION AT ORIOLE PARK

Union Park was rented out from time to time to local teams and for nonbaseball events. After every pennant, a let's-do-something-for-our-gallant-lads sentiment ran high among the rooters. In 1895 they held a trolley party, and in 1895 and 1896 a field day, with admission charge and proceeds to the players. This meant contests of strength and skill for engraved trophies in fungo hitting, distance throwing, running the bases, the 100-yard dash, pitching, and throwing to second base. The 1896 winners on an October day of damp cold and muddy footing and with not all the Orioles taking part, included:

Fungo distance: Jennings, 402 feet, 10 inches
Baseball throw: Kelley, 388 feet, 10 inches
Bases tour: Keeler, 15 seconds
100-yard dash: Kelley and Keeler (tie), 10¼ seconds (whether in full uniform is unclear)
Pitching (nine throws at a cloth, strike-zone target): Hemming, 9
Throwing to second (nine throws at a cloth target about 4 feet square): Robinson, 7

Cup awarded to Walter Brodie for "General Average" in Orioles' post-season Field Day competitions, 1895.

Above: New York photos, 1897. Keeler (*left*) demonstrates his placed hit technique: hands apart on short, light bat. Joe Quinn's stance is conventional (*right*).

Right: Tommy Murphy, grounds-keeper at Union Park (and later at American League Park), and friends. Their work clothes contrast with his Sunday best. There was a strain of the artist in Murphy who, after attending to the diamond's grass, planted flowers over by the stands.

positioning were frequent—today, they help in the dating of photos.

In the later 19th century, photography was a craze. When the Orioles were rounded up for the annual team picture by Busey or Betz or Bachrach (the forerunner of today's portraitists), it was indoors in uniform at the photographer's commercial studio. But in the mid-'90s, photographers such as Jeffres and Rogers lugged their big glass-plate cameras to 25th Street for outdoor shots—simulations of baseball action. And on the road? Some of the best surviving Old Oriole photos were made at New York's Polo Grounds.

The club's payroll included a groundskeeper, Thomas J. Murphy, and assistants. The base coaches were players not in that day's lineup. On many early teams, pitchers not starting were put to work as ticket-takers. Illness was more of a problem then—typhoid fever, in particular—than now. And injuries: as mentioned earlier, legend would have the Old Oriole catcher, whose finger had just been split by a foul ball, treat it by sticking it into the dirt. Hardly. When Henny Reitz suffered a broken collarbone, he was out for months. In 1897 Jennings was beaned by Amos Rusie; the story has it that four days went by before he came to. Nothing helped Sadie McMahon get over his sore right arm until he went to see the society doctor Cary B. Gamble, who applied a hot poker. McMahon pitched again.

Sports medicine isn't all that has improved over the years. A sports brief (in agate type) in the *New York Times* on March 4, 1893, noted: "Manager Hanlon has wagered $500 that his club will finish ahead of Cleveland this year." Ned Hanlon lived to see betting for (or against) one's own team become the strictest of taboos. He also watched Cleveland finish third in 1893 and Baltimore eighth.

Union Park had a clubhouse for the home team. It featured a large wooden tub for hot, dirty men to bathe and cool off in. Most of the visiting teams put up at the Eutaw House, on the northwest corner of Baltimore and Eutaw Streets; the athletes put on their uniforms at the hotel and were accordingly recognizable during the carriage ride to and from the ballpark. Sometimes they were missile targets. Not yet had the seekers of autographs and player regalia descended on baseball; when that did happen, one effect was to soften hostility toward the visiting team.

Photos of Union Park omit the home team's clubhouse (down the right field foul line, apparently), but *Pennant Souvenir*, the 1894 pamphlet, includes this careful sketch. As was customary then, no provision was made for the visiting team; the game over, still in uniform, the visitors went by hired carriage to their hotel downtown.

Many of the pins and badges of the pennant years, in celluloid and enamel, were durably made. Today, the sensible place for such an heirloom is not the coat lapel but the safe deposit box.

At the park, attendance varied greatly. With a small crowd, the raised voice would reach batter or pitcher, and conversely it was possible to make out some of the ballplayer chatter. A large turnout overflowed the double-deck stands and bare-boards bleachers; the solution was outfield standees behind ropes. On a long fly it mattered greatly whether the outfielder was friend or foe, as the spectators quickly dropped the rope and gave way (putout) or stood fast (ground-rule double). Despite the crudeness of the equipment, infield groundskeeping was meticulous (a Tommy Murphy specialty was foul-territory flower beds). The outfield had bumps and sometimes weeds (hence the legend of the extra baseball hidden in the outfield for emergency use). Baltimore was known around the league for its down-slope right field —the bed of an early stream, Brady's Run.

An 1893 *Sun* news note about the grounds reads very much like modern times. Manager Hanlon had just obtained two players from Brooklyn, young Willie Keeler and old but powerful Dan Brouthers, left-handers both. "Hanlon assured Brouthers that he was having the right field fence brought in about 30 feet." The fence consisted of narrow, upright boards, 8 or 10 feet high; used boards were common in the annual repairs. Painted advertising adorned the fence's interior face. One noncommercial sign went up. Against Brooklyn, on May 4, 1894, with Steve Brodie aboard, Brouthers hit one that cleared the fence in right center and landed well beyond—a 400-footer? No tape-measuring in those days, but afterward the rooters persuaded management to allow a painted cross on the fence and the one, all-explaining word "HERE" (a deed recalled in 1966, when the only home run to scale Memorial Stadium's rampart, hit by Frank Robinson, was commemorated with a "HERE" flag.) Be it remembered, nonetheless, that in the 19th century homers were less glorified.

An observation: the individual player is sometimes transmuted into legend (at Cooperstown, N.Y., and at Maryland's Babe Ruth and Cal Ripken museums). Once in a while, so are whole baseball teams. The latter happens less often, especially now that free agency and budget caps encourage the breaking up of lineups. But the *team* as a concept —stars and nonstars who fit together and stay together and outperform all sane expectation—is ever the beloved of sports-page columnists. They have taught the fans to venerate Murderers' Row (the Yankees in the mid-1920s), the Gas House Gang (the Cardinals of the early 1930s), Earl's Pearls (the Orioles of 1969–71), the Big Red Machine (Cincinnati in the mid-1970s). How many such one-for-all and all-for-one baseball teams were there in the 19th century? St. Louis had one, Boston had several, Chicago perhaps—but how often are their names invoked nowadays? The one team that out the windows of baseball heaven shines down on all below is the Old Orioles.

The pennant at the top of this free admission for "yourself and Lady" at 1897's home opener is printed in red, white, and blue. The batter forming part of the scrollwork *BBC* insignia lives on today. The designers of Oriole Park at Camden Yards, wanting to forge continuity with time gone by, reproduced him in iron at the end of every seat row. His name? As determined by a *Baltimore Evening Sun* contest, it's Abner Tripleday.

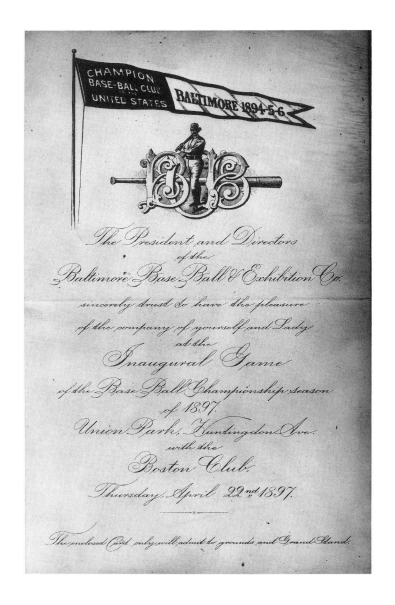

Let us drop a tear and go on, and let it be a hot and scalding tear, for verily Boston is hot stuff.

Baltimore Sun, SEPTEMBER 28, 1897

CHAPTER SEVEN

DOWN FROM THE TOP

Major league baseball has been going on long enough now for every city with an established franchise to have known rapture, however briefly; and also to remember defeat—the sadness of losing, the loneliness, the dark and endless freefall. So in a sense no outcome is new, and no city is so innocent as altogether to let itself go emotionally. And yet . . .

The Baltimore of 1897 had known last place seven times. It had had to wait 24 years for its first pennant. But now its team was universally acclaimed—the brainiest and brawniest anywhere. The whole city was riding high. Arrangements were already made for the Orioles, after the '97 Temple Cup Series, to tour as far as California playing an All-America team of stars from the other clubs.

Maintaining first place in the 12-team National League of 1894, 1895, and 1896 had never been easy, but surely Manager Hanlon and the Big Four (Jennings, Keeler, Kelley, and McGraw) were still superior to the rest of the pack. By skill, by intimidation, surely the Orioles could now attain their fourth consecutive pennant.

The Boston of 1897 had known first place 11 times. It was the only city in baseball that had never been without a franchise since 1871 and the start of the original National Association. And it had never known last place. In 1894, the year when Boston had set out to become the

The Orioles reach San Francisco in their 1897 postseason tour across the continent (at every stop, playing an accompanying all-star team called the All-Americas) and are summoned to one more commercial photographer's studio. Actually, four of the players wearing Baltimore shirts have been borrowed from other NL teams. *At the bottom, Abe Marks, team factotum.* These are the first Oriole caps to be adorned with a cloth bird.

NL's first four-times-in-a-row winner, the city that won instead was Baltimore.

Today's terms for showdown include Armageddon, Troy, Agincourt, the OK Corral, scuffles of that sort. People who are content with such shopworn metaphors show little sense of history. Those three games between Baltimore and Boston at Union Park at the end of September 1897 . . .

Ten other cities hoped to bring about Baltimore's downfall that year, but danger's name was Boston. Frank Selee (pronounced "Seeley"), a nonplaying manager whose big league experience included no losing season, had spent the interim rehabing his 1891–93 champions. Bobby Lowe and Herman Long, infielders, and Hugh Duffy in the outfield (the same Duffy who in 1894 batted .440, still the record) remained on hand, as did the tireless pitcher Kid Nichols. But Selee had nine new men on his 1897 squad, notably third baseman Jimmy Collins and centerfielder Billy Hamilton, early Hall-of-Famers, and an effective young left-handed pitcher, Fred Klobedanz. Until the 1930s they were the last team, those 1897 Beaneaters, to score more than a thousand runs.

Not that Foxy Ned was standing pat. It neither impressed him that Walter Scott Brodie had played in every game for more than five years (at 727, his streak was the 19th century's longest) nor distressed him that Brodie sometimes talked to himself or to the ball. But when Sir Walter's hitting dipped below .300, Hanlon swapped centerfielders with Pittsburgh. The new man, Jacob C. Stenzel (born Steltzle), obligingly batted .353 and stole 69 bases. As to pitchers, Bill Hoffer had one more good year in him, but Esper and Hemming were gone, replaced by two strong-armed 21-year-olds, left-hander Jeremiah H. Nops and Joseph A. Corbett (younger brother of the pugilist Gentleman Jim Corbett). Had Arlie Pond (18-9) just won two more games that year, the Oriole pitching staff would have been history's first with four 20-game winners. It was littered with almosts and if-onlys, 1897.

Opening Day was the most ceremonious yet. In keeping, the Orioles walloped their foe, Boston; better still, they swept the series. But, symbolically, it was only a three-game series, not a four. Next, the Brooklyn Bridegrooms, led by Baltimore's dismissed 1880s manager, Billy Barnie, came to town; it was their pleasure to humble the hosts. The Orioles' first western trip produced only one more win than loss. While Boston was reeling off 17 straight victories, Baltimore jogged along in third place. Road attendance picked up, with people hoping to see the champions stumble. Injuries set in; Kelley and Stenzel alone were healthy all season. Another handicap was internal dissent. By some testimony Dirty Jack Doyle (a playing manager before coming to Baltimore and again after leaving) never felt himself an Oriole and hated McGraw; he was considered the kind of player who, casual about winning, concentrates on posting good personal statistics.

Meanwhile, the league as a whole was at a peak. Amos Rusie, 28-10, had his best year; Cobblestones Klobedanz was 26-7; pitchers were mastering the longer distance. The non-Baltimore rookie crop included Hans Wagner, Larry Lajoie, and George E. Waddell, the fa-

Many photos of William H. Keeler exist; this is as close as he ever comes to smiling.

Opposite page: The sign over the doorway says Eutaw House, the large and well-known hotel downtown at Baltimore and Eutaw streets' northwest corner. On the climactic weekend of the 1897 season, it was host not only to the Boston players but also to two trainloads of Boston fans.

Amid the front row's 15 uniformed Beaneaters is manager Frank Selee. The figure to his left (or elsewhere in the crowd) is John H. (Honey Fitz) Fitzgerald, later grandfather to future president John F. Kennedy. Congressman Fitzgerald had come from Washington.

mous Rube. At the other extreme, Adrian C. Anson, age 45, batted .285 for Chicago's Colts in his 27th and last season—his career and the major leagues had both begun in 1871.

Yet in one individual Oriole, the flame of go-for-broke was never brighter. It turned out to be the finest baseball year any 19th-century Baltimore baseball player ever had, Willie Keeler's 1897. The razzle-dazzle started on Opening Day, when Keeler hit safely twice; he then made at least one hit in every game until June 25. Those 44 games without a zero were an NL record—and, though later tied by Pete Rose, still are. As the majors' mark, Willie's 44 (alas that no fuss was made over it at the time) lasted exactly 44 years, until 1941 and Joe DiMaggio's 56 straight games. Hardly ever did Keeler strike out (whether he holds a record in that regard is unclear, pending the reconstruction of every box score by members of the Society for American Baseball Research). Base hits rattled off Keeler's toothpick bat— 239 altogether, another record. He batted .424. At that, a sore finger held him back in the final two weeks of this 130-game season. He hit 19 triples, stole 64 bases. Meanwhile, his .970 fielding was the best by any rightfielder.

Wee Winsome Willie, a Gilbert and Sullivan parody, went:

A hit-and-run young man,
A take-the-bun young man,
A very foot-loosety, run-like-the-deucety,
Eat-up-the-flies young man.

By September, the two rivals, each playing .700 ball, were alternating in the lead. To stiffen backbones, the *Baltimore American* referred to the Orioles instead as the capital *C* Champions. When Brooklyn's 'Grooms beat Boston behind a rookie pitcher named Jack Dunn, hope flared in Baltimore.

At month's end, the schedule brought the Beaneaters to town for another three-game series and an ultimate confrontation. "Never in the history of the national game has there been such a finish in the pennant race," said the *Baltimore Morning Herald*. Worriedly, league headquarters assigned *two* umpires. Carrying fish horns, cowbells, rattles, and "bazoos," and emitting a form of music, 150 Boston fans arrived via chartered train; the object pictured on their lapel badges was a bean pot. They were led by 34-year-old Congressman John F. Fitzgerald, known as Honey Fitz; long afterward, his grandson John Fitzgerald Kennedy would become president of the United States. They holed up at the Eutaw House, where the Boston players lodged.

The City of Culture, the press said, versus the City of Churches. Baltimore was in turmoil; elsewhere, "the interest [was] so big as to roll like a tidal wave all over the land," in the *Sun*'s words. (It was also high noon for the essayists of rival newspapers.) In that lull between the McKinley-Bryan presidential race and the Spanish-American War, the nation clustered about telegraph-wire news boards.

So still, so silent, so heart-broken. On the worst afternoon of the 19th century in Baltimore, the immense throng at Union Park can only stare and flinch with every additional Beaneater basehit.

Of interest in this classic photograph are the old-style base path configuration, the reused boards forming the outfield fence, the outfield's dense ring of standees, and (if that is indeed a white uniform) the rightfielder, Willie Keeler.

Kid Nichols beat Joe Corbett 6-4 in the first game; twice, "almost supernatural fielding" by the enemy shortstop choked off late-inning Oriole rallies (lyrics by the *Morning Herald*, which noticed that the shortstop, on returning to the bench, "was showered with coins and bills" by the Boston fans seated behind the team). The Orioles seemed nervous, all but McGraw—"he, and he alone, rose to the full height of the occasion."

Next day, Saturday, before a Union Park record paid-attendance crowd of 18,123, Hoffer (22-11 that year) outpitched Klobedanz 6-3, and Baltimore went back to being one percentage point ahead. What a high for rooters perched in the grandstand rafters—and those whose legs were wrapped around the outfield's three pennant poles. Newspapers said the uproar after the final out was audible all the way downtown.

Off day Sunday; then Monday, September 27, and "the baseball game of the century," to quote the *Sun*. Again, the two top pitchers: Nichols (31-11) and Corbett (24-8), though the arm of Brother Joe was said to have stiffened. Much of Bel Air arrived on a special train;

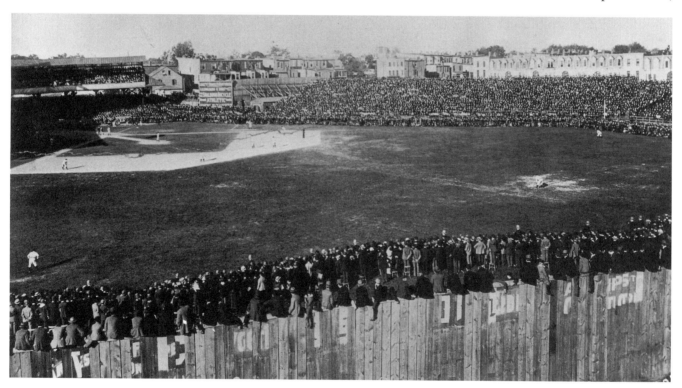

Cambridge citizens chartered themselves a bay steamer. At the train station, another hundred Bostonians arrived to march noisily north to Huntingdon Avenue (today's 25th Street) and the ballpark.

Baltimore's self-appointed "champion rooter," Major (C.S.A.) A. K. Fulton, a downtown hotel keeper, was on hand. Another spectator was Maurice Bloomfield, Ph.D., professor of Sanskrit and comparative philology at Johns Hopkins University (which was downtown then. A decade earlier, Woodrow Wilson, as a Johns Hopkins graduate student, noted in his diary that he had watched a game that afternoon at Oriole Park.) Long before play began, "housetops in all directions were literally black with people."

The admissions figure of 25,390 given out afterward "was not nearly the total number of those who were on the grounds," the *American* reported. When the gates opened at 10 A.M., the general-admission ticket lines stretched to Greenmount Avenue in one direction, Charles Street in the other. Soon the Orioles stopped selling tickets and just took a fan's 25 cents as he pushed on in. (For advance-sale, 75-cent grandstand seats, scalpers were getting as much as $5.) The SRO sign went up. A large gate ordinarily opened only after a game for fast exit went down, and some 5,000 nonpayers swept in before it could be re-erected. Standees, held back by ropes, jammed against the outfield fences with supervision from the 150-man police detail. When the gong rang for play to begin, the human circle ended on either side only a few yards short of the catcher. Three thousand people never did get in but hung around outside. Simultaneously, 20,000 people jammed Newspaper Row (Washington Street) in Boston, following every play as it was posted on the outdoor scoreboards of four daily papers.

This was climax: if you like, the single most dramatic afternoon of the 19th-century major leagues. No 19th-century baseball crowd was larger. And none was more shatteringly disappointed. In the top of the second, Corbett hurt a finger fielding a grounder and used it as an excuse to take himself out of the game. Hanlon, saving Pond for the schedule's next game, sent in Jerry Nops, then Hoffer, then 19-year-old Morris Amole. Nothing worked; the Orioles were "outplayed and outbatted," Boston making 23 hits and every Beaneater scoring at least once. Amid contrasting sights—"a meteoric shower of two-base hits from Boston bats" and "some tiny white-clad champions . . . chasing the leathern balls to the ends of the earth"—a stillness enveloped that vast crowd. It was all too aware of Ernest Thayer's symbol of defeat, Mudville. Repeatedly, raucously, the silence was profaned by the chant of the visitors: "Hit 'er up, hit 'er up, hit 'er up, Boston! Hit 'er up!"

The blamers singled out Hoffer, on duty throughout a hideous seventh inning in which Boston scored nine times. (With three runs in but with two out, Stenzel muffed a crucial fly. Each side made five errors.) Why did Hanlon leave in Hoffer, who had had only one day's rest, through five innings and 17 hits, and use Nops and Amole only briefly? The *Evening News* explained to Championville that Jerry and Morris were left-handers, and Boston's batters were mainly right-handers—one of the earliest printed mentions of baseball's pitcher-batter theory (when both are righties or both are lefties, the pitcher benefits; otherwise the batter has the advantage). Keeler alone was up to the occasion, with four hits, two walks, and four runs. Nichols, "working the batsmen to the Queen's taste," was shaky but adequate. The score at the end was 19-10.

The day, as it happened, was Rosh Hashanah. In Baltimore, unhappy new year. Tuesday's papers told "a tale of woe, of all-pervading, crushing woe." Gloom, solid-state gloom.

Boston went off for a closing series in Brooklyn; Baltimore played Washington at home. The letdown was too much. A loss to Washington, a Boston victory, and the pennant was beyond mathematical reach. At the finish, Baltimore's 90-40 was two full games inferior to Boston's 93-39. The place on the fence behind Joe Kelley, all picked out for the fourth flagpole, stayed bare. Not until the 1920s did an NL team—John McGraw's in New York—win four straight pennants.

A century later, there is a thin consolation in the roll call of major league managers who came out of those Old Oriole lineups. Contemporaries thought well enough of them as individuals to promote no fewer than eight to command rank: McGraw (Orioles, Giants), Jennings (Tigers), Kelley (Reds, Braves), Robinson (Robins, now Dodgers), Gleason (White Sox), Doyle (Senators), Joe Quinn (Cleveland Spiders), and Frank Bowerman (Boston Braves). Keeler declined to manage the Highlanders (now Yankees). McGraw won 10 pennants, Jennings 3, Robinson 2, and Gleason 1.

In the 1897 Temple Cup postlude, Baltimore won handily, four games out of five; Boston (after splitting its season series with Baltimore, six games to six) wasn't giving it much of an effort; to wit: 12-13, 13-11, 8-3, 12-11, 9-3. Public interest evaporated: attendance at the final game, in Baltimore, was about 700. Quietly, the NL wrote *finis* to its ill-considered postseason exercise and sent the Temple Cup back to its donor.

In contrast, the ensuing coast-to-coast tour, Orioles versus All-Americas, went well. It wasn't Europe, about which there had been lightheaded talk earlier; and the Orioles were without McGraw and Captain Robinson, who stayed home (Hugh Jennings was captain instead). But even in October good crowds turned out from Frostburg to Fresno for games on some strange ballfields. After expenses, the players realized $341 each.

The money mattered because among the newlyweds and some of the other Orioles, salary resentment was on the rise. Many NL owners had lost money at the start of the decade, but once the monopoly was secure—with a pay scale lower than that of the late 1880s—the prospect seemed rosy. The historian Robert F. Burk points out the reliable connection in baseball between the excitement of heightened offense (e.g., with 1893's longer pitching distance) and an increase in attendance revenue. Then came, dependably, a corrective: batting feats and the ensuing headline clamor inevitably encouraging batters to seek higher wages. But in the one-major-league 1890s, player power was at its feeblest over against the "indentured servitude" of the reserve clause. The so-called game had become an owners' cartel.

The next season, not the one past, is the one that matters. If his 1897 veterans could no longer do the job, then for 1898 Ned Hanlon would replace the less productive players with others of more promise. In a six-man trade with Washington, he unloaded Jack Doyle, the troublemaker, Pepper Reitz, whose batting had slipped below .300, and Morris Amole; their respective replacements were Dennis L. (Dan) McGann, from Kentucky, Eugene N. DeMontreville, a Minnesotan, and James McC. McJames, a pitcher from South Carolina, and the pick of the lot. When Jake Stenzel's hitting fell off, Hanlon dropped him for a short, burly Iowan, James W. Holmes, known as Ducky; Kelley moved over to center, Holmes playing left. With Hoffer worn out, Corbett gone back to California, and Doc Pond heeding a call to the colors by joining the Army Medical Corps, Hanlon hired still other pitchers: James J. Hughes, a rookie from California, and Albert J. Maul, a Philadelphian who was joining his sixth team.

In April things were looking up as Jim Hughes threw a one-hitter against Washington and then an 8-0 no-hitter against Boston (still the best start ever by a pitcher new to the majors). All three new pitchers went on to win at least 20 games. Twice the Orioles staged 12-game winning streaks; they led the league in batting, base-stealing, and scoring.

But it was not to be. The glory had departed. Even as the NL was offering the nation more baseball, going to a 154-game schedule that no team fulfilled, the nation kept looking in another direction — toward Cuba, the Philippines, the war with Spain. Baseball's war seemed secondary. Baltimore's Opening Day attendance was a mere 6,500; and that, notes the historian Charles C. Alexander, was the Orioles' largest home crowd all year. By midsummer a stern chase, not a pennant race, was going on. The Beaneaters had come up with impressive new pitchers of their own — one, ironically, a Marylander (Victor G. Willis, 25-13, from Cecil County). Willie Keeler's batting average, again the league's highest, nonetheless was down 39 points. At season's end, Boston was six games in front, in contrast with 1897's two-game gap. Baltimore (96-53) was again in second place, out of 12. Yet the year's announced total attendance, 123,416, was less than half what it had been during each of the first-place years. Ned Hanlon, businessman, ceased feeling good about Baltimore.

As 1898 ended, the NL owners, uneasy over their standings' predictability, schemed to shake things up. The big new idea was syndicate baseball—in its extreme form (advocated by the Giants), a heretical pooling of profits and, for annual redistribution, players. Quieter operators pushed through a two-city arrangement. It would be all right for the shareholders in one club to buy into another club; players could then be dealt back and forth, beefing up one team and junking the other.

Unfortunately, Baltimore was ripe for such an arrangement. Its attendance falloff was bad enough; worse, player morale had ebbed. With salaries unchanging year after championship year, the word *strike* was in the air. As rumors bubbled, the public was largely in the dark; its opinion mattered little to the deal makers.

In February 1899 in New York City, the owners of the Brooklyn and Baltimore baseball clubs came to terms: Ned Hanlon and Harry Von der Horst bought a half-interest in the Brooklyn franchise in exchange for a half-interest in Baltimore's. Brooklyn's principal owners were Ferdinand A. (Gus) Abell and Charles H. Ebbets. The historian Burt Solomon points out that the former, a Brooklyn owner since 1883, was on the one hand an operator of gambling casinos and, on the other, a nephew of the late and very proper Arunah S. Abell, founder, owner, and publisher of the *Baltimore Sun*. Ebbets was a self-propelled climber. Behind this malodorous mix were two Baltimore brewery events: the death in 1894 of John H. Von der Horst, father of Harry and (a nonparticipating Californian) John H. Jr.; and the sale of his Eagle Brewery in 1899 to Gottlieb-Bauernschmidt-Straus (a Baltimore attempt to form a city-wide beer trust). Harry moved to Brooklyn, and went on deferring to Hanlon.

In 1898 Brooklyn's team, finishing tenth, nevertheless drew 300,000 spectators; think (the syndicators said to each other) of the receipts a good team would produce. Their announcement continued: in 1899, the foremost Orioles would play for Brooklyn, and Baltimore would be reimbursed with residue. The loss list: Kelley, Keeler, Jennings, McGann, Hughes, McJames, and Maul. Although they were supposed to be on the list, McGraw and Robinson refused to go; McGraw, age 25, was then named manager of what would pass for Baltimore's team. The public outrage and sense of betrayal were every bit as agonized as a modern fan would expect and every bit as futile. Amid it all, what

McGraw and Robinson, partners in two businesses, baseball and booze. The centering of the *B* on their uniform shirts denotes Baltimore's 1899 team.

The 1899 Orioles. *Back row, left to right:* Jeremiah Nops, p; Joe McGinnity, p; Pat Crisham, 1b; George (Candy) LaChance, 1b; Harry Howell, p; Frank Kitson, p; *middle row:* James (Ducky) Holmes, of; Alexander (Broadway Aleck) Smith, c; Walter (Steve) Brodie, of; John J. McGraw, manager; Wilbert Robinson, c; Charlie Harris, utility; James McKenna, p; *front row:* Dave Fultz, util; Eugene DeMontreville, 2b; Bill Keister, ss. *Not shown:* Jimmy Sheckard, of.

Baltimoreans could not refute was that even after salary increases to its players, the syndicate stood to make more money. From Brooklyn's angle, the deal worked. The Bridegrooms, renamed Superbas, left Boston and its unchanged lineup in the dust, eight games out and barely ahead of the Phillies. A 26-year-old pitcher on Brooklyn's staff had his best season ever (23-13): Jack Dunn.

The 1899 standings, however, included at least two teams more interesting than Brooklyn's. One was Cleveland's, fettered to St. Louis in the same wretched syndicate manner. Bereft of Cy Young, Jesse Burkett, and seven other of its best players, Cleveland was left with what proved to be statistically the lowliest team in modern (1893 onward) times. It finished 84 games back, by dint of winning 20 games and losing 134. Shunned in their own park, the Spiders took to the road from July 1 on, managed by Joseph T. Quinn, an Australian, who

had been an Oriole utility infielder from 1896 to 1898. And St. Louis? It rose from 12th place, but only to 5th. (In still another syndicate, Cincinnati was attached to New York and proceeded to finish above it.)

The other team that held attention was Baltimore's. Today, its nostalgia value is at least the equal of the 1989 team's (hoisted by a new manager, Frank Robinson, from last place to visions of first, until a finish-line defeat by Toronto). In 1899, served notice that their great days were over, the remnant Orioles refused the message. John McGraw, now in control, experienced a power surge. After Opening Day, the syndicate owners left him pretty much alone. Energetically, McGraw put together a new set of belligerents: George (Candy) La-Chance and Samuel J. Tilden (Jimmy) Sheckard, Brooklyn discards, at first and in right, respectively; DeMontreville at second; William F. Keister, a Baltimorean nicknamed Wagontongue, at short; Ducky Holmes in left; and in center, back from his travels, Steve Brodie. Behind the plate was the ever-reliable Wilbert Robinson. Two players were outstanding: McGraw himself, leadoff man as usual, who batted a personal-best .391, drew 124 walks, stole 73 bases, and had an on-base percentage of .547, the highest ever until 1941 and still the second highest (the modern-Oriole best is Ken Singleton's .438 in 1977); and a new pitcher, Joseph J. McGinnity, whom Hanlon had simply overlooked. Earlier employed in an Oklahoma iron foundry, McGinnity (born McGinty*) was a 28-year-old rookie who proceeded to win 28 games while losing 16. With Sheckard, too, sprinting around the bases, the Orioles were a close third to Brooklyn and Boston. Fans everywhere marveled.

But then, in late August, Minnie McGraw developed appendicitis. The team was on the road; her husband left it for her bedside. Peritonitis set in; at age 22, she died. For a while, the fire went out in John McGraw. The team finished fourth, 86-62, 15 games back, but it was a remarkable performance. And Baltimore did better than St. Louis.

Whereupon the National League sent Baltimore another message:

---

* Examples of this erroneous additional syllable (to linguists, an interposed schwa) are widespread in common speech: "Atheletics," "Patapsico," and "Westminister." McGinnity seems not to have minded.

good-bye. Finally acknowledging the unwieldiness of a duodecimal league, the magnates lopped off the four cities they thought of as their weakest: Louisville (bled white when syndicated with Pittsburgh), Cleveland, Washington (perennially weak), and Baltimore. Each set of owners was indemnified, receiving $40,000 not to go away mad. And the NL closed out the 19th century with eight teams. Brooklyn repeated as pennant-winner in 1900, edging Pittsburgh thanks to a second infusion of Baltimore Oriole talent: Sheckard, DeMontreville, and especially, Joe McGinnity, who went 28-8. Manager Hanlon thus won his fifth and final pennant. In the reshuffling, McGraw and Robinson had been assigned to St. Louis; this time, they went and played, but off the field McGraw was talking to outsiders. A new plan was in the making for the new century.

The Old Orioles live on in legend as a team. Six or eight individual names remain fixed in the public mind, but most have other attachments as well—McGraw with the Giants, Robinson with the Dodgers, Jennings with the Tigers; all three went on to become memorable managers. The one player nowadays remembered uniquely for his brilliance as an Oriole is Willie Keeler. He is also the one 19th-century Oriole who, as old-timer identities fade in the crowded sports fan mind, somehow holds his own in magnitude of brightness. This is a paradox, since Keeler spent only 5 of his 19 playing years in Baltimore. No print or television biography has been made of Keeler, no docudrama movie, no oral history, no statue. His stats alone speak for him—which may be the way he'd have wanted it.

William Henry Keeler also played for New York NL, Brooklyn, and New York AL. He was a fine rightfielder and a superb second man in the batting order. The bigger the players grow, nowadays, the more people of ordinary size honor this small, deft, nimble athlete, this determined yet unassuming man. Merwin Jacobson, later of the Jack Dunn Orioles, in youth met Keeler and marveled at the smallness of Willie's hands. The bigger the egos, then and since, the more there is to like about an Oriole who generally spoke only when spoken to, whose goal was to be a player, not a boss or a celebrity. Later, when he was with the Highlanders (now the Yankees) and they were doing poorly, the owner thought to install Keeler, the old pro, as manager. Hearing about it from others, Willie took off: he literally hid until somebody else had been appointed.

Most of his fellow Orioles bought or rented places to live in Baltimore. Keeler is unlisted in the annual city directories; evidently, at season's end he went straight back to the Brooklyn of his boyhood, of his relatives and friends. He settled there in retirement. He never married. His investments, in Brooklyn real estate, soured. He was low on funds when at age 50 heart failure killed him. His few interviewers seem never to have got much out of him—which pitchers were hardest to hit, what he thought of Ned Hanlon, what he thought of Baltimore. A hard out, Willie Keeler. Game after game after game, he got on base, he kept on going, he scored—and so he became a star. And also an elusive person, at work or at leisure. The rarity of that combination, perhaps, is what makes him now, a hundred years afterward, even more distinctive and more admired than in his own time.

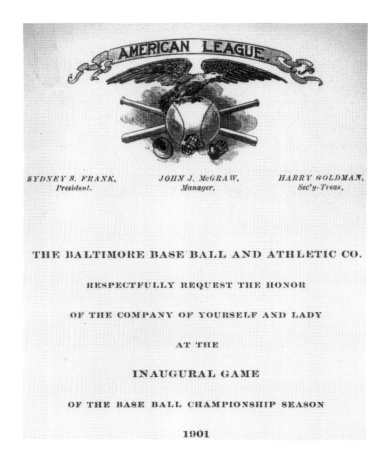

SYDNEY S. FRANK,
President.

JOHN J. McGRAW.
Manager.

HARRY GOLDMAN,
Sec'y-Treas,

THE BALTIMORE BASE BALL AND ATHLETIC CO.

RESPECTFULLY REQUEST THE HONOR

OF THE COMPANY OF YOURSELF AND LADY

AT THE

INAUGURAL GAME

OF THE BASE BALL CHAMPIONSHIP SEASON

1901

The parade celebrating the rejuvenation of ball in Baltimore turned north at Washington's Monument. . . . And to cheer these American League players on to better efforts, the fair students of the Women's College lined the windows of their dormitory on Charles Street, and gaily waved their handkerchiefs. No wonder, with such encouragement, the Orioles won.

Baltimore Herald, APRIL 27, 1901

The future of Baltimore in the American League is very uncertain, stated flatly and plainly. It comes down to this: if the American League can obtain a foothold in New York, the Baltimore franchise will be transferred to Gotham.

Baltimore Herald, SEPTEMBER 10, 1902

CHAPTER EIGHT

NEW CENTURY, NEW LEAGUE

The American League was founded in 1901 as an eight-franchise major, composed of Baltimore, Boston, Chicago, Cleveland, Detroit, Milwaukee, Philadelphia, and Washington. In Boston, Chicago, and Philadelphia, it challenged the National League head to head. In New York, the AL had no team; it wanted one.

The NL had been founded on one man's initiative, and so it was also with the AL. Byron Bancroft Johnson, once a Cincinnati sports writer, exemplified the take-charge mentality. When the NL reduced itself to eight teams in 1900, Ban Johnson and business friends of his created a Western League: a minor league, but one that hired players from the NL's four extinguished clubs. That summer, he lined up four eastern cities preparatory to self-declaration as a major league—the American, equal to, hostile toward, the National.

Johnson's Baltimore agent was John McGraw; in Chicago, Clark Griffith; in Philadelphia, Connie Mack; in Boston, Jimmy Collins. Baltimore's new club president was Sydney S. Frank, a 29-year-old stockbroker. The shareholders included Magistrate Harry Goldman, Judge Conway W. Sams, the Rev. John Boland, James P. Shannon (owner of the Eutaw House), McGraw, and Robinson. The NL had left Union Park vacant but, in the person of Ned Hanlon, still controlled it, and had no intention of letting the AL use it. Having failed at seizure and a lawsuit, the new team built American League Park, $21,000 worth of new home, on the southwest corner of 29th and Greenmount, where the 1889–91 American Association team had played. Wooden one-level stands and bleachers took less than two months to erect and were a bit smaller than Union Park's, but this seems to have been Baltimore's first ballpark containing the club offices.

The AL got most of its players through raiding the furious NL by offering more paycheck money. As he headed back from St. Louis, McGraw brought along Wilbert Robinson, shortstop Bill Keister, and a sturdy young outfielder, Michael J. Donlin, from Illinois. From Chicago NL the manager of the new Orioles abducted a 20-year-old alternate catcher, Roger Bresnahan, an Ohioan; when first base became a problem, Bresnahan filled in there. From Pittsburgh, to play second base, came a Missourian, James T. Williams; from the Giants, to play in right, James B. Seymour, a New Yorker, known as Cy. In center, once more, stood Steve Brodie, who was living at 2321 Barclay Street. The master of showboat, he could catch a fly ball facing away, with his hands behind his back. To rejoin their old mentor, Joe McGinnity and Harry Howell ditched Brooklyn; and Baltimore's well-traveled Frank Foreman came back at age 38 and went 17-7. Altogether, as the Orioles trained in Hot Springs, Arkansas, it was not a lineup to inspire awe; but in the immediate anger and overall confusion, any team might win the first AL pennant.

At this point, a famous incident occurred. McGraw announced the signing of a Cherokee infielder named Tokohoma. Indians in the lineup were no novelty; but this, Chicago club owners soon screamed, was no Indian. He was in fact Charley Grant, a noted black player. Tokohoma, it now appears, was a place name on a map at McGraw's hotel. Earlier, briefly, the color line had been less harsh. In 1884, two blacks had played in the American Association; by 1887, six of the International League's 10 teams had one or more blacks, including George Stovey, a 33-games-won pitcher for Newark. But Stovey was not rehired since white bigots, led by Adrian C. Anson, of the Chicago White Stockings, had set out to exclude all African Americans from Organized Baseball. So Charley Grant never played in the majors, and Baltimore was not the first interracial team in this century after all.

Opening Day against the Boston Puritans was a 10,371-ticket SRO sellout. Ban Johnson, 36, threw out the first ball. McGraw, as leadoff man, made Baltimore's first AL hit (a double) and scored its first run. Next day, Cy Young took the mound to reverse things; the Orioles beat him, too. But when they then went to Washington to inaugurate *its* new park, the Orioles fared less well.

As the season advanced, Baltimore was third, behind Chicago and Boston; its ultimate batting average, .294, was the league's highest, and McGinnity, 26-20 with 39 complete games (in a 136-game season), was the league's hardest-working pitcher. Unassuming and admirable, McGinnity; older than his manager, he operated a shooting gallery at 517 North Howard, alongside the Diamond Cafe. In a pinch, he was good for a two-complete-games doubleheader. (The scholar-author Norman Macht notes that more than once McGinnity let an umpire have it with tobacco-juice spittle.) The iron man went on side-arming in the minors until age 55. Today, Joe McGinnity isn't just a Hall-of-Famer; he is still and always the single-season games-won (26) record-holder for American League Orioles.

But in August, McGraw twice injured a leg (Jack Dunn, now an Oriole and an infielder, replaced him), and by closing day the team (68-65, 13½ games back) had slipped to fifth. Home attendance totaled only 142,000; even so, the Orioles claimed to have lost only $8,000. The NL still refused to recognize the AL, so there was no World Series. And Ban Johnson, the autocrat, pole-axed Milwaukee. Its Brewers, managed by the famous hitter Hugh Duffy, had little to show for their season other than eighth place. Johnson decided to move the franchise to St. Louis and challenge the NL Cardinals, then a consistently weak team. The newcomers, christened the Browns, proved a long-term disappointment, not remedied by the league until 1954. That moveable AL franchise, today's Baltimore Orioles, is correctly viewed as having originated in Milwaukee.

So began 1902, and what in Baltimore should have been better times. McGraw remarried; his second wife, Blanche Sindall, was like

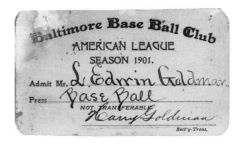

Joe McGinnity models the Oriole coat sweater, corresponding to today's field jacket. Only in 1901 has the identity symbol on Oriole uniforms been the single letter *O*. (The shirts and trousers of road uniforms were a startling black.)

McGinnity still holds the games-won record, among Orioles pitching in the American League.

his first a Baltimorean. The Old Orioles headed a large turnout for the ceremony at St. Ann's Church at Greenmount Avenue and 22d Street. The club had a new president—John J. (Sonny) Mahon, contractor and leader of the city's Democratic machine, which meant that Joe Kelley, having married Mahon's daughter Margaret, jumped Brooklyn for Baltimore: Joe with his (ultimately) 13 consecutive .300-plus years at the plate. (The Kelleys settled in at 2826 North Calvert Street; upon retiring from baseball, Joe took a political job as a racing commissioner.) Also rejoining the Orioles were Dan McGann from '98 and Jimmy Sheckard from '99, plus an Ohioan, Albert (Kip) Selbach, a .300-hitting outfielder. The team looked like a contender.

But dead ahead, disaster waited.

On their way to Savannah, Georgia, for spring training, some of the players stopped in at their manager's place, the Diamond Cafe. Across Howard Street, at the Academy of Music, a musical comedy was playing. Late in the evening, as two groups of pedestrians went by each other in midstreet, words passed between a ballplayer and a chorus girl. The former, taking umbrage, smote the latter in the eye. He was, ironically, the Orioles' best (.347) hitter, Mike Donlin. Arrested, tried, convicted, and sentenced to six months in jail, Donlin never played another inning for Baltimore.

Soon after Opening Day, with Detroit in town, a sliding base-runner aimed not for the base but for McGraw's leg; cleats then were not rubber but sharpened metal. The injured leadoff man was out for a month. Shortly after his return to the lineup, he and an umpire jawed each other savagely. Ban Johnson, as AL president, slapped an indefinite suspension on McGraw.

Meanwhile, the McGraws' house had been sold, and he and his wife were living in the Northampton Hotel on the northwest corner of Charles Street and North Avenue, one rank above a boarding house, a place favored by several Orioles. And McGraw, his team dragging along in fifth place, had been riding trains to and from New York, where he was talking to Andrew Freedman, president of the Giants. A conspiracy was under way. When the details started coming out on July 8, their scope astounded the baseball world. Their meaning staggered Baltimore.

At McGraw's behest, Baltimore's docile owners (who owed him money) gave him an unconditional contract release and sold 51 percent of their stock shares to New York NL for $50,000. That team (with a ballpark seating more than twice as many people as Baltimore's) then signed McGraw as manager and transferred McGinnity, Bresnahan, McGann, and Jack Cronin, a pitcher, to itself. McGraw (whose promise not to tamper with his former teammates was worthless—even the Oriole groundskeeper followed him to New York) took office at once, at the highest on-field salary in baseball, $11,000. Meanwhile, Cy Seymour and Joe Kelley were released from the Orioles and signed by Cincinnati; at ownership level, the Reds were still connected to the Giants. Kelley, too, made out better by leaving Baltimore, becoming the Reds' manager. The document signing at the Stafford Hotel was brief, but the commotion spread over 10 days. And what it did to the pitiful Orioles! Wrecked and plundered, they hadn't enough players left field a team.

(One account has Ban Johnson and John McGraw stage-managing the whole intricate maneuver, but this implies an improbable trust in each other. More likely, as the historian Benton Stark points out, is

The 1902 AL Orioles. *Back row, left to right:* James (Cy) Seymour, of; Harry Howell, p; Frank Foreman, p; Dan McGann, 1b; Jimmy Williams, 2b; Joe McGinnity, p. *Third row:* Charles Shields, p; Joe Kelley, of; John McGraw, manager, 3b; Wilbert Robinson, c. *Second row:* Albert (Kip) Selbach, of; Roger Bresnahan, c; Samuel (Jimmy) Sheckard, of; Tom Hughes, p. *Front row:* Billy Gilbert, ss; Andy Oyler, utility.

that McGraw, starting 1902, had reason to believe he was Johnson's choice to run a New York AL operation, but during their April–June acrimony realized that Johnson no longer wanted him.)

With a roar, Johnson declared Baltimore's franchise forfeited to the league. The AL's founder-president moved in a ragtag of utility men from other teams to play out the season. Wilbert Robinson was left in charge (at ballpark and bistro). Somehow, two other good players remained: Jimmy Williams, who batted .300, and Kip Selbach, who batted .320. (True, on August 19 Selbach—hung over?—somehow committed five errors, which is still the one-game record for an outfielder.)

In August, a second New York event was in effect Baltimore's eviction notice. Andrew Freedman, with close friends running Tammany Hall, could thwart every AL attempt to get the street-closure permits necessary for ballpark-building. But an election occurred at this point and reform voters ousted the machine. The embattled Freedman suddenly decided to sell his steady-loser Giants and to quit Organized Baseball. The crux of it was that the AL could now buy land, lay out a diamond, pick up a weak franchise, and move it into the Big City. And which of the league's eight franchises was weaker than Baltimore's?

Down plunged the team, down went paid attendance, down went civic pride. When the end came, the 50-88 Orioles were last, 34 games behind Connie Mack's first-place A's. For the final game at American League Park on Greenmount Avenue (Boston 9, Baltimore 5), the Coalminers' Glee Club performed to a paid attendance of 138.

That winter, the franchise turned into the New York Highlanders. And the two leagues, NL and AL, made peace. They signed a Basic Agreement like that of the 1880s, respecting each other's player contracts and reserves. In 1903, they played the first modern-style World Series.

So complex were these events, the post mortem still isn't solid. McGraw was an obvious villain; yet he had stood by Baltimore a long, sometimes unrewarded, time, and no great future loomed for him with the team or in the AL. On the contrary, in New York and the National League—on Broadway and at the Polo Grounds—McGraw became "a genuine international celebrity," in the phrase of his able

BALL CLUB GONE

Baltimore Owners Deliver 201 Shares To National League Interests.

BEST PLAYERS LEAVE, TOO

Andrew Freedman Credited With Buying For $50,000.

ANOTHER CLUB TO BE FORMED

---

biographer, Charles C. Alexander. McGraw now managed from the bench, issuing orders on every pitch. With New York capital behind him, he paid high for players. And in his 30-year tenure, Little Napoleon won 10 pennants (although only 3 World Series), which is still the record. After it was all over, his relatives buried him in Baltimore among the constellation of diamond stars in New Cathedral Cemetery: John J. McGraw, who played 941 games for Baltimore, 59 for New York.

Easy for later generations to find fault, of course, and also to misread the times—no 1902 Baltimorean had any way to foretell that franchise-moving, common enough in early baseball, would then stop dead until 1953; that the new AL-NL solidarity would freeze Baltimore out of the big time for more than half a century. All the same, anyone studying baseball times and scenes is likely to form the impression that Baltimore's business community steadily undervalued professional baseball. In those years, the leaders of Baltimore industry, commerce, transport, and banking stood aloof. Common-man Baltimore showed strong if not wholly dependable interest in baseball (a team of chronic losers dejects the fans in any city, and even victory can seem repetitious). But it stands out that from 1871 on, no old-line Baltimorean ever sat in the game's higher councils. Thus Baltimore could be slighted with impunity, and repeatedly it was.

That converted New Englander Ned Hanlon did attain stature in Organized Baseball, though in the early 1900s he was the loser in a power struggle with his fellow-owner in Brooklyn, Charles H. Ebbets. (Fond of Baltimore, Hanlon not only moved back in retirement, living at 1401 Mount Royal Avenue, but until his death in 1937 at age 79, served as chairman of the parks board—and put Steve Brodie, for one, on his payroll). But Ned by himself was never strong enough to get Baltimore back into the big leagues, as became evident when, during his later years with the fading Brooklyn Superbas, he proposed moving the franchise to Baltimore. The cunning Ebbets prevented it, and before long engineered Hanlon's removal from managership and from part-ownership.

In another generation's long view, the 1872–1902 period in Baltimore's baseball experience now casts a double gleam. In visiting-

The genealogy of baseball franchises is a study with few students. All the same, the outcome of 1996's World Series tickled such persons. The Baltimore Oriole franchise started the 20th century in the American League, but since 1903, under other names, its location has been New York City. Boston's National League team, in time rechristened the Braves, was moved in 1953 to Milwaukee and later to Atlanta. Thus, when the 1996 Yankees overcame the favored Braves, it was to some a tiny drop of 99-year-old revenge.

team uniform, almost every top baseball star was there for the watching at a Baltimore ballpark. Among them, already mentioned, were Al Spalding, Al Reach, the Wright brothers, Charles A. Comiskey, Cy Young, Nap Lajoie, Amos Rusie, Hugh Duffy, Adrian C. Anson, Guy Hecker, and Louis R. (Pete the Gladiator) Browning. Other stars not previously mentioned included Dick McBride, Joe Start, John Clapp, George Zettlein, George Bradley, Arlie Latham, Bid McPhee, Chief Sockalexis, Ed Delahanty, Fred Clarke, Jake Beckley, Billy Sunday, Deacon White, Deacon McGuire, Tim Keefe, John and Arthur Clarkson, Pud Galvin, and Eddie Plank. All these, but never, it seems, the famous pitcher for Providence (59 games won in 1884), Old Hoss Radbourn.

Of the players with Baltimore on their shirt-fronts, posterity hails McGraw, Keeler, Bresnahan, Brouthers, Jennings, Robinson, McGinnity, Kelley, and Hanlon—to list them in the order of their election to the Hall of Fame. Some of the nine, to be sure, played longer for other teams and some made it on the strength of later careers as manager. As of 1998, Cooperstown's electors, to their discredit, were still passing over Mathews, Kilroy, and Brodie.

For baseball's many arithmeticians: a few of the season totals posted by the original, AL charter-member Orioles still outrank the best efforts of the 1954-onward AL Orioles. Mike Donlin batted .347; modernity's best is .328 (Ken Singleton, 1977). In 1975, Jim Palmer pitched 323 innings: impressive, but Joe McGinnity's maximum was 382. These two unequaled marks date from 1901. In 1967, Paul Blair hit 12 triples, tops for our times; in 1901, Mike Donlin hit 13 triples, and Bill Keister and Jimmy Williams, 21 each. (In 1902, the disaster year, Williams hit another 21 triples.) Collectively, the 1954 Orioles were good for 49 triples, a mark the team still hasn't equaled; the 1901 Orioles hit 111. And that was during a 128-game season, not today's 162. The supposition is that more triples occurred in antiquity because the outfield played closer in. But what accounts for the discrepancy in base-running? The daring 1976 Orioles stole a record 150 bases. The starveling 1902 team counted 189, and in 1901, John McGraw's last full year as an Oriole, the stolen-base total was 207.

Kid Gleason, an Old Oriole, turns out for the baseball segment of Old Home Week in October 1907. The site is Oriole Park, built by the original 1901–2 American League Orioles. The bench now has a roof, as the evolution of the dugout proceeds. Gleason's subsequent career highlight: managing 1919's Chicago Black Sox.

Baseball is the one perfect game. It is honest, American and manly. It is as invigorating as six fingers of the best old rye and as pure as a bottle of pasteurized milk.

Baltimore Sun, APRIL 30, 1907

CHAPTER NINE

THE HIGH MINORS

Putting a brave face on it, Baltimore in 1903 entered the Eastern League. This high minor dated back to 1884. (A Baltimore team, the Monumentals, was a charter member briefly in that overwrought year of three major leagues and three Baltimore teams.) Flux has been typical of the Eastern League, with its nine different names so far and its more than 50 franchises, 4 of them in Canada or Cuba. Latterly, the name—International League—has been steady but the territory has become mononational.

Baltimore's manager, captain, and catcher was that last remaining Old Oriole, Wilbert Robinson. To work with, he had the Montreal team, which had been bought and moved south by Ned Hanlon. Himself the manager of NL Brooklyn, which was by then a second-division team, Hanlon seemed unhappy at what had been done to Baltimore. With Union Park in disrepair, Hanlon quietly paid $3,000 for the empty American League Park at 29th and Greenmount for these new, lower-down Orioles to rechristen and call home. Moses N. Frank, a retired clothing wholesaler, was named president.

There was no spring training down south in the Eastern League. Of April's 14 Orioles, only 2 were still around at season's end; the fans had had a look altogether at 42 men. (One was Clarence Algernon Childs, a native of southern Maryland and through the 1890s, second baseman for the hated Cleveland Spiders: a roly-poly figure dubbed Cupid in the NL but somehow, in Baltimore, known as Paca. After six Oriole games, Childs was gone.) As the EL years went by, its schedules ranked Baltimore alongside such cities as Albany, Reading (Pa.), Binghamton (N.Y.), and Springfield (Mass.). And this downgrading, this blow to Baltimore's self-esteem, came just as Washington, a younger city but one with a then-solid major league franchise, was passing Baltimore in population, never to be overtaken.

Nevertheless, Opening Day 1903 was ceremonious, to help the fans forget. After a parade, the first ball was thrown out by 79-year-old Henry Chadwick of Brooklyn, inventor of the box score and long the editor of Spalding's *Official Baseball Guide;* Chadwick had been writing about baseball in New York newspapers since the 1860s. But the team wasn't up to the occasion, losing to Buffalo.

Many a Baltimorean assumed that winning pennants in the minors would be a snap, but not so, as the team dragged along in fifth place. In July, Hanlon sent Hughey Jennings, the famous shortstop, down from Brooklyn to be playing manager. In 1899, Jennings' arm had weakened and he was now a first baseman.

Later, Jennings managed the Detroit Tigers during Ty Cobb's greatest years; Hughey looked back on his four Eastern League years (he stayed in Baltimore through 1906) as a low spot in his career. He had reason: in 1905, for instance, he was hit by a pitch that broke his arm; weeks later, in a base path collision, it broke again. He held some of the stock, and was pained when an afternoon's paid attendance dipped below a hundred once in a while. Yet his teams did well, finishing fourth, second, second, and third. In 1906, two Oriole pitchers were league leaders: Del Mason, from New York, 26-9, and Fred Burrell, from New Jersey, with 183 strikeouts. The high point, however, came in '05, when the pennant went by half a game on the last day of the season to the Providence Clamdiggers; Jack Dunn, playing manager. Two other alumni of the American League Orioles were in the opposing lineup—Steve Brodie and Jack Cronin, a pitcher.

In 1907, Dunn left Providence for Baltimore, lured by an offer of part-ownership. The Orioles did poorly that year, finishing sixth. But in '08, everything came together, including the fans, some 20,000 of

Jack Dunn, for some years a playing manager, then sat there on the bench in civilian clothes.

whom turned out for a climactic home doubleheader with Providence. Baltimore (83-57, two games in front) had its first pennant in a dozen years.

Dunn, turning 36, sensed the chance for a big career move. Hanlon, in his fifties and no longer influential in the majors, was ready for a settled, post-baseball life. For $70,000, he was willing to relinquish his last baseball property: the IL park and franchise. Unlisted investors supplied the money; Dunn, the self-confidence. A native Pennsylvanian, later an off-season barrel maker in northern Jersey and an eight-year pitcher-infielder in the majors, John J. Dunn had observed, nay played for or with, his predecessors as Oriole manager: Barnie, Hanlon, McGraw, and Jennings. He had been on three major league pennant-winners, two in the minors. Middle-sized, bald, Dunn himself was still in playing condition. Now if the Orioles would do their part, and go on winning. . . . Jack Dunn toughened early, as his 1909 team, largely new faces, stumbled home in seventh place. Struggle as Dunnie might, a long decade had to go by before he was able to repeat that first quick triumph.

The 1908 Orioles, champions of the Eastern League: Frank Dessau, p; Frank Pfeffer, p; Bob Hall, of; Doc Adkins, p; Tom O'Hara, of; Jack Dunn, 2b, manager; Wilbert Robinson, c; Pearson, ss; John McCloskey, p; Bill Byers, c; Chet (Pop) Chadbourne, of; Hugh Hearne, c; Pete Cassidy, 1b; Sam Strang, of; Jack Knight, 3b. In background, the former American League Park.

Rube Vickers, star pitcher of the 1911 Orioles, was from Ontario. This tobacco card series is of Canadian origin.

In retrospect, the period from 1903 to the end of World War I didn't lack interest. Players of past or future star ranking stayed for a while; outside events affected Baltimore baseball. The first was the calamitous Great Fire of February 6 and 7, 1904. Oriole Park was far to the north of the burnt district, but it seems likely that whatever files and effects remained from the NL and AL Orioles went up in smoke in somebody's office building. The cloth pennants of 1894, 1895, and 1896—nothing has been seen of them since the Great Fire.

In October 1907, proud of its newly reconstructed downtown, Baltimore issued a national call inviting former residents back for a look. Some of the main events of Old Home Week were at Oriole Park; in particular, the Old Orioles rallied 'round, suited up, posed for photographers, and played the current Eastern Leaguers. (The reunion theme continued, in a manner of speaking, even after death, as one by one some of the old-timers were buried in New Cathedral Cemetery out Old Frederick Road: Hanlon, McGraw, Kelley, and Wilbert Robinson.)

On becoming the proprietor in 1909, Dunn moved home plate from near Greenmount Avenue (where batters faced into the afternoon sun) to the lot's northwest corner. He also scheduled Sunday home games. In Baltimore and other major eastern cities, ordinances had long prohibited for-pay Sunday amusements. To get around these so-called blue laws, the Orioles began leaving the city on Sundays to play games in Back River Park in eastern Baltimore County.

The five years starting in 1909 (seventh place, third, second, fourth, and third) may seem a blur at this remove. But they included a moment of sadness unmatched in the experience of the generations of Baltimore baseball fans. A main strength of the 1910 team was its shortstop, Simon B. Nicholls. A farmer's son from Boyds in Montgomery County, Maryland, and a star athlete at Maryland Agricultural College (class of 1903), Nicholls then played several years in the minors. He reached the majors in 1907, starting four years with the Philadelphia A's. When his hitting slackened, Nicholls was sent down to the Orioles, who happily put him to work as shortstop and team captain.

In spring 1911, as the Orioles worked out in a gymnasium (still no southern preseason), Nicholls, who lived at 816 Cator Avenue in Go-vans, came down with typhoid fever. The newspapers' grim headlines warned of the worst. Peritonitis set in, and Dr. J.M.T. Finney oper-ated at Union Protestant Infirmary, but in vain. Si Nicholls, 28, and his Philadelphia wife had two children, the younger born March 6; he bade them farewell and on March 12, died. The world's champion A's came to Baltimore and played the Orioles in a benefit game (which the Orioles won). That year, without Si Nicholls, the Orioles (95-58) missed the pennant by 3½ games.

Standouts in the 1903–18 lineups were often veterans in their twi-light; not much nest egg was awaiting them in retirement from their years of standard major league remuneration. The outstanding ex-ample was Harry P. Vickers, pitcher, a Canadian known as Rube after playing on the same Philadelphia AL team as Rube Waddell. In 1911, when the Orioles were finishing in second place, Vickers was 32-14. Also in public favor—and longer on the team—was "the 500-pound battery" of Doc Adkins and Bill Byers. Merle T. Adkins, from Wis-consin, who had 18-, 20-, 28-, and 21-game-winning Oriole seasons, still went on pitching after receiving his M.D. degree from Johns Hopkins in 1907. James William Byers, from Indiana, was younger but likewise colorful.

Among youngsters on their way up, a name long revered is that of Frederick Charles Maisel, who owned third base at Oriole Park before (and again after) his six-year career with New York AL. Fritz, the Catonsville Flash (he led off and personified the running game),

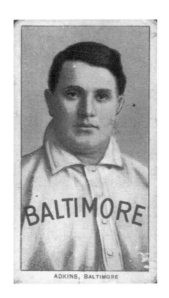

ADKINS, BALTIMORE

Doc Adkins. He had had major league tryouts; things went better in the high minors, and the pay was sufficient to put him through medical school in the off season.

EASTERN SHORE NONLEAGUE BASEBALL

The historian Campbell Gibson has pulled from oblivion Si Nicholls's 1904 nonleague team at Ridgely, an Eastern Shore town whose 1900 population was 713. That team's pitcher and entire infield later made it to the majors: Sam Frock, pitcher; Bill Kellogg, first base; Buck Herzog, second base; Nicholls, shortstop; and Frank Baker, third base. (In 1904, Ridgely, 38-10, won the "amateur championship" of Mary-land. It did not matter, under the prevailing rules, that six players were paid.)

Charles J. (Butch) Schmidt

was 20 when he began his three pre-Yankee years in 1910. That rarity, brothers on the same team, happened in 1912 as Fritz's younger brother George, primarily an outfielder, also played for the Orioles. More on Fritz later, much more.

Two outfielders, Eddie Murphy and Jimmy Walsh, went from the Orioles to Philadelphia AL (another instance of the close relations between Jack Dunn and Connie Mack); in the eventful 1914 World Series, however, this put them into a face-off with Charles J. (Butch) Schmidt, a Baltimorean, who was playing first base for the unexpectedly victorious Boston Braves (descendants of the 1890s' Beaneaters). (It gets complicated: in the big leagues so far, there have been two Charles Schmidts. The Murphys include an Edward and a John Edward—the latter was Baltimore's Eddie. And be careful with the Walshes, James C. and Michael T., respectively outfielder and infielder but both known as Jimmy and both of whom wore the uniform of minor-league Oriole. The second Walsh, also known as Runt, also played for Philadelphia NL—and Baltimore's Federal League Terrapins.)

Three other pitchers are of note for their post-Oriole years: the native-Baltimore Russell brothers Clarence (Lefty) and Allen (Rubber Arm), and James Robert Shawkey. Lefty Russell pitched for the A's; Allen Russell was a solid relief pitcher for the Yankees, Red Sox, and Senators. A Pennsylvanian, Bob Shawkey of the 1913 Orioles joined the 1914 A's, and after 13 years with the Yankees was their manager in 1930.

Still other Orioles of passing note were Jimmy Dygert, pitcher; Sammy Strang, Bill Clancy, Ben Houser, Phil Cooney (original name, Cohen), and Jud Castro (a Colombian), infielders; and Hugh Hearne, catcher. Strang, a much-traveled Tennessean, was known to some as the Dixie Thrush. Did Home Run Baker ever play for the Orioles? The answer is, embarrassingly, yes—five games in 1907, at age 21. Then Jack Dunn let him go. And John Franklin Baker (Frank, back home in Talbot County's Trappe), third baseman and clutch power hitter, went on to greater things in Philadelphia, New York, and Cooperstown.

Nowadays, only the specialist is likely to work up much interest in the long-ago minors, with their parade of little-known names and their scanty coverage (sports writers habitually accorded a player only his last name; Baltimore dailies gave bigger headlines and more space to major league game stories than to minor). Happy is the smile, though, on the family-tree maker nowadays who discovers that "Mom's great-uncle played for the Orioles," even if in the minors for only a part season.

Time abraded some of the scar tissue. One nice touch, in this regard: *The Baltimore Sun Almanac*, distributed gratis to the newspaper's readers from 1876 on and a fixture in Maryland households, published annual baseball summaries starting in 1884. But 1903's statistics—showing Baltimore's demotion to the minors—so disgusted the editors that they refused to print *any* baseball standings, minor or major. Slowly, interest reawakened; from 1907 on, the almanac again contained a baseball page.

For the closest approach now possible to the spirit of that period, the daily sports pages are the place to turn; often, in those days, a player's wife pasted his clippings into a scrapbook. Mary Twombly's treasures were later incorporated into the printed memoirs of her husband, George F. Twombly, who between 1911 and 1916 played five full or part seasons as an Oriole outfielder. As unearthed by the researcher Dave Howell, these examples of Baltimore sports coverage at spring training and during the season add nothing special to the standard Babe Ruth stories, but they do restore life to a flavorsome time.

Here is a composite, rife with slang, cliché, and ways to say *Orioles* without calling them Orioles. (Note: Twombly, a star Massachusetts high school athlete, at age 18 gained a tryout with Baltimore through a relative, Mrs. Jack Dunn. Sports writers did not let him forget it):

(Cousin George) Twombly

The scribes give Manager Dunn credit for having a great crowd of balltossers. Midkiff, Cree and Twombly led the Birds with the stick. Coming up in the second inning with his teammates a marker to the bad, Twombly soaked a screaming double to right center, which put the home talent in the lead. When the fifth rolled around, Cousin George sauntered to the plate; Anderson planted one

Opening Day 1910, at Oriole Park. *Left to right:* Bob Hall, ss; (back to camera) Reddy Treulieb, groundskeeper; Fritz Maisel, 3b, hand to cap; Jimmy Catiz, 2b; Jimmy Walsh, of; Charles (Butch Schmidt, 1b; Alex Malloy, p; Jack Dunn, manager; Doc Adkins, p; Lefty Russell, p; Harry Vickers, p; Bill Byers, c; Jim Frick, 3b.

squarely over the heart of the platter for George and a moment later the fans gazed at the left-field fence, over which a little white speck could be seen sailing. In the seventh, Cousin George again gave the pellet a ride over the fence and this blow gave the Dunnmen a lead which they retained to the end.

Twombly and Daniels pulled off two corking double steals last week. Cousin George knows how to get a lead, and made a rep last year by the number of times he pilfered third base. . . . His work on the paths has been silk-lined.

On Killifer's fly to left, which had a three-base tag hanging on it, George got an early start and speared the sphere with his gloved hand.

Midkiff, Derrick and Ball made swell plays on the infield, while

Twombly pulled a catch of a long fly near the scoreboard. Cousin George was also there with the willow during the matinee, getting three safeties, one a long homer. . . . Yesterday afternoon at Back River, McAvoy [the Oriole catcher] caused a ripple of applause in one of the early innings when he caught one of [Allen] Russell's wild heaves with his bare hand.

Babe Ruth started for the Dunnigans, but was removed in the third inning after the Hustlers had connected with his shoots safely on three occasions. Of the Rochester team's five runs, the majority were made off Ruth before he was hoisted from the box. . . . Jimmy McAvoy, who resides in Rochester, was presented with a handsome gold-mounted umbrella when he came up to bat in the second inning.

In the inaugural stanza, the Flock began straightening out the flinging of Red Oldham, a portsider with a windup like a pretzel. Both teams began their pill-busting early in the game.

Ruth was a real hero. After the game, the Athletics said he is one of the best youngsters they have ever seen for a long time. The Baltimore boy is a natural ball-player and his work today caused Manager Dunn to repeat that he believes the phenom will develop into a star.

Tomorrow the Birds will engage in the opening game of a series with Jersey City. It will be ladies' day at the Greenmount enclosure, and the fair sex will be admitted free.

To protect the crowds from the ravages of pickpockets at the opening of the Federal League season today, Acting Marshal Manning has made elaborate plans. Along the York Road and St. Paul Street car lines policemen will be stationed, one officer at practically every block. If they see anyone jump hurriedly from a car, as pickpockets usually do after relieving someone of his wallet, the policemen will give chase.

Baltimore American, APRIL 13, 1914

CHAPTER TEN

THE FEDERAL LEAGUE

You don't hear much these days about the Federal League — or any putative, rival third major league. Organized Baseball has finally learned to adapt; when the pressure for additional franchises nears flash point, OB simply enlarges its National and American Leagues.

Before World War I, however, stand fast! was the attitude; go away and lie down, the message to cities clamoring for admission. The owners, loosely ruled since 1903 by a three-man National Commission, constituted a business trust, or social club, of galling exclusivity. Any would-be founder of a third league knew that the precedents for it, 1884's Union Association and 1890's Players' League, had lasted a mere one season. Nevertheless, by 1914 angry capitalists in eight cities were ready to take on Organized Baseball, dollar against dollar.

New ballparks were put up, more than 50 AL and NL players were shanghaied by simply offering them salaries closer to their worth, and teams were christened (sometimes commercially): the Brooklyn Tip-Tops, the Pittsburgh Rebels, the Buffalo Blues, the Kansas City Packers, the Chicago Whales, the Indianapolis Hoosiers, the St. Louis Terriers, and the Baltimore Terrapins. Four of these cities had franchises in the existing majors; in the others, the box-office competitor was a high-minors club.

And the city with the warmest welcome, the whoops of loudest

The 1914 Terrapins in spring training at Fayetteville, N.C. Their uniforms (with turtle in silhouette on the shirt pocket) have not yet arrived, so the players are in a motley of previous-team uniforms. *Back row, left to right:* Bernhard (Benny) Meyer, of; George Suggs, p; Otto Knabe, 2b and manager; Frank (Piano Mover) Smith, p; Joseph (Happy) Finneran, p; Harry (Swats) Swacina, 1b; Mickey Doolan, ss; Henry (Ducky) Yount, p; George (Hack) Simmons, of; Jimmy (Runt) Walsh, 3b; Guy Zinn, of; Bill Bailey, p; Harvey Russell, c. *Front row:* Johnny Bates, of; Fred Jacklitsch, c; Vernon Duncan, of; Enos Kirkpatrick, 3b; unknown; James (Snipe) Conley, p; Jack Ridgway, p; Jack Quinn, p.

joy, was surely Baltimore—after a dozen years of being snooted at by Boston, New York, and Philadelphia above it, and Washington below. Baltimoreans put together the $90,000 for Terrapin Park—built new, on the north side of East 29th Street, directly across from Oriole Park—and about $70,000 for a set of players, primarily National Leaguers, assembled and managed by Otto Knabe, previously of the Phillies. The new ballpark's wooden stands were accommodating but, in retrospect, outmoded; in the AL and NL, by this time, the standard was steel-and-concrete construction. The FL was in a hurry (though its Chicago site was built solidly enough to be still in use, as Wrigley Field, today).

As to corporate structure, Federal Baseball Club of Baltimore's biggest individual shareholder was Ned Hanlon. (Leaving Brooklyn at the end of 1906, he had managed Cincinnati for two final, losing seasons and then at age 50 supposedly retired from baseball. But observers saw resentment in a man who had been in control in Brooklyn, only to be shouldered out of office.) Hanlon declined office in the FL club; rather, Carroll W. Rasin, a liquor wholesaler, and Harry S. Goldman, insurance man and ex–police magistrate, were president and secretary, respectively. Club headquarters was in an office building at Charles and Fayette Streets.

After spring training in North Carolina, the Terrapins opened at home, Monday, April 13, against Buffalo. Back in the big leagues! The turnout was immense—30,000 was the paid-attendance figure, meaning that far more stood than sat. Nowhere else had the majors' season begun yet; so when the home team won 3-2, Baltimore was universally first in the standings.

The pitcher that day was John Picus Quinn, a 30-year-old Pennsylvanian (born John Quinn Picus). Otherwise, the Terrapin lineup offered Harry J. Swacina at first; Manager Knabe, 29, at second; his Phillies double-play partner, Michael J. (Mickey) Doolan, at short; Michael T. (Runt) Walsh, a former Oriole, at third; Vernon V. Duncan, Bernhard (Benny) Meyer, and George Washington (Hack) Simmons, outfielders; and Frederick L. Jacklitsch, 38, catching. Other pitchers: George F. Suggs, Irvin K. (Kaiser) Wilhelm, and Frank E. (Piano Mover) Smith. In age, the starters averaged 33½ years.

By May 4 the Terrapins had grabbed the lead, and they held on through June. The *Sun*'s printed box scores were its most detailed ever. A slump dropped the team to third, however, and there it finished (84-70), albeit only four and a half games behind Indianapolis. Fan impatience was reflected in sports page headlines in the *Baltimore News*: the team was being referred to as "the Turtles." Only Meyer, a Missourian, and Walsh, a North Carolinian, had batted over .300. On the bright side, Jack Quinn, a spitballer, was 26-14, and Suggs went 24-14. Quinn ultimately pitched 23 years in the majors, and this was his only 20-games-won season.

All three majors are thought to have lost money, especially as the outbreak of World War I distracted the public; but the Federal League's industrialists could afford to increase their backing. Pennant or no pennant, the Indianapolis franchise was wrenched away, becoming the Newark Peppers—in position for a 1916 move into New York. In Baltimore, the FL team ruled both sides of 29th Street, for the International League Orioles, unable to compete, had lit out for Richmond. As for the 1915 Terrapins, manager Knabe went with the same infield, inserted outfielders Guy Zinn and Louis R. (Steve) Evans and catcher Frank Owens—and, to accelerate the push to the summit, hired the best pitcher in 1914's AL. This was Charles Albert

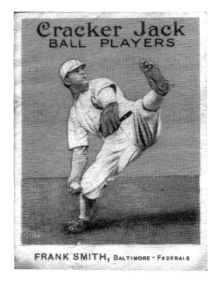

Buy a box of Cracker Jack, look for the free baseball player card in it.

Oriole Park (1914–44), the old timer's palace of enchantment. From the front rows, a spectator could hear the outcries of the combatants. Note size of pressbox.

Guy Zinn, outfielder

Bender, 31, a tall, strong Chippewa from Minnesota who inevitably was dubbed Chief. In 12 years with the Philadelphia Athletics, Bender had been a consistent winner (and went on to become an early Hall-of-Famer).

With the Terrapins, however, Bender lost four games for every one he won; his ERA almost doubled: in sum, his worst year (4-16) ever. Firewater, the fans muttered. Same story with Jack Quinn, whose 9-22 proved to be his only 20-games-lost season. Evans, from Ohio, and Walsh hit .300; everybody else was down: Swats Swacina, Knabe himself, and Doolan (who, hitting .186, was dumped). What demoralized the Terrapins? No single factor or circumstance now stands out. Other FL teams went at it vigorously in a hot pennant race; Joe Tinker's Chicago Whales churned across the finish line one percentage point in front of Fielder Jones's St. Louis Slofeds, and only 16 games separated first place from seventh. Then came another, 24-game interval. And who dwelt in this cellar, waiting to be boiled alive? The terrible 47-107 Terrapins. The Terps were last, and it was the last of the Terps.

The Federal League talked publicly of moving its Newark franchise into New York City; it proposed a three-way World Series. (Organized Baseball, alarmed, sent back a cold no.) But the big talk was bluster. A key FL owner died; other magnates, having lost money

even as AL and NL attendance improved, gave up and sent out sur-
render feelers. Offered good terms for their players and some of their
parks, the Federal League then disbanded. The single exception—the
one franchise ignored in the indemnifying payoffs—was Baltimore. It
was, in a way, 1902 all over again.

The majors took it for granted that Jack Dunn would move his
Orioles back, that Baltimore would quietly resume its place in the
minors. They reckoned without Hanlon and Goldman, who rocked
the boat. Alleging a $300,000 loss, and invoking the Sherman Anti-
trust Act, they sued Organized Baseball in U.S. District Court, asking
triple damages. On first instance, the claim was denied, but in 1916 a
circuit court, on appeal, found for the plaintiff—$80,000, trebled.
Organized Baseball, prospectively out of pocket even more when ordered to pay both sides' legal expenses, took it to the Supreme Court.

There, with Justice Oliver Wendell Holmes Jr. speaking for the
court, a unanimous decision ended seven years' litigation by holding
that baseball is not, after all, interstate commerce and therefore is not
subject to regulation by acts of Congress; lower-court verdict and
award were thrown out. The legal scholar G. Edward White finds
Holmes's ruling "strikingly out of touch with its subject matter," albeit
consonant with "the jurisprudential and economic assumptions of the
time." Today, to Baltimoreans with a sense of perspective, that 1922
verdict remains sentimental as well as asinine.

An even 50 years later, a similar suit was brought under the Clayton
Antitrust Act by the NL outfielder Curt Flood; the Supreme Court,
7-2, still endorsed special status for Organized Baseball. Thus, over
the years, all three groups—players enraged by owner collusion;
owners irate over agent and player greed; and fans disenchanted by
hidden profits, swollen salaries, rising ticket prices, and seating that
favors the privileged—could be confident that any new call for impar-
tial oversight would be unheeded.

Today, the many other professional sports are universally acknowledged as a sector of the entertainment business and therefore subject
to regulation. Organized Baseball, the one monopoly that still man-
ages to fend off regulation, continues on its special-exemption way.

Otto Knabe, second baseman and
playing manager of the Baltimore
Terrapins. About to turn 30, this
veteran National Leaguer was one
of many players happy to spite
Organized Baseball by leaving for
the better pay and work atmosphere of the new third league. But
Knabe persuaded few of his fellow
second-place Phillies to join him,
and the manpower otherwise provided was inadequate.

A Babe Ruth museum treasure—this snapshot of the famous ballplayer during a visit to St. Mary's Industrial School, his alma mater. He has agreed to hit a few fungoes to the next generation's would-be outfielders. He has dropped his suspenders. Sink out, fellows.

I guess I could have written two books of my life—one for the adults, one for the kids.

BABE RUTH, IN *Baseball Shorts*, BY GLENN LIEBMAN

CHAPTER ELEVEN

THE KID FROM EMORY STREET

One day early in 1914, Otto Knabe opened a letter from a local bar-tender. You should give my son a tryout, the message was; my son is a terrific pitcher and would win lots of games for your Federal League club. Knabe, the Terrapins' manager and head talent-seeker, gave the new league's standard response: thanks, but we're not interested in a growth team; we're hiring the proven major leaguers who can deliver now.

This recollection emerged during a conversation with Knabe in his Philadelphia retirement (he died in 1961). The pitcher in question was a 19-year-old left-hander, the star athlete at St. Mary's Industrial School, at Caton and Wilkens Avenues in southwest Baltimore. Si-multaneously, one or another of that school's administrators was try-ing to interest Baltimore's International League club in him. A third undercurrent: when Jack Dunn, the Orioles' manager and talent-seeker, then went out to St. Mary's to see for himself, he may have done so partly on his own. Young George Herman Ruth Jr. had been getting great press, as anyone following local-game box scores closely would have noticed.

A lengthy set of biographers has struggled to retrace the route that Babe Ruth took in youth, from the apartments above a series of blue-collar southwest Baltimore saloons to a church-operated training

216 Emory Street is the second doorway. Photo was made before restoration of these houses in the early 1970s. Today's Babe Ruth museum occupies the whole four-unit building.

school for the orphaned and the wayward. The saloonkeeper's oldest child had an olive complexion, broad nose, impressive ribcage, and thick, straight black hair. As boy and as man, Ruth loomed over others (in his prime, when many pitchers and fielders measured less than 6 feet, Ruth stood 6 feet 2 inches; his weight was from 215 pounds up). Also, the Ruth boy was unruly, carefree, nonacademic, and startlingly well coordinated. His mother was busy with younger siblings, his father with bar trade. The boy's younger sister, Mamie, later recalled, "He wouldn't mind Daddy, that was the problem. Daddy used to whip him something terrible." By age seven, "Little George," as the family spoke of him, had been packed off to St. Mary's. (The cost to parents was $15 a month.) Occasionally young Ruth was reprieved, but after a few days or weeks at home, he always returned to the custody of the school's operators, the Xaverian Brothers, attendance records show.

St. Mary's, home to some 800 boys, was run by a staff of 22. With such a ratio, the only salvation was strict rules and routines. (Memories of that disciplining may have intensified Ruth's delight later in flouting the conventions of baseball management and polite society.) While at St. Mary's, young Ruth was taught a work skill (shirtmaking), instructed in penmanship (he later gave beautiful autographs), and turned loose on the playing fields with their 43 separate baseball teams. At first, Ruth was a left-handed catcher using a right-hander's glove; after playing every position, he concentrated on pitching. The largest role in showing him how is traditionally assigned to Mathias Boutilier, C.F.X., a big man in size, athletic skill, and student respect. Ultimately, Ruth and a few other boys were allowed out to play on nearby teams in Baltimore's many sandlot leagues. Searching for Babe Ruth's 1912–13 games is a select pursuit for today's readers of newspapers on microfilm; photos of him as a St. Mary's player excite sports collectors.

Many of the circumstances of Babe Ruth's upbringing had become obscure even by the time he joined the New York Yankees. There were 50-some families of Ruths among 1895 Baltimore's many German Americans. Supposedly, this set of them had moved down from Pennsylvania. In 1895, John A. Ruth and his sons John A. Jr. and George H. were running a saloon and grocery store and selling lightning rods at 622–25 Frederick Avenue Extended. Ancestors on Babe Ruth's father's side were Protestant, on his mother's Roman Catholic. In 1996, the researcher Paul F. Harris Sr. located the record of the Ruths' wedding, June 25, 1894, at Fulton Avenue Baptist Church. Their first child was born slightly more than seven months later, at 216 Emory Street, a three-story brick rowhouse. Then the home of Kate Ruth's parents, Mr. and Mrs. Pius Schamberger, today it is the home of the Babe Ruth museum, the foremost baseball exhibit space north, east, south, or west of Cooperstown, New York. The Schambergers had lived there since the 1880s. He was an upholsterer and a labor union activist.

Young Ruth was baptized March 1 at St. Peter the Apostle Roman Catholic Church, on South Poppleton Street—perhaps, in that time of denominational intransigence, without his father's knowledge. Young Ruth was baptized again August 7, 1906, at St. Mary's Industrial School, which listed him as a convert. As an adult, George Jr. thought he had been born February 7, 1894. The city's Bureau of

Above: "Little George" learns a trade at St. Mary's. *Left:* Half a dozen surviving photos show Babe Ruth as a ballplayer at St. Mary's Industrial School; this is one of the best. Ruth, holding mask and glove (*top row, left*), has been catching—with a right-hander's glove.

Scorebook showing Babe Ruth's first game in Organized Baseball, April 23, 1914, at Oriole Park (south side of 29th Street, at Greenmount Avenue). He shuts out Buffalo 6-0.

The Oriole order that afternoon: Bert Daniels, rf; Fred Parent, 2b; Neal Ball, 3b; Birdie Cree, cf; George Twombly, lf; Claude Derrick, ss; Ed Gleichmann, 1b; Ben Egan, c; George Ruth, p. The scorer was Charles L. Schanberger, Baltimore correspondent for *The Sporting News*. This prize document is now in the Babe Ruth museum.

Vital Records lists only an unnamed male born and midwifed February 6, 1895.

Supposedly, Babe Ruth's father, "Big George," and his mother, Kate or Katie, went on to have eight children, but the only other one to survive childhood was Mary, known as Mamie. While "Little George" was big like his father, Mamie was small like her mother but had her father's and brother's face. (Mary Ruth Moberly spent her whole life in Maryland, cheerfully responding to innumerable interviewers until 1992, when she died just short of age 92, a Lutheran.) In 1912, Kate Ruth, ill from "exhaustion" and tuberculosis, went to a sister's house to die. George Sr. remarried shortly after.

The picture clarified once Jack Dunn took the strapping teenager under his protection in 1914. Off went Ruth and the Orioles to spring training in Fayetteville, North Carolina. (The preseason southern sojourn, as an IL Oriole tradition, had finally begun the year before.) Supposedly, Ruth's nickname originated there, where a team coach, Harry Steinmann, spoke of him as "Jack Dunn's babe." Ruth held attention from the start for his fastball, curve, and control (the

Orioles found little to teach him about the game's mechanics), and for the wetness behind his ears. His first-ever train ride was followed by his first-ever elevator ride, in a hotel. Practical jokes abounded, not all at the greenhorn's expense; the morning a horse was discovered in the hotel lobby, incontestably having been tethered there most of the night, Dunn could not vent his anger. Jack Dunn Jr. proved to be one of the perpetrators.

Babe Ruth's first run as a pro was scored on an intersquad game double by Rodger Pippen, then a sports writer for the old *Baltimore Star* and a fill-in outfielder. Soon Pippen's rival, Jesse Linthicum, on the scene for the *Sun*, had a bigger story to file: Ruth's first home run, a huge wallop, some 420 feet, that has been commemorated in Fayetteville by a plaque at the site. In exhibition games, Ruth as pitcher faced and beat Brooklyn, the Phils, and the world-champion A's. (Baltimore also beat 1913's NL pennant-winner, John McGraw's Giants.)

That year's Orioles had many strengths. In the outfield were George F. Twombly in left, William F. (Birdie) Cree in center, Bernard E. (Bert) Daniels in right; at first was Ed Gleichmann, at second Cornelius (Neal) Ball or Freddy Parent, at short Claude Derrick, at third Ezra Midkiff. Ralph Capron and 18-year-old Jack Dunn Jr. were utility men. Catcher and captain was Arthur A. (Ben) Egan; second catcher, James E. (Wickey) McAvoy. The pitching staff was unusual for its three/three right-hander/left-hander balance: Dave Danforth (a left-hander with some strange pitches, who later joined the White Sox and Browns and then became a well-regarded Baltimore dentist on Greenmount Avenue); Ensign (Lefty) Cottrell, from Syracuse University; two Baltimoreans, Allen E. (Rubber Arm) Russell and Bill Morrisette; and, once college was out, a 23-year-old North Carolinian, Ernest G. Shore, at 6 feet 4 the tallest man on the team. Finally, there was the big kid from St. Mary's whom, from reading the excited newspaper stories out of spring training, the fans already knew as Babe Ruth.

For the home opener (as with the Federals across 29th Street) it was Baltimore versus Buffalo, the home team winning. On April 23, the season's second game, Jack Dunn started Ruth, and the newcomer, nervous at first, pitched a 6-0, six-hit shutout. Joe McCarthy, long afterward Ruth's manager in New York, was the Bisons' second baseman; he went hitless while Ruth got two singles. "Fewer than 200 people were in the stands," the standard biography of Ruth notes (*Babe: The Legend Comes to Life*, by Robert W. Creamer). A full box score of that momentous debut in Organized Baseball still exists at the Babe Ruth museum, as kept in pencil that day by Charles L. Schanberger, Baltimore stringer for the *Sporting News*.

A former pitcher himself, Dunn was astonished by this rookie who, Mamie recalled, wore rings on three fingers of his pitching hand and who won his first 10 starts. His batting average was unexceptional; still, Al Schacht, the baseball clown but then a Newark pitcher, remembered throwing one that Ruth hit against the outfield fence so hard that it was fielded on the rebound by the second baseman. Ruth's pay rose from $100 a month to $250. He bought a bicycle and then a motorcycle and gave rides to his kid sister. The family saloon by then was at 552 West Conway Street, about where the centerfielders stand now in Oriole Park at Camden Yards. Babe Ruth was happy; Baltimore, with its Terrapins and its Orioles simultaneously in first place in their respective leagues, was happy.

Jack Dunn was unhappy. The respective schedules did not ordinarily have both 29th Street teams at home the same afternoon; nevertheless, attendance at the minor league park was not just down, it was dismal. The *American* noted, "The crowds attending games here just pay for the ground[s] help"—not for the players, who formed a relatively high payroll. No marketing strategies were available then; no souvenir-giveaway days or group-ticket deals. Why didn't Dunn just get a mortgage or line of credit and wait out the three-majors fight? There was an unexplained urgency in his maneuvers; behind them, the researcher Dave Howell sees Dunn's unpublicized debtor position remaining from his 1909 purchase of park and team. He had promissory note payments coming due. (The frequency of 1909–14 player exchanges with AL Philadelphia suggests that the creditor was

Connie Mack or his backers.) A Baltimore rumor had the Terrapins inviting Babe Ruth to broad-jump 29th Street and join them. Dunn went to New York to plead for help from Organized Baseball, but in vain. Dunn also asked the IL to let him move his franchise to Richmond in mid-1914, but the league, which would have had to pay off a lower-league local team, said no.

In that era, the owner desperate for cash had one recourse: sell his best players. Dunn wired Connie Mack in Philadelphia, but Mack had a first-place team already. A Cincinnati agent was seen in the stands. Dunn went to Washington, where the Red Sox were playing.

On July 7, the situation caved in. Cree (the top hitter at .356 and top earner at $400) was sold back to his old team, the Yankees. Next day, Cincinnati bought Twombly and Derrick. The day after that, Ruth, Ernie Shore, and Ben Egan as their catcher became Red Sox property. Two more players followed, ending with eight altogether. The Orioles had been 47-22, 5½ games in front (Ruth, 14-6); with what was left, they slid to sixth place and finished 72-79, 21 games back. (The final "home" games of these "remnant Orioles," as the sports writers called them, were played in Wilmington, Del.) Then, going about it more methodically this time, Dunn obtained authorization to move, and his 1915 team played out of Richmond.

Over the years, Ruth sometimes invited his kid sister Mamie, who was still living in Baltimore, to New York or Washington, to watch him play.

The price for Ruth, Shore, and Egan (Boston soon traded Egan away) was about $20,000. The three-way AL-NL-FL war had reduced virtually every owner's bank balance. In Baltimore, the wave of Oriole sell-offs touched off sports-page lamentations; the abrupt departure of Baltimore's young native son did not happen quietly: "He is a wonder and his performances have been followed by fans all over the country," C. Starr Matthews wrote in the *Sun* that black Friday. "During the past four months, his shoots have made the whole baseball world sit up and pay attention."

Babe Ruth did not hit a home run as an Oriole. He did, however, play the outfield in several games. In September—a sad postscript—the Babe reappeared in enemy uniform. Not quite ready for the majors, he had been sent down to Providence, a Boston farm club. Pitching for the Clamdiggers, he did once homer. And they won the 1914 IL pennant.

Thoroughly urban, quite lacking in inhibitions, and soon famous for his creature appetites, Ruth was quickly at home in other big cities. In Boston, he befriended a waitress from Texas named Helen Woodford and brought her to Baltimore to meet his father and sister. Little George, age 19, and Helen, 17, were married late in 1914 at St. Paul's Roman Catholic Church in Ellicott City. He spent one or two winters helping his father tend a bar, which is still at the northwest corner of Eutaw and Lombard Streets. But his father had remarried, and in 1918 was killed in a fist fight on the sidewalk outside the bar. After the funeral, Babe Ruth never came back to Baltimore to live. He liked Boston during his five-plus seasons there; it was a Boston newspaper that dubbed him G. Hercules Ruth. Traded to the Yankees for the 1920 season, he loved New York.

But Ruth made occasional appearances at or for the benefit of his alma mater, particularly after a fire in 1919 destroyed almost all its buildings. (St. Mary's Industrial School, founded in 1866, shut down in 1950.) And with Red Sox or Yankees, Ruth turned up at northside 29th Street's Oriole Park in exhibition games, mostly but not all pre-

Babe Ruth remained loyal to his alma mater and, by appearing at fund-raisers, helped it rebuild after a destructive fire in 1919. Here, at Oriole Park, he poses with the St. Mary's Industrial School Band. That he could play a tuba is in doubt.

season—a dozen games altogether. The earliest was in 1916, the final one on May 1, 1930. On April 18, 1919 (Boston 12, Baltimore 3), Ruth walked, homered, walked, homered, homered, and homered. Four in one game: the feat of feats that he never pulled off in a big league box score. So far, researchers have found no other exhibition-game instance of four Babe Ruth home runs. The following day his first two at-bats were additional homers, which made it, spread over two games, five homers in five consecutive batter's box appearances. (Without detracting from Ruth's feats, it should be noted that the Red Sox were on their way up from spring training in the South; no such momentum for the Orioles, whose few practices had been in chill and muddy Baltimore.)

His last visit was in July 1948. Wasted with cancer, Babe Ruth nonetheless kept his pledge to come to Baltimore, staying overnight at the Lord Baltimore Hotel, for that year's IL Oriole Interfaith Game, which was then rained out. Back in New York a month later Babe Ruth died at age 53 and was buried in a New York suburb.

Babe Ruth's last Baltimore visit was in 1948, an appearance at Municipal Stadium to help increase the attendance at 1948's Interfaith Night ball game. It rained; no game. Ruth went back to his New York hospital bed. Tickets were untorn.

The sense of someone and something extraordinary remains. He was in youth a superlative athlete. The columnist and speaker John Steadman rouses after-dinner audiences with his account of the tests that Columbia University physiologists once put Ruth through; his reflexes registered at the top of the scale. Ruth's .690 slugging average is still 56 points ahead of the nearest competitor's. In 1920 and 1921, his slugging average was .847 and .846, respectively; no one else has ever reached .800. With 1,330, he is by now 40th on the strikeout list; with 2,056, he is still first on the walks list. The 714 home runs overshadow his speed feats—the 705 doubles, the 136 triples.

The decades since Ruth's death have seen baseball become more comparative than ever, what with expanded score-keeping, computerized analyses, and huge, overweight, 2,750-page baseball encyclopedias. One by one, Ruth's showiest records have been surpassed: one-season homers, lifetime homers, lifetime runs batted in, on-base percentage, and consecutive scoreless innings pitched in the World

George Herman Ruth Jr. in his 20's. The first, and still the most dazzling, of baseball's superstars. Moreover, a man who enjoyed having his picture taken. For this one, no cap? But there it is, in his coat pocket.

Series. But the process offers a more complex, more comprehensive category: Total Baseball Ranking. What long-ago player (followed in order by Nap Lajoie, Willie Mays, Ty Cobb, and Hank Aaron) is still tops by many points? That's right: Babe Ruth, the kid from Emory Street.

Stats are for the studious; nouns, verbs, and adjectives get it across in ordinary talk. "This odd, appealing, truly unique man," in Robert W. Creamer's words, "was the best baseball player who ever lived."

Red Smith was equally succinct: "He changed the rules, the equipment, and the strategy of baseball." His Maryland biographer, Lois Nicholson, calls him "an authentic hero"—as distinct from a role model, which he was not. "The most colorful figure ever to appear on the American sports scene," obituaries said.

In 1969 the city government, led by Mayors Theodore R. McKeldin and Thomas D'Alesandro III, rescued the house where Ruth was born, which was on the brink of demolition, for reconstruction and use as a museum. Today, The Museum: The Babe Ruth Birthplace and Baseball Center is operated by a nonprofit foundation. In 1992, when the site of major league games in Baltimore was moved downtown, by happy chance the new Oriole Park at Camden Yards was within a few hundred yards of 216 Emory Street—the distance of "a long fly ball." In 1995, when Baltimoreans and others far beyond whooped it up commemorating the centennial of Little George's birth and erecting a statue of him (wearing a right-hander's glove) on the Camden Street side of the new ballpark, the museum, headed by director Michael Gibbons and curator Greg Schwalenberg, was the celebration's busy and resplendent focal point.

All this while, the legend of Babe Ruth's three-month sojourn as a minor league Baltimore Oriole has lived on: meteorlike in its flash, but a gaudy good time for all.

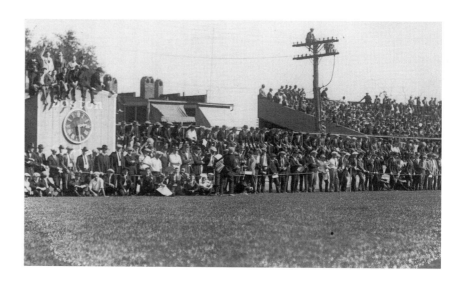

Did you ever hear of a left-side hit and run? We had one, on the seven-straight Orioles. [Fritz] Maisel, leading off, would get aboard; [Otis] Lawry would sacrifice; I was up next, the heavy hitter, and I'd bunt, toward third. Maisel, off with the pitch, would round third, never slowing. While the third baseman was running in after the ball and trying to throw me out, Maisel would score, most often standing.

MERWIN JACOBSON, IN 1976 INTERVIEW
WITH DAVE HOWELL AND AL KERMISCH

CHAPTER TWELVE

THE ENDLESS-CHAIN CHAMPS

The quiet in 1916 must have seemed otherworldly to Baltimore's baseball fans. In the distance, only two major leagues: the old, familiar, condescending National and American. In Baltimore, the same old minor league Orioles, now occupying the ballpark built two years earlier by the Terrapins of the newly extinct Federal League. It was business (i.e., the national pastime) as usual.

With no other bidders, the FL club turned over the newly renamed Oriole Park to Jack Dunn for a song: $25,000. It was going to be less simple moving his 1915 Richmond team back from self-exile; Dunn's solution was to sell Richmond, buy Jersey City's franchise, and transfer it.

Unsure what to expect, unwilling to care greatly after the rollercoaster rides of 1914–15, the fans were pleased to see the Orioles contending; fourth-placers, finally, only 7½ games back. And the lineup featured three young, promising Marylanders: a Baltimore infielder, Wilson L. Fewster; from Montgomery County, William H. Lamar, outfielder; and John N. Bentley, left-handed pitcher–first baseman. Chick Fewster and Bill Lamar soon afterward left for the majors, but seven years had gone by and Jack Bentley was 28 years old before Dunnie let go of him.

These, it turned out, were the first steps toward glory. This was the start of an Oriole team that would rise to the top of the high minors and stay there, almost indefinitely. The 1916 team (75-66) was first in batting, last in fielding (in 140 games, 312 errors); 1917's third-place team (88-61) was only 2 1/2 games back. Dunn's mind was ever on pitching, and 1917, which saw the arrival of an outfielder, 135-pound Otis (Peanuts) Lawry, from Maine, also produced two 21-year-old, 6-foot pitchers. One was Herbert E. Thormahlen, a 25-game-winning left-hander who then went on up; the other, James A. Parnham, one more of the many ballplayers stuck with the nickname Rube, stayed eight years off and on. (One day in August, he pitched—and won—both games of a doubleheader, the first game running 15 innings.)

By this time, the nation's thoughts were on World War I. In 1918, all minor leagues ceased play by September 1; IL teams played only 128 games. With many players in military service, the IL's leading pitcher was an Oriole left-hander, 19-year-old Ralph Worrell, a Bal-

The patriotic 1917 Orioles, with three servicemen ready to testify in their support. The poster at top center promotes a World War I Liberty Loan.

timorean, who went 25-10. But then, calamity—as influenza swept North America, Worrell was one of its fatalities. Also that year, Dunn signed a 17-year-old second baseman fresh out of City College, Max F. Bishop. Again the Orioles (74-53) finished third.

In any other city with a baseball franchise, mention of 1919 is good for a scowl. That was the year when certain Chicago AL players, underpaid, took money from New York gamblers and, it is accepted, set out to lose the World Series. In Baltimore, however, 1919 is a good number—make that a great one. That was the year Baltimore started counting consecutive pennants in the International League: one, two, three, four, five, six, seven. The big time it was not; but it was more championships in an unbroken row than any other team had rung up in majors or high minors. These proud Orioles were the seven-straighters; or "the endless-chain champs," as people sometimes spoke of them in other, less favored cities. For all who like numbers, it was also the first time Baltimore's baseball team won a hundred games. Tell it in Gath, publish it in the streets of Askelon: uniformly, throughout The Streak, the Orioles won a hundred or more games.

Three of 1919's newcomers fit in beautifully: Joe Boley at short, Merwin J. W. Jacobson in center, Fritz Maisel (a returnee from the Yankees, actually) at third. A Pennsylvania Pole, born John P. Bolinsky, known by his teammates as Zitz, Joe was one of four players from the 1919–25 Orioles who then figured large in Philadelphia AL's three straight pennants, 1929–31. As for handsome Jake from Connecticut, he was quickly a fan idol. And Fritz, leadoff man and base-stealer, was John McGraw over again without the truculence and chicanery. Also, Maisel as team captain took charge whenever Dunn went off to a lower-league city to have a look at some vaunted prospect there. Zitz and Fritz played on every one of the pennant teams, and Fritz Maisel was ultimately associated with the Orioles (successively as rookie, regular, shareholder, team captain, manager, director, and scout) for almost half a century. Another personnel note: both Jack Dunns, *père* and *fils*, were in a few of the box scores (apparently never in the same game). For Dunn Sr., age 46, it was the last such outing—and also for the eager but less talented Dunn Jr.

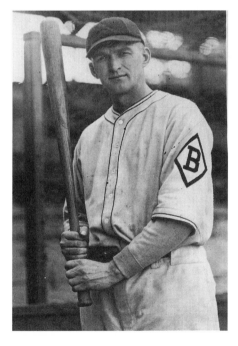

Joe Boley, the coalfield Pole and quiet shortstop who played as if the Orioles were in the majors.

The strikingly uniformed Baltimore Dry Docks of World War I. *Top row:* Johnny Baldwin; unknown; unknown; Dave Danforth; unknown; Ginger Settan; Lou Rehak; unknown; Jim Carter. *Bottom row:* Tony Citrano; John Pedone; unknown; J. M. Willis, Baltimore plant manager, Bethlehem Ship Building; Frank Wade; Jim Kelly; Johnny Eackle. Deferred from the draft because of being on the payroll of a war industry, players from majors and high minors fielded a strong team.

The Orioles took over first place early in June that first year, and stayed there. Peanuts Lawry's .364 made him the league's leading batter (an honor that one or another Oriole—never the same man twice—would grab throughout the streak, except in '22 and '25). At the same time, Rube Parnham's 28-12 made him the league's leading pitcher. The IL was back on a peacetime schedule, and Baltimore's 100-49 was good enough to beat out Toronto's Maple Leafs, pennant-winners in 1917 and 1918, by 7½ games.

There followed a strange, postseason series—for the city championship. During World War I, the government tried to boost morale by encouraging the formation of teams at war industries' local plants; some major leaguers, sidestepping the draft, were thus employed. This still went on in 1919, after the Armistice was signed. Accordingly, to the fans' excitement, the champions of the Bethlehem Steel League and of the International League now went at it, best of seven: the Baltimore Dry Docks versus the Baltimore Orioles. And the Dry Docks—managed by Sam Frock, a Baltimorean who after four NL years was one of Dunn's 1911 pitchers, and starring on the mound Dave Danforth of Dunn's 1912–14 Orioles—upset the proud IL champs, four games to three.

Then came 1920, competitively the most lustrous of all Oriole seasons in the minors. Down from the hills of western Maryland strode a youth barely out of his teens, long and lank, with an arm like a flail: Robert Moses Grove. He was overshadowed that first year by the veteran Harry Frank, a Baltimorean, and by the Swarthmore College newcomer, Jack Ogden, who were 25- and 27-game winners, and by Bentley, who won 16, mostly in relief. In crises, Bentley moved over from first base, his regular assignment. Bentley led the IL in the wildly disparate categories of ERA and RBI. Meanwhile, Jacobson's .404 was the league's first .400 batting average in a quarter century; the team average was .318. (Jacobson said afterward his bat was a war club—46 ounces.) Toronto, too, was strong that year, winning all but two of its last 26 games. Baltimore, never flustered, won every one of its last 25 games. At the end, they were 2½ games apart, and the Orioles were 110-43. Their winning percentage was .719, then and still the highest ever attained by an Oriole team.

That fall, the Junior World Series resumed. Begun in 1904 but held only four scattered times before 1920, the postseason playoffs of the International League in the East and the American Association in the Middle West then became a fixture (until 1936, it was best five out of nine). Baltimore, in eight appearances, split even. In 1920, the foe

Rube Parnham (*left*) was a townie, not a country hick. But with memories of the Philadelphia Athletics' great pitcher and drinker Rube Waddell still fresh, the nickname was applied to convivial Jim Parnham, and it stuck. Jack Ogden (*right*) was a tall, strong pitcher, otherwise Parnham in reverse, being dour, stern-faced and a college athlete. In 1921, Ogden was 31w-8l and then pitched all three Oriole victories in the Junior World Series.

Max Bishop, second baseman, was one of the three local high school players (Fritz Maisel and Tommy Thomas) who became key members of the Seven Straighters. Sportswriters called him Camera Eye; six times in one 1936 Oriole game, Max walked. Afterward, he coached the Naval Academy baseball team for 24 seasons.

was formidable: St. Paul, which had won its pennant by 26½ games. Along came Baltimore: the proud Saints were converted into erring sinners, five games out of six. Dunn was so pleased he put Baltimore's entire receipts into the player pool: $1,800 apiece. Back home in Lonaconing, Grove, 20, married his sweetheart.

A few days before, during an American League pennant climax, the second-place New York Yankees had stopped off for an exhibition game at Oriole Park. New York's roster included five former Orioles—Fewster, Thormahlen, Shawkey, Ernie Shore, and, at the height of a sensational 54-homer season (almost twice the previous record), Babe Ruth. So, against Parnham and the minor league Orioles, Ruth struck out three times and haughty New York was whitewashed 1-0.

For 1921, the IL lengthened its schedule to 168 games (the Pacific Coast League had been playing as many as 230 games in a season). All being daylight games, this meant many a doubleheader, its second game limited to seven innings. Another City Collegian, Alphonse Thomas Jr., universally called Tommy, joined the pitchers and won 24 games; Grove won 25; and Ogden's 31-8 took league honors (for more than 15 decisions). Bentley led the league in singles (246), doubles, homers (24), hits, total bases, and batting average—a superb .412. Simultaneously, Bentley's 12-1 record was tops in pitching percentage. For this, his pay, the team high, was $4,500. In mid-May, Baltimore started winning and kept on through 27 straight to tie the Organized Baseball record. That was the pennant that the Orioles (119-47) won by 20 games. Their victory total remains the IL record.

The Junior World Series, however, was a letdown. Injuries having removed three of their starters, the Orioles bowed, five games to three, to Joe McCarthy's Louisville Colonels. Conspicuous in the AA lineup were outfielder Baldomero Acosta (little Merito, from Cuba, in 1917 had been an Oriole) and infielder Charles L. Herzog, better known as Buck, a former NL infielder and manager and a Baltimorean.

When the Orioles made it four in a row in 1922 (115-52, 10 games in front), the majors grew restive. They wanted Dunn's stars. But during the World War I crunch, the majors had looked out only for themselves, while all minor leagues save the IL foundered. Coming to life again in 1919, the minors avenged this abandonment by withdrawing from the National Agreement of 1903, the pact that had regularized the drafting of players at set prices. For some years, accordingly, Jack Dunn was free to dicker or to turn down an offer altogether. In 1922, when Dunn let the New York Giants have Jack Bentley, "the Babe Ruth of the minors," the bill was for $72,500. Baltimoreans whistled. Meanwhile, the Orioles had ingloriously lost a best-of-three series to the New Haven Profs, pennant-winners in a mere Class A league. But they were able to tarnish the American Association's year by beating St. Paul again, in eight games.

Other clubs had won four years in a row, but not five. The 1923 Orioles, facing the big one, were jolted by the death in early March of Jack Dunn Jr. from pneumonia at age 27. An athlete, Little Jack was an only child and, as club secretary-treasurer, the heir apparent. Despondency enveloped his father. But all hands gave it the Old Oriole

John Needles Bentley, a Montgomery County lefthander. The Orioles' first baseman between his pitching starts (in 1921, he led the IL in both batting and pitching), Bentley as pitcher still batted fifth. When Jack Dunn began letting go of his stars, Bentley was the first one sold (to New York NL in 1923, aged 28)—as a pitcher.

Oriole Park, on the northwest corner of Greenmount and 29th; built in 1914 as Terrapin Park. Where, in this crowd at an entrance, are the women? Home, to have supper ready when the game is over.

One advantage of all those flammable boards was their availability for signs. Legend above automobiles advertises the start of a new season. Opening game: Buffalo Bison vs. Baltimore Orioles. Sidewalk gas lamp contrasts with electric light pole for new-fangled night games.

try, and in proper course (i.e., 111-53, 11 games ahead of the closest pursuer), the record was Baltimore's. Clarence Pitt, acquired in mid-season, narrowly won the IL batting championship. The replacement at first base, Clayton Sheedy, a Bostonian, had joined the Birds on graduation from Georgetown College; he and a utility player, Richard T. Porter, from Princess Anne and St. John's College, topped .300. But the real joy, as usual, was the pitching. Lefty Grove (he and his wife Edith lived at 708 East 23d Street) rang up 330 strikeouts. Parnham, called "the dumbest man in the world off the field but the smartest, on," had his best year ever. His 33-7 included a season-ending 20 in a row (exceeding Ogden's 18-straight games won in 1921). To do it, Parnham, on the last day of the season, came back from being AWOL to pitch and win a doubleheader.

Here and there, baseball people were saying that Baltimore's team was of major league dimensions. After IL play had ceased, the Orioles scheduled a week of exhibition games with major league teams. The all–New York (or Subway) World Series of 1921 and 1922 (winner: the Giants) were about to be followed by yet another (winner: the Yankees). But first, the Giants came to Oriole Park, where the IL champs beat them in 10 innings, 4-3. (Next were the second-division Philadelphia A's, who won.) Climactically, the New York Yankees arrived for three games in three days, which Baltimore swept thanks to Parnham, then Grove, then Thomas. Babe Ruth played only in the first game, Sunday, September 30 (20,000 paid attendance; 5,000 other fans turned away); with the bases loaded, Ruth belted one clear out into Greenmount Avenue, but the game ended Orioles 10, Yankees 6.

And now the critics' theory could be put to a test, of sorts. On October 3, at the Polo Grounds in New York, Jack Dunn's stars took the field against John McGraw's Giants, whose lineup was reinforced by three of Miller Huggins's Yankees, including Babe Ruth (to heighten big-city interest in what was only an exhibition game, though also a benefit: the resulting attendance, "approximately 7,000"). For the visitors, the pressure was too great. Lefty Grove, pulled after three innings, had allowed five runs, including two homers, and the New York–New York team went on to win, 9-3. The fine shortstop Joe

Robert Moses Grove, an Allegany County lefthander brought up from the Blue Ridge League at age 20. In his five years as an Oriole, Grove averaged 22 wins a year, 7 losses. In 1923, he pitched 303 innings, walked 186 men, struck out 330. His specialty was the very pitch favored by Jack Dunn—the cannonball.

The 1924 Orioles. *Top row:* John Alberts, utility; George Brown, p; Ed Tomlin, utility; trainer Eddie Weidner; Bill Clymer, coach; Lefty Grove, p; Clifford (Stonewall) Jackson, of; Clayton Sheedy, 1b; Jack Ogden, p; *middle row:* Rube Parnham, p; Fritz Maisel, 3b; Lew McCarty, c; Bill Henderson, p; Homer Jenkins, p; Merwin Jacobson, of; Tom Connelly, of; Charles (Buck) Foreman, p; George (Moose) Earnshaw, p; *bottom row:* Lawrence Fischer, of; Tommy Thomas, p; Otto Greenae, c; John Jacobs, of; Earl Clark, of; Sewell Dixon, utility; Joe Boley, ss. *Not shown:* Jack Dunn, manager.

Boley was out, hurt; his replacement made errors. Ruth homered off Jack Ogden. That anticlimactic afternoon, the SABR researcher Al Kermisch notes, the IL Orioles were up against eight future Hall-of-Famers. In a summary of these and other exhibition games, Kermisch counts 11 pitcher-batter high noons: Grove versus Ruth, left-hander versus left-hander. Nine times, Ruth struck out. (Later, with both in the majors and Ruth on his way to hitting 60 home runs in a single, 154-game season, number 57 was off Grove.)

Letting down after New York, the 1923 Orioles went on to play, and lose to, Hartford, the lower-league New England champs; and to Kansas City, five games to four, in the Junior World Series. This latter was the series in which Jack Dunn lost his temper off the field, firing a pitcher and a catcher for, well, warming up too soon: down-

town at the Emerson Hotel, during a fifth-pennant banquet, Chief Bender, who had recently begun playing for Baltimore again, and William G. Styles, known as Lena, were a bit too happy as they threw the bread rolls back and forth. This was also the series in which the announced attendance for game eight was 373. It was October 24 and 51 degrees; the bases umpire that day, whose name was Chill, wore overcoat and gloves. Afterward, Dunn got back to business: for $25,000 and two players, Max Bishop, informally Tilly, became the property of the Philadelphia Athletics.

In 1924, the Orioles swept smoothly on to still another triumph. Filling the vacancy was Dick Porter, also known as Wiggles or Twitchy Dick to sports writers eyeing the wibble-wobble in his batting stance. Whatever, it worked: he won that year's IL batting title. Grove, per-

The two most important figures in early Oriole management were adoptive Baltimoreans: Ned Hanlon and Jack Dunn (*above*). The name Edward Hanlon is now enrolled at the Hall of Fame; the name Jack Dunn goes on and on in Baltimore—Jack Dunn V's turn is coming, in the twenty-first century.

fecting his control, had his finest year, 26-6; and the pitching staff was buttressed by one more hard-throwing 6-footer, George L. Earnshaw. Instead of just blowing it by 'em, Earnshaw, from Swarthmore College, was a 1919-25 novelty in also having a first-rate curve.

The one position Dunn could never fill with a standout player was catcher. Half a dozen men gave it a try, the best of them perhaps Lena Styles, and he stayed only two years. Also worthy of mention: Babe Ruth's old catcher, Ben Egan, in the third and last of his tours of Oriole duty; Wickey McAvoy, down from the A's; and Joe Cobb, whose last name was originally Serafin. As for the outfield, an even longer parade: a dozen regulars performed there during the seven great years. Jacobson and Lawry alone stayed more than two years. (After Jake was beaned twice, Dunn figured he was through and traded him —only to watch Jake become a major leaguer.) But Dunn got many a .300 year out of Bill Holden, Johnny Honig, Tom Connelly, Maurice (Comet) Archdeacon, John Roser, and Curt Walker.

The first two years, it had been Toronto that floundered in Baltimore's immediate wake; then, three times, Rochester; in 1924 (117-48, victory by 19 games), Toronto again. After the 1924 season, all seven other clubs rejoiced as Lefty Grove, too, took the A's train. The price? All of $100,600, the extra hundreds to make it a sum greater than what the Yankees had paid Boston for Babe Ruth. Not even then did the younger (by five years) of these two Marylanders confirm the careless error by both the front office and the sports writers in pluralizing his last name. Later, in Philadelphia, the correct spelling came out: not Groves but Grove. With his best years still ahead of him (IL totals: 109-36; in 17 years as a major leaguer: 300-141, a better ratio than Ruth's as pitcher; home runs: 15), the Lonaconing sycamore said little, did much. As just one example, Grove led the IL in strikeouts in all but the first of his five Oriole years. He also walked a few. In his Baltimore years, Grove got by on two pitches: fastball and vestigial curve; his change of pace was "hard and harder."

All this while, as Dunn slowly allowed his stars to advance, one by one, Baltimore's IL rivals waited for the Orioles to weaken. Not in 1925, though. How splendid a sight it would be—rather, it was—for seven pennants to be flapping from the centerfield flagpole. One final time, the season plan of overpowering pitching worked. Thomas led the league with his 32-12 and 268 strikeouts; Earnshaw was 28-11 and Ogden went him one better, 29-11. Even so, Toronto this time was only four games behind the 105-61 Orioles. But what matter, when Louisville then went down, five games to three (Earnshaw thrice the winning pitcher)? And if only Jack Dunn, afterward, hadn't gone and sold Tommy Thomas to the White Sox. . . .

They did their best in 1926, the patchwork remainder; from the bench, Dunn (profane even when happy) drove his players as hard as ever; but a degree of ennui had set in—empty grandstand seats said it, too. In August, the Birds once more took the lead. But they couldn't hold it and, at 101-65, ended up eight games behind Toronto—which had the Baltimore rejects, Lawry and Styles, in its lineup. Whom would Dunn put on the block this time? Joe Boley, going off to join Grove and Bishop in Philadelphia. And who felt left behind, and griped at not being sold? George Earnshaw, who had to pitch two more seasons before he, too, became an Athletic (for $80,000 to Jack Dunn). Grove and Earnshaw, in the majors, were soon Mose and Moose, respectively. Maisel and a few others were past the selling age. That left a single prime name unspoken for—at that, one more of the tall, strong pitchers: Rube Parnham. Parnham, from western Pennsylvania, was on the team eight years, won 88 games, and lost only 34, and drank. With Parnham, it was Dunn who had the control problem. The majors rejected a player who, at the start of one more spring training, was reliably absent.

Did Dunn, by holding his star players back, deprive them of added glory in the majors? No answer is provable, but the loss in playing years can be underscored by comparing their ages with those of other players simultaneously entering the big time. These eight Oriole graduates—ultimately, five pitchers, three infielders—averaged slightly under 27 years old; the other starters on Connie Mack's 1929 champion A's averaged 24 on arrival in the majors. To raise again that topic dear to the arguefiers: were the Seven-Straighters as good as, even better than, the major leagues' bottom-feeders during the early '20s? One day, yes indeed; another day, perhaps no.

And so, as 1926 concluded, the jubilee was over. Gone, the annual

A young Baltimore bookseller, Aquilla B. Hanson, used to take his best girl, Dorothy, to the ballgame on Lefty Grove days, buying seats directly behind home plate. When a pitch got away, hurtling on the fly straight into the screen, Dorothy would shriek and clutch Quill. Theirs was one long and happy marriage.

pennant-clinching day when downtown's dailies for once made more fuss over the Orioles than over AL and NL doings. No more, the days of exhibition games in which the opposing big-time teams had to bear down hard if they were to stave off bumptious Baltimore. Fortunate, as 1927 began, that Baltimoreans had no inkling of the many annual disappointments ahead, the tedious procession of lackluster seasons, before a set of Orioles would once more scramble back on top of the IL heap.

Many of the Seven-Straighters were long lived, but by the 1990s none was left to give an insider's account of those times. Grove, the only one of them so far to enter the Hall of Fame, died in 1975 at age 75 and was buried in Frostburg. Long ago, Grantland Rice called him "in my book, the greatest left-hander that ever lived." Bill James, superstatistician to the videoscreen age, concurs. Since 1931, when Grove went 31-4 for Philadelphia AL, no left-hander and only one right-hander has equaled that games-won mark; no one has surpassed it. (Remember that in a 154-game season, when everything goes well, a pitcher gets about 36 starts; in a 162-game season, about 38.) Grove remains the AL's only left-hander to have won as many as 30 games in one season. Several pitchers have outdone his 300 career wins, including the left-hander Warren Spahn. But the Total Pitcher Index, compiled by John Thorn, Pete Palmer, and Michael Gershman, ranks Grove fifth, behind Walter Johnson, Cy Young, Pete Alexander, and Christy Mathewson—who were not just old-timers, but right-handers all.

Grove's parents were English-born; his father worked 54 years in the coal mines. Grove, a ninth-grade dropout, worked in a silk mill, a glass factory, a B&O track gang—anything but the mines. In boy-hood, he recalled, the big thing was rocks—"we threw at anything, moving or stationary." As an adult, he was a 6-foot 3-inch 190-pounder; what impressed John Lardner about Grove was his "vast sloping shoulders." Martinsburg of the Blue Ridge League signed him out of the semipros; the same year, 1920, Dunn bought him for $3,500—the cost of repairs to Martinsburg's outfield fence. In 1941, after 17 years in the majors, still a man of few words and a sometimes vile temper, he went back to Allegany County, to Lonaconing. Fond of hunting, cigar-chewing, and pool-shooting, he operated Lefty's Place, with pool tables and duckpin alleys. To the hill people, he was Bob. He gave away most of his trophies one by one. His introversion waned; Mose Grove voiced one of the best descriptions ever of player joy: "After the game was won, I used to take my shower and swallow an ounce of whiskey slow and get a rubdown. I'd go to sleep right there on the table. It was real damn good."

Of 18 key players during the 1919–25 IL championship years, the last survivor was Tommy Thomas, 88 when he died in Dallastown, Pennsylvania, in 1988. Thomas's mark on Baltimore baseball is one of the deepest cut. In 1921, he lost the game that broke off the Orioles' winning streak at 27 straight, but he made up for it by winning the 117th game, which broke all previous records. In 1927, one of Babe Ruth's 60 homers was off Grove; three were off Thomas, yet Thomas won 19 games for a losing set of White Sox. After the 1925 season, Thomas was finally allowed to advance to the majors, and the Orioles won no more pennants—until 1944, with Thomas as manager. Long after, Thomas passed his own judgment on teammates, calling Parnham "the best pitcher of all of us in Baltimore." In contrast, "if you were to leave Grove in for only 85 pitches" in his first Oriole years, "he might not yet have finished the first inning."

Grove moved to Ohio late in life. Four of the Silver Age Orioles, in retirement, remained Marylanders: Fritz Maisel, Jack Bentley, Max Bishop, and Dick Porter; and Merwin Jacobson became one. Jack Dunn and nine others were long ago elected to the International League's Hall of Fame.

The champion 1929 Baltimore Black Sox. *From left, top row:* Robert (Eggie) Clarke, c; Jesse Willis (Pud) Flourney, p; Holsey (Scrip) Lee, p; Ollie Marcelle, 3b; Jesse James Hubbard, of; Merven J. (Red) Ryan, p; Pete Washington, of; Bill Force, p; *bottom row:* Herbert A. (Rap) Dixon, of; James (Jay) Cooke, p; Domingo (Harry) Gomez, c; Francis X. (Frank) Warfield, 2b, manager; Jud Wilson, 3b; Dick Lundy, ss; Laymon Yokeley, p. *Not shown:* Knowlington O. (Buddy) Burbage, of; Jesse (Nip) Winters, p.

I recall, only too vividly, this past season at Maryland Park, how blue-coated officers of the law would stand in front of the press box, shutting off any possible view of home plate.

BILL GIBSON, *Afro-American*, SEPTEMBER 28, 1929

CHAPTER THIRTEEN

YEA, BLACK SOX!

Separate baseball, as played by black players in Baltimore in the first half of the 20th century and enjoyed by black spectators, is a story with great moments and, as in any competitive team sport, also some desolation. During 25 years of Baltimore franchises in one or another Negro League (between 1923 and 1951 inclusive), three times Baltimore won a championship. That glory is the more memorable for having come at equal intervals—in 1929, 1939, and 1949—and each at a point when Baltimore's all-white International League team was in the doldrums. Later, following integration, three of the players on those Black Sox and Elite (pronounced "EE-light") Giant teams were young enough and good enough not just to play in the majors but to win fame. It is an enviable distinction in Baltimore today to be able to say, "I saw games played at Bugle Field" or "I was there, at Westport Stadium."

After black players had been harshly turned away by Organized Baseball in the 1880s, entrepreneurs seeking to form clubs and to construct schedules went on using the model of the late 1860s: independent traveling teams. By 1910, Chicago was the power center, and a massive Texas right-hander, Andrew (Rube) Foster—pitcher, manager, owner—had become black baseball's most prominent figure. In

Maryland, numerous semipro clubs flourished in one or more seasons: for example, the Baltimore Sluggers, Catonsville Social Giants, Easton Blue Sox, Coleman Brown Sox, Cambridge Orioles, Elkton Giants, Pennsylvania Avenue Eagles, Aisquith Giants, and Lincoln A. C. (Athletic Club) of Ellicott City. The two strongest teams were in Baltimore: the Baltimore Black Sox, founded about 1913, and the Weldon Giants.

As World War I ended, Rube Foster made the dream real. Invoking the authority that came with having outpitched major leaguers (e.g., Rube Waddell and the Philadelphia A's), Foster, from Chicago, convened the Kansas City organizing meeting that brought into being a viable Negro National League. Most of its member clubs played in parks of their own, but sometimes, as popular interest rose, they rented big league parks for the day. Meanwhile, Baltimore's Black Sox began hiring NNL-level players. In 1920, the historian Robert Leffler records, came an unpublicized crisis: a Black Sox challenge to the Baltimore Dry Docks, the team of Bethlehem Steel war workers who had just beaten the International League Orioles in a so-called city championship series. In response to the challenge, silence.

Black Sox as a Baltimore team name was in use well before 1919's Chicago-Cincinnati World Series and the scandal of its New York–gambler fix; afterward, Baltimore's team went right on using the name with honor and respect. The owner was white—Charles P. Spedden, a barkeep and then a traveling salesman. Toward 1920, George Rossiter bought into the operation. Age 35, a former semipro, Rossiter owned a seafood business (later, a restaurant) at Hanover and Hamburg Streets.

The team's home field was Westport Park, small and rundown, at 1701 Russell Street (the intersection with Bush Street) in Southwest Baltimore. In 1921, the Black Sox Baseball and Exhibition Co. built and fenced, across the street, roofed stands with first- and third-base line bleachers, for a seating capacity of about 3,800. Called Maryland Park, it was on a main streetcar line.

Management's immediate goal was to fill the calendar. Sometimes, this meant a 1920 Westport game matching Rube Foster in person and his Chicago American Giants (no longer quite the aggregation that in 1910 had won 106 games, lost 7) against the Bacharach Giants of Atlantic City, New Jersey. But far more often it meant local, black semipro nines or prizefight cards. Fan support, long before season tickets, was undependable. Sometimes the Black Sox made more money by taking to the road and playing before larger crowds in the larger parks to the north.

The first player of national standing signed by the Black Sox seems to have been Buck Ridgely (or Risley), a shortstop, in 1915. In 1920 came the outfielder and cleanup hitter Blainey Hall and Doc Sykes, with his three-speed spitter ("slow, slower, slowest"). Sykes, an Alabama graduate of the Howard University School of Dentistry, in 1922 not only no-hit the Bacharachs but went 18-4. (In retirement, he built up a dental practice in Baltimore, where he died in 1986 at age 93.)

In 1922 came Jud Wilson, infielder, and Holsey Scranton Scriptus (Scrip) Lee, an underhand pitcher (according to his teammates, "his curve broke up; his fastball, down") and Purple Heart veteran of World War I; in 1923, Julio Rojo, catcher, a Cuban; in 1924, J. Preston (Pete) Hill, "the first great outfielder in black baseball history," in the judgment of James A. Riley, encyclopedist; also in 1924, John Beckwith, infielder and epic slugger, and (Crush) Christopher Columbus Holloway, rightfielder; in 1926, Benjamin H. Taylor, first baseman, another who settled in Baltimore afterward, holding the scorecard concession of the subsequent Elite Giants; and again in 1926, Laymon Yokeley, a tall, slender, 22-year-old right-hander from Livingstone College, in North Carolina, who was about to become the most accomplished of all African-American pitchers so far in Baltimore uniform.

More should be said about Ernest Judson Wilson—now Jud, now Boojum for the sound his base hits made, smacking into the board fences. Built like the contemporary white outfielder Hack Wilson (short, with barrel chest and pile-driver arms), Jud Wilson excelled at either first or third and, at the plate, Riley reports, "could hit anything thrown to him." During his occasional rages, strong men backed off. Jud Wilson was there in the lineup for nine straight years, the Black Sox record.

Crush Holloway, 1920s outfielder, also later played for the Elites.

Holloway, too, was memorable. He said Crush was his real name, not just a comment on his base-running style, which he once described for the historian John Holway: "No, I didn't hurt [the catcher], I didn't cut him. I just knocked his mitt and mask off, turned his chest protector around and left him sitting there on home plate."

Playing managers were customary in that economy. For the Black Sox, the succession began with J. Burke Hairstone (1916–20; some sports writers listed him as Harristone), outfielder; Charley Thomas (1921–22), catcher; Robert J. (Eggie) Clarke, catcher (1922–23); Pete Hill (1924–25), who, as an outfielder on Rube Foster's 1910 team, had batted .428; Ben Taylor (1926–28), first base, whose three brothers were also in the league; and Francis X. (Frank) Warfield (1929–32), second base.

By 1922, clubs that were natural rivals were loath to come to Maryland Park, with its relatively small ticket revenue. To ensure games, Rossiter and Spedden helped found a rival to the Midwest's Negro National League—the new, six-team National Association of Eastern Colored Baseball Clubs (ECL). League play must have

The 1924 Baltimore Black Sox. *Top row, second from left:* Neil Pullen, c; Crush Holloway, of; Preston (Pete) Hill, of and manager, in sweater; Jud Wilson, 1b, *sixth from left.* *Bottom row:* Wade Johnston, of; Bill Force, p; Mouse Morcell, mascot; John Beckwith, 3b, *fourth from left.* Others, uncertain.

puzzled Baltimore fans: the 49-12 team that called itself "champions of the South" in 1922 then won only 19 of its first-year ECL games and lost 30, to finish last. While 36 players came and went in 1923, at least Jud Wilson batted .373, leading the league.

Thanks to Spedden's other-city visits and aggressive hiring, Baltimore then did better: in 1924, second place (30-19); in 1925, third place (31-19); in 1926, sixth of eight (18-29); in 1927, a split season, third place (35-35). Jud Wilson's .412 outdid all other batters. Attendance reached 8,000 for home games with the champion Hilldale (Philadelphia) team. In 1928, however, the ECL collapsed amid owner contention and rowdiness on-field and off. To that point, nary a pennant for the Black Sox, despite their imposing roster.

One source of trouble was the bootleg-liquor era. The big man, Beckwith, led the ECL with his .404 batting average in 1925; what's more, Babe Ruth was quoted as saying, "not only can Beckwith hit harder than any Negro ballplayer, but any man in the world." (Then Josh Gibson arrived.) At the time, though, Beckwith was making the Negro League rounds, in the uniforms ultimately of 13 teams. Arrived in Baltimore and named team captain, Beckwith as batter pulverized the ball but loafed at practice, and during games drank some of the alcohol handed out to him from the stands. He beat up an umpire, and was the reason why Rojo, no violet, was traded away at his own request. By 1927, Beckwith was gone to his next town. Most pro baseball teams black or white could expect to include one or more alley fighters, but Beckwith was a standout, "his character deficiencies often negat[ing] his player value," in the words of the *Biographical Encyclopedia of the Negro Baseball Leagues*.

In 1929, Black Sox management joined a new American Negro League composed largely of familiar rivals from New York (Lincoln Giants), Philadelphia (Hilldale), Pittsburgh (Homestead Grays), Atlantic City (Bacharach Giants), and New York again (Cuban Giants). Over the winter, Rossiter and Spedden had pulled off two large trades, bringing in second baseman Frank Warfield, shortstop Dick Lundy (a World War I veteran), and third baseman Oliver Marcelle. All were well traveled; Weasel Warfield, 5 feet, 7 inches and the new team manager, ruled by intimidation. Together with old-reliable Jud

Wilson, who had held down first base since 1922, they constituted the Negro Leagues' version of a million-dollar infield.

The outfield included Pete Washington in left, Herbert (Rap, as in Rappahannock) Dixon in center, and Knowlington (Buddy) Burbage or Jesse Hubbard in right. Dixon, formerly with Baltimore's old rival the Harrisburg (Pa.) Giants, batted .432 that year. Spelling Laymon Yokeley on the mound were Jesse W. (Pud) Flournoy, a left-hander, and a small knuckleballer, Merven J. (Red) Ryan. Behind the plate, Eggie Clarke was relieved occasionally by Domingo (Harry) Gomez. Not one rookie in the lineup.

The 1929 season was played in two parts—the Black Sox won both (24-11, 25-10), and finished seven games ahead of the Lincoln Giants, their nearest pursuer. Yokeley won 17 games, including two double-headers and a no-hitter (Leon Day remembered Yokeley as his boyhood hero.) Flournoy and Ryan went, respectively, 9-5 and 7-4.

Was there euphoria up and down Pennsylvania Avenue? Hard at this distance to gauge Baltimore's rejoicing. A World Series against the Negro National League's formidable, white-owned Kansas City Monarchs? It was not to be, not when the two leagues were raiding each other's rosters—and the new ANL's owners couldn't even quiet their internal discord. What did happen was a postseason series against barnstorming big league All-Stars. At least once, attendance reached 11,000. The Black Sox won handily, six games to two. In the 1930s, when his arm went sore, Laymon Yokeley was deemed to have been overworked in youth; but he walked away from 1929's postseason in the glow of having beaten Robert M. Grove—Lefty himself—twice.

But in 1930, home and away, the Black Sox were back to all-comers scheduling.

The so-called Negro Leagues spanned little more than a generation, from 1920 to 1954—from segregation and Rube Foster to Branch Rickey and the integration that drained off their young stars. At least 36 cities, of all sizes, held Negro League franchises. Many of the owners were black; many of them as primary occupation were big locally in the young but growing illegal numbers lottery. Star players lived well and were idolized in the black community; but an occasional team wasn't much above the level of semipro. Usually, the manager doubled as a player. In the absence of a reserve clause, many an established player started a new season with a different club.

Working conditions were inevitably inferior to those in white baseball. The seven-passenger sedan of conventional Negro Leagues travel gave way late in the 1920s to the team bus (denied gasoline ration stamps in World War II, the Negro Leagues began using trains and were less able to barnstorm). Many players wintered in Cuba, paid to play in its thriving leagues. As Latin American baseball broadened, however, its season lengthened. The Negro Leagues lost players to clubs in the Dominican Republic in the late 1930s and, during and after World War II, to the Mexican League. Stateside, the money was never exciting. In 1946, Burnis (Bill) Wright, heavy-hitting outfielder for the Baltimore Elite Giants, said the club was paying him $3,000, roughly half what he could have been making in Mexico.

Advancement from high school or semipro teams could come early; Jim Gilliam, also known as Junior, was an infielder for the Elites at age 17. If he kept himself fit, a player could also continue in the lineup: Raleigh (Biz) Mackey, 1937–38 catcher for the Elites (and Roy Campanella's mentor), was still playing regularly a decade later, at age 50. Be it long remembered that in 1965 Satchel Paige pitched three innings—one hit, no runs—for the AL Kansas City Royals, at age 59.

Many of these African-American stars were born in the South, few in Maryland. One prominent exception was William J. (Judy) Johnson, born in 1900 in Snow Hill (though the rest of his life he lived in Delaware). A third baseman, Johnson had an 18-year career, mostly with Hilldale and the Pittsburgh Crawfords. In 1975 he became the sixth Negro Leaguer elected to the Hall of Fame. The pitcher-outfielder Leon Day, born in Virginia, started his career in 1934 at age 17 in a Baltimore Black Sox uniform; was long a Newark Eagle; played the championship year 1949 as a Baltimore Elite Giant; and, finally, was living in Baltimore in retirement when in 1995 his overdue election to the Hall of Fame came through six days before his death.

There seems to be no surviving overall photo of Maryland Park, home to the Black Sox for more than a decade. At that, a photo would

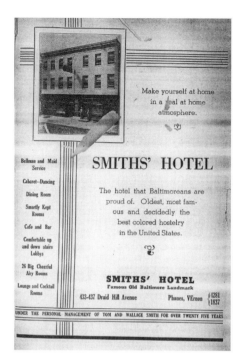

The Smiths' Hotel was owned and operated by Tom and Wallace Smith. At 435–437 Druid Hill Avenue, Smiths' occupied part of a row house block since torn down. Tom Smith, a public figure, was heavily involved in ward politics. His brother, Wallace, attended more directly to the hotel and its sports and entertainment guests, who included visiting Negro League teams.

not closely portray the condition of the wooden and weathered premises—their chronic dustiness irked the fan turned out in his or her Sunday best—or noise levels in the stands. During Prohibition, the vendor of concealed pints or half-pints moved about at will. The peak crowds were for Sunday afternoon's doubleheaders, sometimes between teams that were both from out of town. Many of black baseball's greatest stars took the field in South Baltimore. (They, and many of the Black Sox, stayed at Smiths' Hotel, 435-37 Druid Hill Avenue. Tom Smith, owner, was the city Democrats' most prominent black political boss.)

Twice Maryland Park was the venue for games in the traveling black World Series, between winners in the NNL and ECL. The Kansas City Monarchs and Hilldale played two close games in 1924; in 1926, it was the Chicago American Giants versus Atlantic City's Bacharach Giants (dubbed the Seasiders by sports writers). Almost every October, a touring set of ad hoc All-Stars (players from the white majors, looking to make a few more dollars before winter) would stop off to play the Black Sox. For such an occasion, management would spiff up the park with rented folding wooden chairs.

How many whites were in the stands at Maryland Park? No way to know. Some said Rossiter was offering white spectators a separate section, but in a 1930 newspaper interview he denied it. Since a ticket bore no seat number, fans were free to congregate as they pleased, Richard D. Powell points out. (Powell was a boy then, the excited guide showing new players the route between hotel and ballpark; as an adult, still in baseball's thrall, Powell was ultimately general manager of Baltimore's Elite Giants.) At Maryland Park, the box-office ticket-sellers were white. In the 1920s, the home team supplied the umpires, and until 1930 Baltimore's were white (notably, for some years, Bill Byers, a beefy former catcher for the International League Orioles). How many African Americans were thereby alienated? No way to know.

For news of the Black Sox, nonspectators could read Bill Gibson (later, Sam Lacy and Art Carter) in the *Baltimore Afro-American*. In most of these years, however, the *Afro* was a weekly; published on Saturday, it was more interested in tomorrow's games than in the previous Sunday's. No newspaperman was along on road trips, and the coverage of Baltimore's away games was skimpy, sometimes nonexistent. As for the city's white press, the *Evening Sun* and the *News* (forerunner of the *News-Post*) printed pregame publicity releases (George Rossiter is thought to have had an arrangement with the respective sports editors), but they often failed to report game outcomes. The *Sun* ignored black baseball.

The *Afro-American* liked the team, disliked the club. The historian Mark Ribowsky cites a 1932 *Afro* article referring to the "sewer known as Maryland Park, which featured broken seats, holes in the roof, nonworking toilets, and weeds on the field." Management was indifferent to the disgust voiced by the occasional sports writer from an out-of-town black newspaper, whose own home team played in larger, finer premises. George Rossiter's daughter, interviewed years later by Robert Leffler, said that his living came from the store and restaurant; the Black Sox were "his hobby," and in some years her father lost money on them. His partner, Charles Spedden, ultimately withdrew; also, the ballpark was sold, and Rossiter then rented it. One theme stands out: the owners put their money into player personnel, and finally in 1929 they got results. In ironic retrospect, the zenith of this policy may have come the year after, when, without an eastern league and standings and averages, team excellence was mostly a matter of opinion. The unaffiliated 1930 Black Sox were a powerhouse.

Wearing the catcher's mask was Macajah (Mack) Eggleston, in the second of his three separate tours of Black Sox duty. Jud Wilson moved to third (Ollie Marcelle had been injured—in a card game, by his own manager). And there were three new faces: George (Mule) Suttles played first; the new leftfielder was Clarence (Fats) Jenkins. (Both Suttles and Jenkins achieved fame—the one a homer-hitter, the other a manager, elsewhere and later on. Suttles swung a 50-ounce bat, and witnesses said one of his Havana homers carried 600 feet. Jenkins, 5 feet, 7 inches and 180 pounds, was a leading base-stealer.) The other addition was a pitcher, on some sort of loan from Birmingham in the Negro National League, where he was already a star. Tall and lanky, this newcomer was named Leroy, but everybody called him Satchel.

A 1923 sports page cartoon in the *Baltimore Afro-American*, following a doubleheader between the Black Sox and the Brooklyn Royal Giants. Jud Wilson's home run technique —hit the ball *under* the fence— baffles Tom Fiall and Robert Scott of Brooklyn. Other home team players mentioned are left fielder Lefty Smith and pitcher Tony Mahoney.

How Satchel Paige got his nickname, as a boy in Mobile, Alabama, is a study in contradicting legends. But it is accepted that he learned to pitch while in reform school (cf. George H. Ruth Jr.). No beginner when he came to Baltimore, Paige was, according to Ribowsky, already "a born and shameless self-promoter" whose career goal on a long series of teams was "to make a name and a buck for himself." At times, he was wonderfully, mock-seriously funny.

At age 23, Satch specialized in heat, not the Bat Dodger or the Hesitation Pitch of later years. Not yet did the advance ads promise he would strike out the first nine batters to face him. Baltimore was his first northern city and, it seems, he was "shunned as a hick and an interloper . . . by more educated, snootier" teammates. Richard D. Powell, who attended many a Black Sox game as a boy, points out that in doubleheaders Yokeley was regularly given the honor of pitching the first game, Paige coming in only for the second (which could be shortened, as the sun sank). Second fiddle? Stuff that, was the attitude of the athlete listed in 1930's white press as Kid Satchells. Part way into the season, with a won-loss record listed as 9-4, Paige abruptly went back to the Birmingham Black Barons, without repaying money advanced to him against salary. (Be it noted that he was far from the first player to have left or joined the Black Sox, or any other Negro League team, during the season.) A photo of young Leroy Paige in his Black Sox uniform would agitate today's collectors.

But he left his mark, to wit in that year's *R. L. Polk & Co. Baltimore City Directory:* "Paige, Leroy (Alice), baseball player, r [residence] 632 W Lanvale." The address is just west of Pennsylvania Avenue, around the corner from a statue of the singer Billie Holiday. No building stands there now.

Without Paige, on July 10, 1930, a doubleheader between New York's Lincoln Giants and the Baltimore Black Sox marked the first use of Yankee Stadium by African-American teams. Before 20,000 fans, Laymon Yokeley won the first game, 5-3; Rap Dixon's three homers were a big help.

The Depression impaired (and complicated) African-American baseball. The American Negro League skipped 1930, operated with four teams in 1931 (Black Sox 18-31, third), and then expired. For Baltimore, 1931 is memorable as the part-season when its roster included not only John Beckwith (again) but Martin Dihigo. A large, pleasant, immensely talented Cuban (variously, Dihigo played every position—well), El Maestro then went south, and is now the only player in three nations' baseball halls of fame: United States, Mexico, and Cuba. Ultimately, Martin Dihigo was Minister of Sport in the Fidel Castro regime.

Black baseball's only organized play in 1932 was by a new East-West League of 10 teams, including Pittsburgh's always powerful Crawfords and Homestead Grays. But in June, breakup—just when the Baltimore Black Sox, 20-9, were in first place. Besides the old reliables (Yokeley, Flournoy, Hayes, Clarke, Lundy, and Washington), the lineup included Dave (Showboat) Thomas and Dick Seay.

In 1933, the Negro National League came back to life briefly; the Black Sox joined and, at its disintegration, were a distant third. Times were not improving. Parenthetically, a 1933 nonleague team, the Baltimore Stars, which played home games on one of the public diamonds in Druid Hill Park, had a rookie named Walter (Buck) Leonard. His manager, the old Black Sox player Ben Taylor, taught him how to play first base—well enough to stay there 17 years with the

Homestead Grays, batting just ahead of Josh Gibson. Leonard, one of the first Negro Leaguers elected to the Hall of Fame, testified that with the Stars he made $125 a month plus 60 cents a day meal money; by 1948, his pay was $1,000 a month, perhaps black baseball's third highest, behind Paige's and Gibson's. But back in 1933, cash was scarce. The public diamond having no fence, the only way to collect from spectators was by passing the hat. In his autobiography, Leonard recalls having roomed on Druid Hill Avenue, at the Ben Taylors'. One day another club made Leonard an offer. But he was prevented from jumping the Stars by his wily landlady, who had hidden his street clothes. Worse followed: that summer, the team set out for away games in two automobiles: nine men in a seven-passenger Buick, five in a Ford coupe with rumble seat. Unable to pay a Harlem hotel bill, they sold the two cars; the Stars thereupon foundered.

In 1934, a team in the NNL standings called itself the Black Sox, but was based in Chester, Pennsylvania, and sponsored by a local numbers operator named Jack Farrell. For what it mattered, at last an African American was in charge. The manager was Rap Dixon of 1929's pennant-winners. After part-season play, however, the team withdrew and broke up. And that proved to be, unhappily, road's end for Baltimore and its honored Black Sox in league play.

As far back as 1926, the postseason at Maryland Park had included games against local, industry-sponsored white nines. Early in 1930, the Black Sox twice visited Bugle Field in East Baltimore to play a white team representing the Bugle Coat, Apron and Towel Supply Co. (a laundry and garment supplier at 1501 North Chester Street). The firm, the ballpark (at Federal Street and Loney's Lane—later Edison Highway), and Bugle Athletic Club were controlled by Joseph Cambria. Later in 1930, Rossiter began occasionally sending his team over to Washington to play in Griffith Stadium with its major league seating capacity. And in some years, autumn saw the Baltimore Black Sox heading out for a long tour of cities and towns in the South.

The end of 1931 meant the expiry of George Rossiter's lease on dilapidated Maryland Park. Moreover, he was evidently losing hope that black baseball would settle its disputes, organize for keeps, and realize a profit. The historian Robert Leffler pictures him as finally just walking away, after inviting Joe Cambria to take over the operation. Cambria's Bugle Field was in good condition; and the new head man had ideas for taking people's minds off the Depression. He installed floodlights for night baseball. Another innovation was less successful. After the National Negro League's collapse, he tore up all contracts. Instead of salary, players were paid a share of the gate. A player was thus free at any time to seek a better offer elsewhere, and many did.

Where more than one of Baltimore's identities in big-time white baseball had been lost through corporate violence—expulsion, franchise revocation, league collapse—the Black Sox just faded away. Fans mourning that proud name could do so, mostly, only to themselves.

Neither the Black Sox, it should be said, nor the Elite Giants after them, had a local monopoly. Teams of less than city-wide status competed for attendance. Among their sponsors, Leffler records, was Dr. Joseph Thomas, who in 1939 took out a franchise in an abortive Negro International League. His team called itself the Original Black Sox and then the Edgewater Giants; it played at Edgewater Park in Turner's Station. In 1943, that long-ago Black Sox stalwart, Laymon Yokeley, returned as an Edgewater Giant. (In later years, Dick Powell recalls, Yokeley was so relaxed, or narcoleptic, that sometimes after his team had finished batting, Yokeley, eyes closed as he sat on the bench, had to be wakened to take his place on the mound. He also formed Yokeley's All-Stars, played until age 53, and retired to operate a shoeshine parlor at Madison Avenue and Dolphin Street across from the York Hotel—by then, the stopping place both for Elite players and for black teams from out of town.)

Many baseball teams have represented Baltimore, more players than the unaided mind can summon. Events noble and vile have occurred, more than a few overlooked by or outside the scope of the present chronicle. This is to avow that the public mind's largest area of unawareness, the phase of Baltimore baseball that calls out the loudest for closer inspection, is the Baltimore Black Sox. Without surviving players to interview, without business records to examine, the best hope for recovering box scores and game-by-game highlights is probably the nation's array of African-American periodicals. Good fortune to anyone who takes up the cause.

The champion 1949 Baltimore Elite Giants. *Top row, from left:* Joe Black, p; Leroy Ferrell, p; Charles (Specs) Davidson, p; Lenny Pearson, of; Bill Byrd, p; Al Wilmore, p; Bob Romby, p; Johnny Hayes, c; Jim (Junior) Gilliam, 2b; Jesse (Hoss) Walker, manager; *bottom row:* Butch Davis, of; Lester Lockett, of; Silvester Rodgers, p; Henry Kimbro, cf; Vic Harris, coach; Henry Bayliss, utility; Henry (Frazier) Robinson, c; Frank (Junior) Russell, utility; Tom (Pee Wee) Butts, ss; Leon Day, of.

The Elites had gone from Nashville to Cleveland to Columbus to Washington to Baltimore; it was a while before they got used to the idea of staying put. But finally, they put Baltimore on their shirtfronts, and Maryland on their license plates—in time for the 1949 pennant.

RICHARD POWELL, IN 1997 INTERVIEW

I've hobnobbed with major leaguers for three years now, and I've yet to see one who could play more shortstop than Pee Wee Butts.

SAM LACY, *Afro-American*, MAY 24, 1943

CHAPTER FOURTEEN

YEA, ELITES!

Three years went by before Baltimore again held a franchise in the black majors. Occasionally, unsatisfyingly, out-of-town teams stopped off to play an exhibition game at the whim of out-of-town promoters. When the fans did again have a team to cheer for and players to idolize, in 1938, the changes were vast: new league configuration, new team name, new ballpark, and new management.

To start with the owner: Tom Wilson, age 55, was an African American, an out-of-towner (from Nashville, Tennessee, where he owned a night club and dance hall), and, unlike the Black Sox owners, a power, being secretary of the NNL, later vice president, and ultimately its president. Wilson's club was the Elite Giants. Rebuffed in their first efforts to use Oriole Park at Greenmount Avenue and 29th Street when its white team was on the road, the Elites rented Bugle Field from Joe Cambria. (Beyond the eastern edge of Baltimore's African-American community, Bugle Field was reachable by cross-town bus; also, it had ample parking, with space for charter buses.) A business office was set up at the York Hotel, 1200 Madison Avenue. And the franchise was in the Negro National League, which in still another reversal was by this time an eastern group, while its former midwestern and southern members now constituted a Negro American League.

YORK HOTEL

Most up-to-date Colored Hotel in the South—newly renovated—running water in each room—13 baths, 38 rooms, maid service.

BALTIMORE'S FINEST HOTEL

It took a while, but offices of the Elite Giants eventually moved from the Nashville of their owner to the Baltimore of their home games. Headquarters was then in the York Hotel, at Madison and Dolphin streets. In the 1930s and 1940s, visiting Negro League teams stayed at the York Hotel.

No less tortuous was the Elite Giants' road to Baltimore. Organized in 1921, NNL members since 1929, they left Nashville in 1931 for Cleveland and then returned. Their 1935 base was Columbus, Ohio. One more year and they were gone to Washington. But in 1937, Pittsburgh's powerful, exciting Homestead Grays began playing much of their schedule in Washington. So the Elites moved once more—to Baltimore. In 1938, Wilson made it official: the Baltimore Elite Giants.

The bad impression left by low attendance figures in the final Black Sox years had been countered, happily, by one more new circumstance: support from Baltimore's small but growing African-American business community. The leading role in advancing baseball's cause with the Frontiers Club and other civic organizations was taken by Richard D. Powell, a Black Sox spectator in boyhood, by this time a Social Security official. Then Powell persuaded Smiling Tom Wilson and Wilson's business manager, Vernon Green, to move their team to Baltimore. They themselves became part-time Baltimoreans.

Another plus was Joe Cambria's willingness to lease Bugle Field. Cambria took no direct part, his flamboyant baseball energies by this time spread wide, as variously the owner of clubs in the Class D, C, B, A, and double-A minors. (Ultimately, Cambria sold them all, disposed of his laundry, left Baltimore, and became a scout for the Washington Senators, specializing in Cubans.) Cambria's ballpark, seating 6,000, was built roughly to the same standards as Maryland Park: roofed grandstand with seats, uncovered first- and third-base-line bleachers, and wooden outfield fence.

Losers on arrival in a seven-team league dominated by the Homestead Grays, the 1938 Baltimore Elite Giants improved to 12-14 in a season that turned out to have no second half. But name players showed their stuff—George (Tubby) Scales, manager-infielder; Jim West on first; Sammy Hughes at second; Jesse (Hoss) Walker at short; Felton Snow at third; in the outfield, Bill Hoskins, Henry Kimbro, and Burnis (Bill) Wright; Bill Byrd, the number-one pitcher, plus Jonas Gaines, Andrew (Pullman) Porter, and Woodrow (Lefty) Wilson; catching, Raleigh (Biz) Mackey (a Texan on his way to a record, 30-year Negro Leagues career, 1918–47), and a 17-year-old rookie just out of a Philadelphia high school, Leroy Campanella.

In 1939, the Elites were finally accepted as occasional Sunday afternoon tenants of Oriole Park. Personnel changes proved equally invigorating. Felton Snow became playing manager; an old Black Sox star was on hand—Crush Holloway, closing out his career. (He then settled in Baltimore, as a tailor, dying in 1975.) In midseason catcher Biz Mackey was traded away, so good was his teenage understudy. James (Red) Moore took over at first, Thomas (Pee Wee) Butts, 19, was at shortstop. Gaines and Tom Glover, left-handers, were backed up by Willie (Bubber) Hubert and Emery (Ace) Adams.

The Elites lost their first four games, but Bill Wright got hits—so many, by season's end, that his .488 far led the league. Meanwhile, the celebrity-laden Grays, breezing along in the first half, slowed in the second. The Elites' 25-21 was good only for third place, but it admitted them to four-team playoffs (in a six-team league). In successive, best-of-five series, the Elites first eliminated the Newark Eagles in three straight (11-3, 7-3, 5-2)—the first game in Philadelphia, the others a Sunday doubleheader at Oriole Park. Newark's lineup included some Baltimore favorites: Mule Suttles, Leon Day—and Biz Mackey.

Then came a pennant showdown against the hulking Grays. First, a Sunday home double-header was split. The score of Homestead's victory has been lost; in the other game (7-5 Elites), Josh Gibson, the famous catcher, added his name as hitter to Oriole Park's list of way-way-way-out home runs. Game three was at Parkside Field, Philadelphia: a 10-5 Baltimore triumph, broken up in the seventh by five runs. The game's star, with homer, double, two singles, and five runs batted in before a crowd of cheering fellow-Philadelphians, was young Leroy Campanella. The fourth and final game was at Yankee Stadium in New York—a pitchers' showdown, Jonas Gaines versus Roy Partlow. In the eighth, with the bases loaded, Bubber Hubert relieved Gaines and preserved his 2-0 shutout. The public, beyond the stands' 15,000 spectators, took limited notice; in Europe, World War II had just broken out. No World Series against the Negro American League's dominant Kansas City Monarchs followed. Nonetheless, it was a capital *E* Event, this dumping of Josh Gibson and Buck Leonard and

East's players in the 1939 East-West All-Star game in Chicago. The three Elite Giants are (*standing, fourth from left*) Sammy Hughes, 2b; (*second from right*) Burnis (Bill) Wright, of; (*kneeling, left*) Bill Byrd, p. *Standing, left,* is Buck Leonard; *third from right,* Josh Gibson.

Vic Harris and Sam Bankhead (of the Negro Leagues' five Bankhead brothers). Tom Wilson's smile was never broader.

In 1940, the Elite Giants' record improved to 25-14, and Pee Wee Butts, hitting .390, led the league; but Homestead (by this time Washington-based) was never headed. In 1941, Homestead led again, as Baltimore slipped from second to third. Then, as the United States entered World War II, came a season of success: first place, 37-15, far ahead of Homestead, which, however, reversing the 1939 outcome, won 1942's NNL playoffs (and went on into the first NNL-NAL World Series). Missing from the 1942 NNL playoffs was Roy Campanella, who, after a fuss with Tom Wilson over a $250 fine, had jumped to the Mexican League; with him went Pee Wee Butts, the Elites' small, deft shortstop. For Baltimore, accordingly, 1943 was a

losing, fifth-place year—assuaged by the two stars' return in 1944 and second place once more. (A midsummer event, the fire that destroyed Oriole Park, meant playing Baltimore games entirely at Bugle Field, with its smaller capacity and revenues.) As VJ Day went by, the Elites slipped to third. In any event, Negro League play had continued throughout wartime, uninterrupted.

Then came the breakthrough in Organized Baseball's color line. For the Negro Leagues' younger, better players (e.g., Jack R. Robinson, previously of the Kansas City Monarchs), desegregation meant a chance at the big time at last. For older players and the franchises behind them, the great change was a hard, in time fatal, blow. To start with, Baltimore's black fans went to Municipal Stadium to watch International League Montreal, whose second baseman in 1946 was Jackie Robinson; when he joined Brooklyn, they went to Philadelphia

Catcher for the Baltimore Elites:
Leroy Campanella.

for National League games. From 1948 on, they were going to Washington to watch African-American players in the American League.

A second, personal setback before the start of 1946 play: the Elites lost Roy Campanella to the Brooklyn organization. How much dollar reimbursement was there from Branch Rickey when he took away Baltimore's star catcher (assigning him to a league lower than the International)? For Campy, who across part or all of seven seasons with the Elites had become their top star, nothing. While with the Elites, Roy Campanella had batted .344; then in his 10 Brooklyn Dodger seasons, he hit 242 home runs, was three times the National League's Most Valuable Player, and played in five World Series. With no delay, Campanella was voted into the Hall of Fame.

In his subsequent autobiography, Campanella mentioned that his mother, formerly Ida Mercer, was from Cecil County. He told of growing up in the Nicetown section of North Philadelphia, of dropping out of Simon Gratz High at age 15, and in a Harlem hotel signing a contract with "the really big, really colorful" Elites, pay $60 a month. Nicknames followed him: Half-breed as a boy, Pooch or Poochie in the Negro Leagues, Camp or Campy in the majors. He married at 19, had two daughters, was divorced. Catching (or batting) wasn't easy in a league that tolerated tricky pitching—the spitter, the shine ball, the emery ball. By 1939, Campanella had become a 5-foot 8-inch 200-pounder, his pay had doubled, and he had grown used to life aboard "the great, big blue-and-white bus" that was "our home, dressing room, dining room and hotel." Winters, he played in the Caribbean. Of Baltimore, he had little to say.

So in 1946 it was another team that at last terminated Homestead hegemony—Newark's Eagles, among them Biz Mackey, Leon Day, Larry Doby, and Monte Irvin. For the Elites, 1947 was a winning year again, and third place; but 1948 ended in disorder, as black baseball's revenues crumbled. So many teams dropped out that the NNL schedule was never completed.

Meanwhile, Tom Wilson's health was failing. In 1947, before dying, he sold the team to Vernon Green, his general manager. Once a catcher, he, too, was from Nashville. Then, two years later, Green died. His widow, Henryene, turned over the running of things to

Dick Powell, the lifelong Baltimorean who had become the Elites' business manager. His was a hard prospect—the loss not only of players to the belatedly penitent majors but also of a place to play. The Elites' 10-year lease was running out; renewal was out of the question, the owners having a purchase offer for Bugle Field from a printing firm eager to build there.

Regardless of all this woe, a final burst of glory was in store. Two Elites, joining as teenagers, were turning into top-quality players: Joe Black, pitcher, and Jim (Junior) Gilliam, second baseman. The former was from New Jersey and Morgan State College; the latter, out of a Nashville high school. (Black went on to half a dozen years in the majors; Gilliam, to 13 years and seven World Series.) Meanwhile, the lone league operating, the Negro American, reorganized into eastern and western divisions, setting up postseason playoffs. Baltimore, New York Cubans, Philadelphia Stars, Indianapolis Clowns, and Louisville Buckeyes comprised the NAL East.

The 1949 lineup included 1939's shortstop, Jesse (Hoss) Walker, now the manager, and three others from the last previous champions: Pee Wee Butts (angry later on when the majors signed his double-play partner, Gilliam, but not Butts himself), centerfielder Henry Kimbro, and Bill Byrd. A spitballer, Byrd was from Ohio; he joined the Elites when they were in Columbus, accompanied them to Baltimore in 1938, and was still with them in 1951 when the team left town. Byrd, the old dependable, won more than 100 games for Baltimore, losing some 65. In 1949, when Byrd was 42, his 12-3 led the league in percentage.

In addition, Leon Day, late in his 20-year career, returned to the Baltimore of his Black Sox start for a year and a half as Elite pitcher-outfielder. Also on that 1949 team were pitchers Leroy Ferrell, Alfred (Apples) Wilmore, Bob Romby, Sylvester (Speedy) Rogers, and Charles (Specs) Davidson; outfielders Lester Lockett, Lenny Pearson, and Robert (Butch) Davis; infielders Ed Finney, Henry Baylis, Frank (Junior) Russell, and Clinton (Butch) McCord; and catchers Johnny Hayes and Henry (Frazier) Robinson. The team had a coach—Elander (Vic) Harris, from the Homestead Grays.

There was no stopping the '49 Elites. After winning both halves of a split season, Baltimore for the first time played in a Negro World Series. The best of the West (Kansas City Monarchs, Birmingham Black Barons, Houston Eagles, Memphis Red Sox, and Chicago American Giants) in that year's NAL was the Monarchs, in percentage; but at Series time they passed, asserting that no adequate home field was available to them. So the American Giants substituted, only to be drubbed in four straight: 9-1, 5-4, 8-4, 4-2. The winning pitchers, in order: Byrd, Black, Ferrell, Wilmore. The first two games were played in Baltimore, the last two in Chicago. Game two was on a September Sunday. There was no farewell ceremony, then or the next morning, as wreckers moved in to demolish Bugle Field. That 1949 clean sweep turned out to be, also, the farewell Negro World Series.

Bugle Field, in East Baltimore, from 1944 onward home to the champion Elite Giants. Few photographers went there when all was well; they came on the run when the news was bad. Bugle Field in 1949 was being demolished.

That same winter, Municipal Stadium, home to the International League Orioles, was likewise torn down, for replacement by Memorial Stadium in its first stage (one level, 19,000 seats). The city's Rec-

reation and Parks Board agreed for the Elites to rent it—at a ruinous rate, four times what the board was charging the white team. Hurriedly, Elites general manager Dick Powell put together a new home field: Westport Stadium, alongside Old Annapolis Road, well south of 1915's same-name ballpark. The stands were roofed bleachers; the infield, bare ground; capacity, perhaps 5,000. With Henry Kimbro (an Elite since 1938) promoted to manager, 1950's Elite Giants finished second to the Indianapolis Clowns. Elsewhere attendance fell, but crowds made the trip to Westport, owing in part to the continuing all-whiteness of the International League Orioles. Off went Black and Gilliam to the Dodger organization (this time, for $10,000 each).

Then the owners, the Green family of Nashville, decided to sell the Elite Giants. No Baltimorean was willing to invest in black baseball; another Tennessean, putting up $11,000, took over. A team bearing Baltimore's name played the 1951 season, largely on the road (it finished 28-36, fourth and last). In 1952, gone south, the team barnstormed as the Nashville Elite Giants. Then the operation disbanded. Nationally, the final year of Negro League play, with only six franchises, was 1954.

Joe Black at Bugle Field

Memories of black baseball grow dimmer, but also fonder. The one white Baltimorean of prominence who could be counted on for a home-opener appearance was Mayor Theodore R. McKeldin. In the 1990s, when interest in black baseball's fading trail finally flared, legatees and collectors presented some associational objects to the Babe Ruth museum, in Baltimore, others to the Negro Leagues Hall of Fame, in Kansas City. The remaining Baltimorean with an insider's recollections is Powell, who, in his 80s, has enthralled come-lately scholars with recollections going back to the errands he ran for the Black Sox in his boyhood.

The many road trips could be wearing; Roy Campanella recalled playing as many as four games in one day. Sometimes, Elite home games were played at Washington's Griffith Stadium, which could seat 30,000 fans. Road games, with their higher attendance at some cities' larger parks, helped Tom Wilson considerably in meeting his payroll. In scheduling, the emphasis was on weekends; sometimes, in a Sunday doubleheader, four different teams played. No doubt the

To some, the best place for watching a game at old Oriole Park was atop the grandstand roof. Bit of a slope and no guard rail, but individual chairs and a glorious panorama. George Bennett, M.D., the Hopkins orthopedist who attended to the bone and joint miseries of many a major leaguer, used to sit up there.

JOHN STEADMAN, SPORTS EDITOR AND COLUMNIST, IN 1997 INTERVIEW

CHAPTER FIFTEEN

YEARS OF UNSUCCESS

Meanwhile, back in the International League . . .

It was long and it was harsh, the letdown from those seven years of 1919–25 Baltimore Oriole glory. Not once, from the start of 1926 to the end of 1943, did the Orioles finish first; worse, in 9 of those 18 years they flapped about disconsolately in the second division. A parade of managers plus several general managers developed a handful of individual stars but never a truly successful team. After being pennant-sated, Baltimore went back to being pennant-hungry.

Jack Dunn's last years were unhappy. The eye for young talent was still sharp, but by then he was up against the manifold dollars of the majors' spreading farm chains. In '27 and '28, his teams won barely as many games as they lost, to finish fifth and then sixth (85-82, 82-82; only eight games back, that final set of Dunnie's Orioles). He liquidated the last of his Seven-Straighter assets, Jack Ogden going to the St. Louis Browns, Joe Boley and Moose Earnshaw to the A's, Dick Porter to the Cleveland Indians. (The while, six Orioles from the so-called Silver Age went on to be the manager or general manager of an International League team: Ben Egan, Fritz Maisel, Jack Ogden, Dick Porter, Tommy Thomas, and Jimmy Walsh.) Dunn cast about for player replacements, hiring several superannuated major leaguers. Dunn himself, who had been sitting on the bench in business clothes,

Throwing out—and catching—
the first ball, on Opening Day at
old Oriole Park (1932). As Manager Fritz Maisel stands by, Ned
Hanlon rehearses signals with
Mayor Howard W. Jackson, who
will crank up and let it go.

put on a uniform again for coaching and umpire-arguing; but nothing
availed.

Dunn lived first at 3509 Greenmount Avenue, then at 5217½ York
Road, finally at Lake and Chestnut Park (now Pinehurst Road)
Avenues. For years, as an off-season hobby, he had trained hunting
dogs; one day in October 1928, while out riding to put his setters
through field trials, Jack Dunn was felled by a sudden, terminal heart
attack. He was 56. The encomiums were flowery: Dunn had force
and he had style. He could be harsh (Al Kermisch, Baltimorean and
Library of Congress baseball researcher, tells how one day in 1916,
irked at his out-of-shape pitcher, Ford Meadows, a Baltimore native, Dunn left him in a lost game for two full innings—during which
Meadows walked 11 batters). Dunn could also be generous. When the
Orioles were playing in Newark or Jersey City, he booked his team
into a hotel in Manhattan. If, then or later, it was sometimes suggested that Dunnie, having such a good thing going as sole owner and
operator, was of no help in the fitful effort to lure a major league franchise Baltimore-ward, well, Organized Baseball and its so-called czar
were all too clearly set against the idea anyway.

A structural reorganization followed Dunn's death. Charles H.
Knapp, a corporate lawyer who had been seeing to Dunn's legal needs,
headed Baltimore Baseball and Exhibition Company. Knapp, a native
of Western Maryland, was then also elected president of the International League. Following Knapp's death in 1936, George W. Reed, a
banker, became club president; then Mrs. Jack Dunn Sr. (a female ex-
ecutive was a rarity in that era's Organized Baseball); and finally, from
1943 on, Jack Dunn III. That testamentary moment in 1936 also provided Bird watchers with a financial sighting. Probate showed Knapp
owning only 50 of the club's 1,250 stock shares (by his time of death,
Jack Dunn owned 998 shares); extrapolated, the stock produced a paper value—club and park—of $106,250.

The second newcomer, in 1929, was George M. Weiss, 33, the
sharp-eyed entrepreneur who had put together that pesky New Haven team; he became the Orioles' first general manager. Fritz Maisel
("May-zel," in fan speech), captain and third baseman, took over as
manager, and turning 40, retired as an active player. (Active, indeed;

back in 1914, when Babe Ruth arrived in the majors, who was the first to welcome this teenage rookie pitcher by homering off him? Fritz Maisel, the Catonsville Flash, in New York Yankee uniform.) Every bit as solid a baseball man, Maisel was less arbitrary and less dominant than Dunn. His '29 team rose to third place, and no Maisel team finished lower than third. But the skill or luck with pitchers vanished. In four years, the triumvirate of Knapp, Weiss, and Maisel had only one 20-game winner: Montgomery M. Weaver, from North Carolina. (Scouts had pulled him from the faculty of the University of Virginia, where Monte Weaver was teaching analytic geometry.) Weaver the Oriole was 21-11 in 1931—and, in 1932, a Washington Senator. That first year, 1929, Maisel's first baseman was a 29-year-old fellow–Baltimore German, John H. Neun (pronounced "Noon"). While with Detroit, Johnny Neun had achieved an unassisted triple play; after that one Oriole year, he was back in the majors. Later, he managed the rival IL Newark Bears and then the Cincinnati Reds.

On Maisel's Orioles, the batting was strong, far, and insufficient; none of it stronger and farther than that recorded in 1930 by a 30-year-old first baseman let go by the Philadelphia A's after breaking his kneecap (and after being replaced by James Emory Foxx, a formidable teenager from Sudlersville, on Maryland's Eastern Shore). This new Oriole was Joseph J. Hauser—Unser Choe, they called him in his native Milwaukee. When that 168-game IL season began, the any-league home-run mark was Babe Ruth's colossal 60, set three years earlier in a 154-game schedule. When 1930 was over, the record was 63, set by lighter, smaller, likewise left-handed Joe Hauser. The inexactness of the comparison was evident to all (furthermore, many an IL park had nearer fences than did Yankee Stadium); and 63 itself lasted only three years, or until Joe Hauser, by then with Minneapolis in the American Association, proceeded to hit 69 homers. But Joe did have a remarkable year, what with his 173 runs scored and 443 total bases. He was not alone: the 1930 Orioles hit 231 homers (John W. Gill, 34; Vincent D. Barton, a Canadian, 32) and, improving from 90-78 to 97-70, rose to second place.

Then Hauser, for whatever reason, had an off year, his batting average dropping from .313 to .259, his homers from 63 to 31. As in

A pleasant, long-lost annual ceremony was the Orioles' departure
from Penn Station (here, in 1931)
for spring training in the South.
The departure time having been
published, out came the fans. How
to tell which ones were ballplayers?
Someone had handed each a cane.
George Weiss, general manager,
holds business files.

Philadelphia earlier, he was mistakenly written off, and replaced.
And 1931's Orioles, though only six games out, slipped back to third
(94-72) as Rochester won its fourth consecutive pennant. The team
was notable for one of its bit-players: Joseph T. Cascarella, a pitcher-
crooner from Philadelphia who, after five subsequent years in the majors, became a Maryland horse-track official.

At this point, General Manager Weiss moved up to the majors (for
a distinguished career with the Yankees and then the Mets). The Orioles promoted a scout, Henry P. Dawson; for 1935, he was replaced
by Jack Ogden. Knapp's son, Charles H. Jr., held the job from 1939 to
1943. Tommy Thomas then recombined the roles of manager and
general manager; and the final GM of the minor league years was Jack
Dunn III, who had been one year old at his father's death, six at his
grandfather's.

In 1932, Baltimoreans had another slugger to lionize: a colorful,
switch-hitting outfielder–first baseman, Russell L. Arlett, 33. Buzz, he
was; a beefy Californian and Pacific Coast League veteran. When he

duly hit 54 home runs, that was tops in the IL, and so were his runs, runs batted in, and total bases. Twice, Buzz Arlett hit four homers in one game, something no other International Leaguer had done. It happened on June 1 and again on July 4—in Reading, Pennsylvania, and then at Oriole Park. (Record-checkers found that a Pacific Coast League slugger had once hit five in one game, but two fours, by the same player in the same year, remains unequaled.) As the pitchers came and went, Arlett swung now left-handed, now right. In the second game, played at home, Arlett struck out; then, boom! boom! boom! boom! A great way to celebrate the glorious Fourth. The Reading Keys may have found all of this too discouraging; an IL member since 1919, Reading dropped out at the end of 1932.

Baltimore ended the year in second place (93-74). But it was also 15½ games behind—Newark, rather, was the team that extinguished Rochester's threat to the seven-straight streak. And the general manager's first year proved to be the manager's last. For, dissatisfied with

Charlie Dressen (*left*), third baseman, and other 1931 Orioles sport birds both on their hats and on their round shirt patches.

four years of no championships and thinking to save money by hiring a playing manager, Jack Dunn's heirs ousted Fritz Maisel. (In later years, he headed the Baltimore County Fire Department, and appeared in print as "a little round man" in many a moment of fond recall by his son Bob Maisel, *Sun* sports editor and columnist.) The new manager was Oriole centerfielder Frank B. McGowan, age 31, a New Englander known to the big leagues as Beauty (for his fancy footwork).

As the nation's economy worsened, Oriole baseball did little to take people's minds off their problems. Buzz Arlett wasn't much of a fielder; even though his runs and homers still led the league in 1933, afterward he was discarded. Like Joe Hauser, Arlett then performed splendidly elsewhere; his career including only one year in the majors, Arlett ranks close to the all-time top among minor league batters. Alongside McGowan was an upward-bound, 25-year-old Pennsylvania newcomer, Julius J. Soltesz, whom baseball rechristened Moose Solters; in Baltimore, he immediately topped the league in batting

The Oriole Park of time gone by. Waverly, St. John's Episcopal Church, City College and a lane between mound and plate.

(.363), total bases, and runs batted in. One such year, and Solters was off to the majors. A pitcher stood out: William Henry Smythe, known as Harry, a left-hander and a Georgian, whose totals were 21-8. Regardless, the 1933 Orioles finished 18 games back; third, but only 84-80.

That was the year the IL protracted things by establishing the Shaughnessy Playoff, named for the league president, Frank J. Shaughnessy. The first-place team would play the fourth, while the second-place team played the third, four games out of seven; then the two winners would play. The governors of Maryland, New Jersey, New York, Ontario, and Quebec put up a silver cup for this ultimate victor. The Birds were quickly beaten.

Then, with a clang, the bottom fell out. The '34 team started in last place; a month of this and playing manager McGowan was fired; another month and playing manager Joseph I. Judge (20 years in the majors, mostly with Washington) was fired; at season's close, under playing manager Guy R. Sturdy, 35, also a first baseman, the Orioles (53-99) were still last. And their paid home attendance all year totaled 78,343. What had gone so glaringly wrong? Why, 32 seasons out in the IL, was Baltimore finally reduced to eighth place? No clear answer, then or now. That was the year the league retreated to a 154-game schedule, matching the majors'. It was just as well. A footnote: 1934 was also the year the Orioles had older-and-younger-brother pitchers: Jack and Curley (Warren H.) Ogden, whose home town was Ogden, Pennsylvania. Each was on his way down from the majors; neither thrived.

The regime of Sturdy, a Texan, lasted through 1936, with fifth- and fourth-place finishes. Again, success was isolated, not general, particularly in '35, the year of George L. Puccinelli. A tall, brawny outfielder, Pooch bestrode the league in every batting category except triples: hits (209), runs (135), runs batted in (173), doubles (49), homers (53; 43 of them at Oriole Park), total bases (435), and batting average (.359). San Francisco George was voted the league's most valuable player (a competition begun in 1932), the first such in Oriole uniform. Puccinelli's sunburst 1935 earned him, of course, a major league 1936. Another grace note was Puccinelli Night at the ballpark—an instance

Woody Abernathy heads the parade of all 1,109 IL Orioles — alphabetically. From 1934 through 1937, he played first and second bases and outfield. Twice he led the IL in homers, once in runs scored.

of that occasional, late-season way of saying mass thanks, back in the age of low salaries and no bonuses. Only 4,000 fans turned out and Newark won the game, but the club had leaned on other businesses to contribute. Mayor Howard W. Jackson presided; the *Evening Sun* itemized Puccinelli's loot: "One hundred cigars, a case of whiskey, five cases of soda pop, two gallons of paint, flowers, bathing suits, passes to the movies, passes to a golf course, a ham, a year's worth of haircuts, and an automobile."

Another right-hander, first baseman William J. Sweeney, meanwhile had the second-highest batting average (.357) and hit safely in 36 consecutive games, an IL record. Pitcher Harry E. Gumbert was 19-10 (and, at age 25, likewise off to the majors). But . . . 78-74, and not even in the first division.

One glance was enough to affirm that 1935 team's identity. IL Oriole uniforms, until then, had been utilitarian and drab. Sewn onto caps was the outline of a small bird; as for shirts, the black shoulder-sleeve diamond with enclosed *B*, of Babe Ruth's era, was about as startling a sight as the front office would allow. Suddenly, here were bills and feathers — two sizable birds, perched at either end of a shirt-front bat above the team name, in color. Little matter that the design had been copied from the St. Louis Cardinals.

On came 1936, and Orioles who at last looked more like a set of equals, instead of one or two stars against a shifting background of third-raters. An 81-72 record and fourth place meant Cup play; Baltimore not only eliminated first-place Buffalo but nearly won the silver trophy. The offense included Virgil Woodrow (Woody, sometimes Woodley) Abernathy, age 21, a left-handed outfielder from North Carolina (who led the league with 42 homers) and, in his last hurrah, 36-year-old Max Bishop (in one game, old Camera Eye came to bat six times and drew six walks); the defense featured Clifford G. Melton, a 20-14 North Carolina left-hander (Cliff, burdened with the nickname Big Ears, was en route to a New York Giants career).

A poor 1937 start — 10 losses in a row — canceled all this; out went Guy Sturdy, in came Clyde E. Crouse, an Indianan, White Sox alumnus, and lumpy-fingered career catcher. Bucky Crouse led by example: a relatively slight man still playing at age 40, he brought the

Above: Clyde E. Crouse, catcher
and manager, 1937–38. A small
man, a natural leader, aged 40 and
with beat-up hands, Bucky Crouse
enjoys his loot after winning the
IL's 1937 most valuable player
award: trophy, key to the city, and a
bag of silver dollars. That year,
Bucky's Birds almost won the Governors' Cup. *Left:* Safe or out?
George Puccinelli during 1935,
when he led the IL in seven batting
categories, still a record.

Orioles in fourth and, for his guts, was voted the league's most valuable player. An Oklahoman, outfielder Albert O. Wright, Ab to his
admirers, led the IL in homers (37), runs batted in, and total bases.
Puccinelli, back again from the AL (his true home turned out to be
the minors—eight cities' worth), could lead the team only in batting
average; William L. Lohrman, from New York (before following Melton to the Giants), posted 20 wins, 11 losses. The Orioles opened the
playoffs by losing four in a row.

Alphonse (Tommy) Thomas (1899–1988). A life devoted to baseball. Thomas was a full-time pitcher (in the IL at age 18, five of the Seven Straight years, 12 years in the majors with four teams), and then coach, manager, general manager, and scout. A quiet man, reflective, purposeful.

A shadow loomed over Crouse; the front office had brought in, as third base coach and 42-year-old pinch-hitter, Rogers Hornsby. Texas's gift to batting (across 23 major league seasons, a .358 average, the highest ever for right-handers), Hornsby, a second baseman, had by then shown an additional knack: for martinet managing and unsuccessful teams. But the sports writers called him Rajah, and when the 1938 Orioles nose-dived (last place, 52-98, worse than in 1934), Crouse turned over his job to Hornsby. Posterity would like to white-out an experience such as 1938's; yet once again, in retrospect a season may be interesting as much for who was on the team as for what he then did, or didn't. That year, Sydney H. Cohen was an Oriole pitcher. Syd, and his older brother Andrew H. (never an Oriole), were Baltimoreans. A left-hander, Syd earlier spent several quiet years with the Senators; Andy for three years had been New York NL's second baseman—almost, not quite, the answer to John McGraw's out-loud prayer for a Jewish star who would excite the Giants' many Bronx fans.

So 1939's team, with its elders dreaming regretfully of the mild-mannered Maisel, McGowan, Sturdy, and Crouse, rose, but only to sixth (68-85). With a 20-man IL roster limit, Hornsby wrote 45 names into his lineups, first day to last: not an exceptional number. The contrast that hurt was his salary over against his results. Standing there this time in the third-base coaching box was old reliable Tommy Thomas, winner of 106 games for the Seven-Straighters, then 112 more in the majors—reserved in manner, but a reasonable man and a keen play analyst. And so for 1940 Hornsby gave way to Thomas, the Orioles' seventh manager in nine years. (When in 1942 the Hall of Fame electors tapped Rogers Hornsby, their minds may not have been on his Baltimore interlude.)

One other large change: after all the years of independence, in 1940 the Orioles agreed to affiliate with a major league club—NL Philadelphia. In practice, this accelerated the player turnover: an influx of young men sent to Baltimore to gain experience balancing an outflow of top players whenever in mid- or late-season the Orioles' parent club sought help. Among these promising youngsters who, unlike others earlier mentioned, left scant mark in Baltimore before going on to solid careers in the big time, were Joseph A. Kuhel, to the Senators, first baseman and manager; Daniel Webster Litwhiler (Phillies, Cardinals, Braves), outfielder; Roberto F. (Bobby) Avila (Indians), second baseman; John A. Antonelli (Braves, Giants), pitcher; Gus E. (Ozark Ike) Zernial (White Sox, A's, Tigers), outfielder; and Edward M. Kasko, age 17 (Cardinals, Reds, Astros), infielder and Red Sox manager. At least five minor-league Orioles were later with AL Baltimore in various roles: Howard F. Fox and James A. Wilson, both times pitchers; native Marylander Robert G. Young, both times second baseman; Elmer (Swede) Burkart, pitcher (relieving in a 1942 game, he struck out Rochester on 10 pitches, the extra pitch owing to a foul), subsequently ticket manager; and George W. (Stopper) Staller, outfielder, subsequently a coach. Another of these hopeful young men was Edward T. Collins Jr., whose story is the opposite of cheerful. Looking over his shoulder was Eddie Sr., a Hall of Fame second baseman and 25-year player with the A's and White Sox. But young Eddie, a 1940 Oriole outfielder, never made it in the majors.

In a companion hiring change, the emphasis on youth meant a quiet end to the hiring of big-name players who, past their major league prime, needed the money and who occasionally flashed their old skills. Between 1903 and 1910, at least five Old Orioles took the field (mostly in token appearances) in minor-league Baltimore uniform: Steve Brodie, Hughey Jennings, Sadie McMahon, Wilbert Robinson, and Cy Seymour. Other name players, between 1903 and 1919, included Thomas J. (Buttermilk Tommy) Dowd, former NL manager-outfielder; Cornelius (Neal) Ball, infielder, formerly of the Indians; and Freddy Parent, former Red Sox and White Sox shortstop. Between 1920 and 1940, the formerlies included Richard W. (Rube) Marquard, Hall of Fame left-hander who once won 19 games in a row for the Giants and who on retirement settled in Baltimore, a race track employee; Sherwood R. (Sherry) Magee, outfielder, and Mickey Doolan, shortstop, from the Phillies (who had also played for the lamented FL Baltimore Terrapins); L. Everett (Deacon) Scott, shortstop, from the Yankees (whose consecutive-games streak Lou Gehrig broke); Charles W. (Chuck) Dressen from the Reds, a 5-foot 5½-inch

Opening Day parade, 1935, with the players in the top-down convertibles. Department stores had awnings then; and this intersection, Howard and Lexington Streets, had department stores.

The scoreboard reads:

YOU'LL FIND GUNTHER'S DRY BEERY BEER IS SMOOTHER GOING DOWN!

STRIKES   BALLS   OUTS

= GAMES TOMORROW =
INTERNATIONAL LEAGUE
1 2 3 4 5 6 7 8 9 10 11 12

ORIOLES A.B. VISITOR	AMERICAN R.IN.	NATIONAL R.IN.
BUFFALO	2 SS CF 23	PHILADELPHIA	ST. LOUIS
SYRACUSE	3 RF SS 20	NEW YORK	CINCINNATI
MONTREAL	12 1B RF 9	DETROIT	PITTSBURGH
NEWARK	0 LF LF 27	ST. LOUIS	CHICAGO
ROCHESTER	7 3B 3B 4	WASHINGTON	NEW YORK
JERSEY CITY	1 CF 2B 14	BOSTON	BROOKLYN
	11 2B 1B 25	CHICAGO	BOSTON
	10 C C 21	CLEVELAND	PHILADELPHIA
	21 P P 19		

WORLD'S LARGEST   TORONTO ORIOLES   SCORE BOARD

"World's largest" claims are hard to prove. But in 1938 scoreboards in other International League cities didn't have room for the returns from major league cities.

third baseman who managed the Dodgers to pennants in the 1950s; John H. (Heinie) Sand, shortstop, from the Phils; Chalmer W. (Bill) Cissell, second baseman, from the White Sox; Lawrence J. (Larry) Benton, pitcher, from the Giants; John F. (Sheriff) Blake, pitcher, from the Cubs; and Ralph (Red) Kress, shortstop, and William C. (Baby Doll) Jacobson, outfielder, from the Browns.

A final list: native Marylanders who never played for the Orioles, but still attained renown in the majors. They include Homer Smoot, from Galesburg on the Shore, outfielder for St. Louis NL; Charles L. (Buck) Herzog, from Baltimore, infielder for four NL teams, Cincinnati's manager for three years; Edwin Americus Rommel, from Baltimore, knuckleballer for Philadelphia AL (one year, a 27-game winner; afterward, an AL umpire); Ernest G. (Babe) Phelps, from Odenton, Brooklyn catcher; Walter I. (Peck) Lerian, a Baltimorean who at 26 was the Phillies' main catcher—until killed in the off-season while walking along West Baltimore Street by a car that jumped the curb; D'Arcy R. (Jake) Flowers, NL infielder, from Cambridge; William B. (Swish) Nicholson, Cubs outfielder, 16-year man, from Chestertown; Charles E. (King Kong) Keller, Yankee outfielder, from Middletown; Albert W. Kaline, outfielder from Westport in Baltimore, who after leading the AL in batting at age 20 and making 3,007 hits in the course of 22 years with Detroit, entered the Hall of Fame; and Robert E. Robertson, Pittsburgh first baseman, from Frostburg.

The 19th-century catcher, manager, and umpire William H. Holbert, born in Baltimore, is a favorite of quizmasters as the only major leaguer with more than 2,000 at-bats who never hit a homer. And two NL pitchers widely overlooked today are Victor G. Willis, in birth and death a Cecil Countian and in 1995 a Hall-of-Famer (between 1898 and 1910, Vic Willis won 249 games, lost 205, with an ERA of 2.63); and, rescued from oblivion by the Baltimore sports authority John Steadman, Nicholas Maddox, born in Govans, who in 1908 with the Pirates was 23-8.

How dear to my heart are the seats of my childhood—in the backless bleachers at Oriole Park, when boys wore neckties and knickers, and hoped to capture a home run ball.

What can be said of the fans in those years? Afterward, with Baltimore back in the American League, it pleased great numbers of elderly males to assert spectator memories from boyhoods before or after the 1944 fire; how then could paid attendance, as announced at the time, have been so small? Totals were helped by the use of night lighting starting in 1931. In wartime, the proportion of young men—and young women—gained vastly, thanks to night-game dating.

Immediately, in 1940, the new presence of a major league player source—and drain—was beneficial. Excitement arose such as Baltimore hadn't felt since the '20s—and suspense as to the standings. This .500 baseball team with neither a great pitcher nor a fence-buster at the plate had, notwithstanding, a chance for fourth place, and made it on closing day. Then 81-79 Baltimore took on 96-61 Rochester in the playoffs, and won again. The Cup finals went to seven games, and the seventh-game score was 3-2, as Newark's Bears (Johnny Neun, manager) finally overcame the Orioles. That winter's hot-stove league relived the exploits of the bellicose outfielder Murray D. Howell, second baseman William T. Nagel, and first baseman Nicholas R. T. Etten, league-leaders all: Red in batting, .359; Bill in home runs, 37; and Nick in runs batted in, 128.

During World War II, Oriole Park was rented to the Boston Red Sox for their spring training. The IL Orioles moved north, to Gilman School and its gymnasium. Here are Manager Tommy Thomas and members of his 1943 squad, some of them under draft age.

But then another downslide set in: three unrelieved second-division years. Little went right, on teams finishing seventh, then fifth, then sixth. The best way to distinguish a team such as 1941's is perhaps to point to an outfielder, G. James Honochick—his success later was as a big league umpire; and on a team such as 1942's, to point up at Michael J. Naymick, a pitcher whose 6 feet 8½ inches made him to date the tallest Oriole.

Also in 1942, the Orioles changed their affiliation from the cellar-prone Phillies to the Indians (a first-division team). And three of AL Cleveland's rookies were assets to the 1943 Orioles: Edward F. Klieman, Stephen J. Gromek, and Robert G. Lemon, whom the Indians then remorselessly called up. (On a day in June, Gromek stood off Rochester for 18 innings, only for rain to arrive. The game ended as a tie, 0-0.) Ed Klieman, 23-11 as an Oriole, went nowhere; Steve Gromek stayed 17 years in the majors; Bob Lemon, a Californian, made it into the Hall of Fame (ironically, as a pitcher; in Baltimore, he had played third base, wearing number 5) and also managed Kansas City, Chicago, and New York AL. Small beer, to be sure, when the nation was increasingly preoccupied with World War II. Amid daily eight-column battlefront headlines, Baltimoreans could shrug off such irritations as 58-94, 75-77, and 73-81 Oriole seasons.

But then came 1944 and, in Baltimore, some cr-r-r-azy, look-for-me-on-the-first-base-side baseball.

Team of Destiny? The 1944 Orioles look like one more standard set of ballplayers. But a city of war-workers adored them, and they won—big. *Top row, left to right:* Fred Pfeiffer, ss; mascot; Lloyd Shafer, of; Ambrose (Bo) Palica, p; Rolland Van Slate, p; Sherman Lollar, c; Blas Monaco, 2b; *middle row:* Ken Braun, ss; Stan West, p; Harry Imhoff, c; Charles (Red) Embree, p; Frank Skaff, 3b; George Hooks, p; Sam Lowrey, p; Frank Rochevot, p; John (Specs) Podgajny, p; Felix Mackiewicz, of; Eddie Weidner, trainer; *bottom row:* Howie Moss, of; Patrick Riley, of; Milt Stockhausen, c; Hal Kleine, p; Tommy Thomas, manager; Stan Benjamin, of; Bob Latshaw, 1b; Lou Kahn, c.

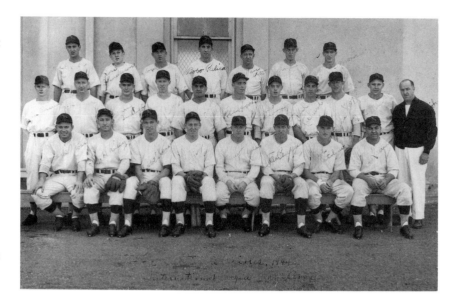

Stick with them Birds!

Municipal "motto," City of Baltimore, 1944

CHAPTER SIXTEEN

THE YEAR OF DOUBLE FOURS

Until recently, years that end in a four have tended to be big ones in Baltimore baseball. The city had two home teams in two major leagues and one in a minor (1884); it won its first-ever pennant (1894); it had two teams playing on opposite sides of 29th Street and Babe Ruth was an Oriole (1914); it won its sixth straight International League pennant (1924); and it re-entered the American League (1954). Impressive stuff. For an old-timer, though, 1944 was the season closest to fable, the manna least expected, the grandest time of them all (well, until 1966 and its World Series sweep). The ball club caught fire in 1944 (in the pervasive pleasantry) and so did the ballpark. It was the year of 52,833 paid admissions to a minor league playoff game in Baltimore—16,625 more than to any game in that year's World Series. That year, the winner of the IL pennant was a team so scruffy, it entered closing day in second place and proceeded to lose the second game of a doubleheader. Simultaneously, the first-place team was losing two.

All hail 1944's champion Baltimore Orioles!

How bad a team was it, really? The collective batting average, .259, ranked it fourth in that eight-team league; in fielding, though, the Orioles ranked seventh. A 25-year-old North Carolina outfielder, Howie Moss, led the league in homers (only 27), and second baseman

If Baltimore's wooden, one-decker ballpark had somehow survived, today it would doubtless be on the National Register of Historic Places. And the sight of 1890s and 1920s trophies would charm us all. But that night in 1944, one match too many lit up.

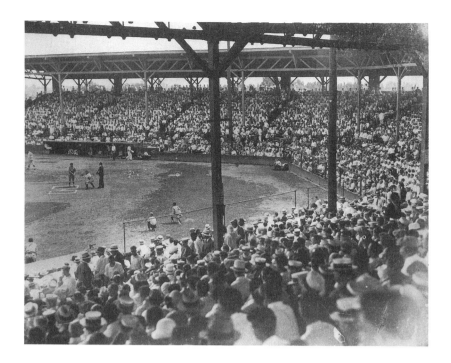

Blas Monaco drew 167 walks, an IL record. But the Birds couldn't even win their season series with last-place Syracuse. Twice, for lack of better, Tommy Thomas as manager sent his 44-year-old self in to pitch. Bobbysoxers idolized an 18-year-old, 130-pound shortstop, Kenny Braun, who batted .167.

It was a year of teenagers and 4-Fs (and everywhere, teams debilitated by military call-ups); in Baltimore, a year of Orioles cheered on by war workers and armed forces personnel from out of town in a ballpark with no roof, seat backs, or armrests from mid-July on.

On, brave Oriole team!

In the early IL years, spring training was fairly informal: Manager Dunn leading his men, for instance, in a brisk walk up the right-of-way of the Maryland & Pennsylvania Railroad. By 1913, the club could afford a preseason trip south (or could no longer stand the sight of rival teams thus getting into shape). From then on, the only interruption to the IL Orioles' annual remove to warmth and sunshine came in 1918 and 1919, owing to World War I. Over the years, and in calendar order, the spring-training dispatches bore datelines from North Carolina, Georgia, Florida, Texas, Mississippi, and South Carolina. Most frequently, the site was Hollywood, Florida, but in all there were 21 minor league Oriole localities: an atlas's worth of pine and palm.

Then came World War II, during part of which the O's couldn't work out even in their own muddy, chilly Oriole Park, having rented it out to the Boston Red Sox. Instead, the club arranged to use Gilman School's gymnasium and fields.

The lineup assembled for 1944 under these conditions wasn't a whole lot different from the year before (when the Orioles finished in sixth place, 23 games back). But in the afterlight of many a disappointing postwar IL season, something heroic must've crept in there somewhere. At first base was Bob Latshaw, a Baltimorean and a sound performer but one of many who never made it to the majors; at second, Monaco, a Texan who did have a 17-game career in the big time; at short, Braun, from Kentucky; at third, Frank Skaff, from Wisconsin, previously with the A's (and later, manager of the Tigers); in right, the team captain, Stan Benjamin, a New Englander who had played football at Western Maryland College; in center, Felix Mackiewicz, a star athlete while at Purdue; and in left, Moss—to his many admirers, Howitzer Howie. The pitchers included Charles W. (Red) Embree, a Californian who started 1944 with Cleveland but, sent down in May, proceeded to win 19 games for the Orioles; Sam Lowry, from the A's; Milt Stockhausen, Stan West, Ambrose (Bo) Palica, and Rolland Van Slate, for all of whom the IL was career apex; and Johnny (Specs) Podgany, a relief pitcher down from the Phils, a Pennsylvanian whom Oriole fans rechristened Fireman Johnny "Pa-GOHN-ee." The one name player—subsequently—was the first-string catcher, John Sherman Lollar, 19, from Arkansas (Sherm's career rounded off with 18 years in the AL).

The team started off with something of a rush in and out of first place. On July 3, just back from the road, it engaged the Syracuse Chiefs in a night game. After nine innings, the score stood Baltimore 4, Syracuse 4. After 10 innings it was Syracuse 11, Baltimore 4 (the Chiefs had their own 18-year-old shortstop, who hit a grand slam). Then everybody went home, leaving groundskeeper Mike Schofield to hose down the stands as usual.

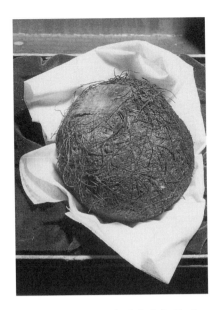

The fire that wrecked Oriole Park ranks second in 20th-century Baltimore fire legend only to the Great Fire that burned out the heart of downtown in 1904. Typical of the internal destruction was this indeterminate baseball (*above*).

The next day, a glare from south and east awakened Tommy Thomas in his home at 3313 St. Paul Street. Bright sunlight, his mind said—a good omen for our Fourth of July sellout. But no; his clock said a few minutes after four. This was firelight—from Oriole Park, a structure entirely composed of 30-year-old beams and boards. Soon the fire department had sounded eight alarms, the maximum. Before the first engine arrived, Schofield had awakened and opened the vehicle gate. The fire engine drove out onto the diamond; one good look at a circle of fire and the driver wheeled around and got out. Grandstand, pavilion, bleachers, batting cage, and underneath, the offices, locker, and storage rooms: all were doomed. Patches of sideline turf were aflame; so also were trees and utility poles near the stands. Police went from door to door in the neighborhood, ordering some 1,500 people out of their homes. Firefighters (in all, 31 companies) turned their hoses on these brick rowfronts and none burned down; but dozens of windowpanes blew out and molten roof tar dribbled down many a wall. The club later indemnified a number of householders; no one sued.

That night, three men had bunked down inside the enclosed machinery shed: Schofield, his assistant, Howard Seiss, and Charlie Price, a reserve outfielder. Price, having been cut from the team the day before, was all packed to leave for his home in Louisville. All three escaped, but Price lost even his civilian clothes.

The fire—its dense-packed spectators "in various stages of dress" —burned itself out in little more than an hour; it had been "visible from all parts of the city," newspapers said. (Afterward, the best supposition was that some fan had absentmindedly flicked a lighted cigarette into an obscure corner of the stands.) Once the newly tarred roof ignited, total destruction became inevitable. Club officials estimated the loss at $150,000; Jack Carpenter of the *News-Post* quoted them as putting the insurance coverage at $80,000. But the club's business records, archives, trophies, pictures, even the receipts in its safe were gone—its players' very bats, shoes, gloves, and home-game uniforms, as well. The Chiefs, too, lost their uniforms and equipment. One day earlier, it transpired, the Orioles had taken delivery on 40 dozen new baseballs. Vendors had freshly stocked their stands against holiday hungers and thirsts. Only the Orioles' road uniforms were spared, having been sent off to a cleaner.

Mayor Theodore R. McKeldin arrived. When a kid asked for his autograph, the mayor complied; soon he was searching his pockets for campaign photos to pass out to the reaching hands. The important thing was that McKeldin immediately offered the club a new home in Municipal Stadium, eight blocks to the north and east; he ordered his department heads to help convert its ground pattern from football to baseball.

In Baltimore fire lore, the burning of Oriole Park has taken second place to downtown's Great Fire of '04. In retrospect, however, the destruction of that quaint but inadequate ballpark—it had no off-street parking whatever—proved beneficial. The team's plight stirred emotions: Baltimoreans who hadn't been to an Oriole game in years went for a look at this set of waifs using unfamiliar equipment. Attendance, flat in May and June, soared in July and August. (No deterrent, somehow, the absence of beer, a long-standing ordinance barring its sale on city property.) To an extent, the team responded, trying harder. To cynics in a later age, burning down the ballpark in midseason rates as an (unplanned) public relations master stroke.

It was two weeks before the Orioles, forced to go back on the road and obliged to use gloves, bats, and shoes bought in haste (and in

Externally, all connection to the business of baseball had been expunged, other than turnstiles, outfield fence, and night-game light standards. The fire became a conversation piece: where were you the night that Oriole Park burned down?

Baltimore Municipal Stadium may have been built on a dirt embankment and may have lacked roof and seatbacks and restrooms under the stands, but its entrance from East 33d Street, with offices, had the look of architecture. And starting in July 1944, it provided the Orioles with a site for home games.

wartime), had a home to come back to. Herbert W. Armstrong, the Oriole business manager, organized a drastic redesign of Municipal Stadium's playing surface. Light poles and exterior ticket booths, the only salvage from Oriole Park, were lugged over.

The players, on their return to Baltimore, walked out into a vast wood, cement, and earthen arena, on East 33d Street, that had been built by the city in 1922 to attract intercollegiate football (particularly, Army vs. Navy). Its tiered, roofless, backless benches had room for 60,000 spectators. The open, southern end of its horseshoe was closed off by fencing and a pillared administration building with space for management's offices; hard by were two sets of enclosed showers and lockers. In the stands' long arc, the best place for home plate (not facing the sun) was where north and west intersected. The effect on hitting was dramatic—a 270-foot fly down the left-field line went into the stands; a hit over right field's 406-foot fence could roll unimpeded until next inning. (These distances were later modified.) No dugouts; rather, an on-field shed with benches. The catcher going to his left for a high foul had to beware a light pole. (Lighting, for the postwar IL's many night games, was never good. In 1949, when the annual convention of the minor leagues was held in Baltimore, the commissioner called Municipal Stadium's illumination "worse than what some Class D teams provide.") Outside the stadium, portable ticket booths and scattered enclosed, wooden toilets awaited the public. The grandstand had no entrance tunnels; on the Ellerslie Avenue side, fans had to mount high, wooden external stairs and arrived at the top of the seating. Behind home plate was a reserved section; otherwise, the rule was pretty much anybody anywhere. Under the stands were supporting timbers, earth, and anything that slipped out of your hands. No realist, he or she nowadays who gets teary over that ballpark.

Afar, the Orioles had slumped to fourth place; at home, they inaugurated the new park with a doubleheader victory. Cheered by the turnouts, they inched on up. Bad weather required, ultimately, the playing of 40 doubleheaders; it helped, winning four of them in a row from Montreal. But then the Newark Bears, last on July 6, shot past and on August 20 seized first place. On down to closing day itself, the tension never let up. Both teams were to play away-game doubleheaders—Baltimore against Jersey City, Newark against Syracuse. The Orioles, frantic, somehow lost their last game—and backed into the pennant (84-68) as the Bears (85-69) lost both games. Baltimore's percentage superiority was all of .0007. And its .553 season, for an IL pennant-winner, was history's least impressive. The players were as amazed as anybody. They kept right on hanging from the cliff by their glove-loops, beating the fourth-place Buffalo Bisons and then Newark in the Governor's Cup playoffs—each time, in the seventh game.

Here is a sampling of 1944's histrionics, from the Newark series. With Newark leading the series two games to one, and the game, 3 runs to 1, it was the bottom of the eighth; so far, only two Oriole hits: Weasel Braun walked. Lou Kahn, batting for Bo Palica, walked. Blas Monaco bunted safely; bases full. Bob Latshaw singled (one run in). Stan Benjamin's roller was thrown home for the force; catcher dropped it (second run in). Howie Moss lifted a sacrifice fly (third run in; one out). Felix Mackiewicz's grounder was fumbled twice (fourth run in). Pitcher, trying to pick Benjamin off third, threw wild (fifth, sixth runs in). Frank Skaff fanned (two outs). Sherman Lollar walked. Braun walked, again. Kahn, pinch-hitting again, struck out (three outs). No greenhorn, that pitcher; rather, he was Joe Page, a 26-year-old left-hander who was soon to be the Yankees' number-one relief pitcher.

Only 10 minor leagues functioned that wartime year; only one postseason, interleague series was held: the Junior World Series. It pitted Louisville of the American Association against IL Baltimore; three

Part of the tieclasp presented to the winners (each also received a ring).

games there, three games if needed at Municipal Stadium, the seventh game if needed in Louisville, to be played on consecutive dates starting October 6. The Colonels, an old foe, won the opener, 5-3; the 12,000 spectators (the park's capacity) cheered for hometowner Braun, who went hitless. The Birds, refusing to worry, responded with an 11-0 laugher. Red Embree pitched not only a shutout but a complete game. A helpful touch was Sherm Lollar's grand slam during an eight-run fourth.

Thus the third game promised to be a tide-turner. The two teams went at it in all earnest. In the top of the 13th, Baltimore went ahead 4-3, only to watch the Colonels tie it up. Three more in the 14th, however, sufficed: Orioles 7-4. Stan West, though giving up 15 hits, pitched the whole game.

In Baltimore, newspapers and radio called for a big turnout for game four, because it would be the last one included in the players' pool. (Their salaries had ceased after the Cup playoffs; management promised instead to turn over 60 percent of the first four games' proceeds.) The resulting head count reached 52,833, mostly people arriving via public transit. In seats behind home plate were Ogden Nash, the poet, and Alfred G. Vanderbilt and Harry A. Parr, horse breeders. Signs aplenty exhorted, "Stick With Them Birds!" But Louisville refused to flinch. It ran up a five-run lead against four Oriole pitchers, and held on to win, 5-4.

On to game five, and this time the tide did roll. Red Embree reappeared, to present 19,463 fans with a second complete-game shutout, 10-0. Louisville's four hits in nine innings contrasted with Baltimore's six runs in one, the fifth inning. Wednesday, October 11, with 22,536 witnesses and the temperature at 49 degrees, the home team wrapped it up, 5-3. But not before Louisville took a three-run lead; and then with two out in the top of the ninth but one man on, Louisville watched one of its sluggers hit a home run—which an American Association umpire ruled foul. Palica, the third of three Oriole pitchers, was the winner. After the last out, "the crowd tore the night apart with a continual roar," wrote C. M. Gibbs, of the *Sun;* "pandemonium reign[ed], with bands blatting and fans forming in impromptu parades." The players, trying to reach the clubhouse across the field, were mobbed, particularly the battery of Embree and Lollar. To go with the former's 18 scoreless innings, Lollar had batted .423.

In the International League, it was the first time since 1928 that the same team had won pennant, Cup, and Series. Baltimore was ecstatic. Older residents, sensitive to the double slight of minor league status and even there the 19-year-long inability to come out on top, felt a core satisfaction. Young people, as the monotony and the restrictions of wartime stretched on and on, exulted in a victory both clear and present. The *Sun* shone imperially: "For this series, Washington is just a suburb of Baltimore." Ned Hanlon's family gave the Orioles a silver loving cup (the same one originally presented to the winners of 1923's playoff between the Eastern Shore League and the Blue Ridge League). The Dunn family, previously prosperous, was suddenly rich.

In the big leagues, it was the year of St. Louis versus St. Louis—an unexciting World Series in ballparks barely able to seat 35,000 people. A fig, if that, for the dull and distant majors.

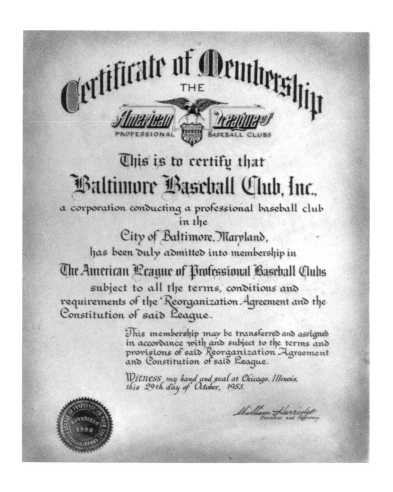

It's fine to have the Orioles back in the big leagues again.

New York Herald Tribune, SEPTEMBER 30, 1953

Oh, somewhere men are laughing, and somewhere children
   clown;
That somewhere, friend, is Baltimore; the Browns have come to
   town!

Time, OCTOBER 17, 1953

CHAPTER SEVENTEEN

THE ROAD TO THE MAJORS

Was it too much, a Baltimore loyalist reflected as the summer of 1945 went by, asking for victory in World War II and maybe also in the International League? The makings of a pennant-winner were there: most of the celebrated 1944 team plus, at first base, a part-season present from the Cleveland Indians, W. Edward Robinson, a big, handsome Texan. Sherm Lollar, the catcher, was hot again that year, working in all but 14 games and batting .364, the league's best by 26 points. Frank Skaff was hot, leading the league in runs (128), home runs (38), and runs batted in (126). Johnny Podgany was hot—or, coming on in relief, cool—recording 20 wins, 11 losses in 66 appearances. But the rest of the team was cold (and Howie Moss was in the armed forces). No one other than Lollar batted .300. An old jinx cost the Birds 17 of 22 games with Newark; it did not revive them, coming out ahead of Syracuse 20-18 one 55-hit day in August. Finishing fourth (80-73, 15 games back), Baltimore lost to Montreal in the play-offs, four games to three.

As regards World War II, the Orioles counted nearly 20 players or former players on active military duty, considerably more than in World War I. In that war, none was on the combat-fatality lists. In the second world war, two were killed: the 1940–41 pitcher Earl Springer and the 1944 catcher Harry Imhoff. Neither was old enough to have had so much as a day in the majors.

At Municipal Stadium, general admission was for a section rather than a numbered seat; friends heading for a game could expect to sit together. Day games could be cold or wet—or, as here in 1946, blazing hot. Shorts? Bare chests? Come back in ten years.

Then came peace, and the year of a 27-year-old Army veteran from Georgia and California, Jack Roosevelt Robinson, who was now playing second base for the Montreal Royals. How would Baltimore, as the IL's southernmost city, react to the sight of Jackie Robinson on the playing field? The answer was, sometimes, with abusive profanity. In the stands, ordinary-looking people screamed filth at him. Baltimore newspapers covered this big story—big-time baseball's first black player in the 20th century—in discreet, general terms. Meanwhile, Robinson, enjoined by his employer, Branch Rickey, to live the role of stoic for two full years, did so, never acknowledging, much less responding to, the personal insults. (All the harder, since Robinson "had little sense of humor," Thomas Boswell notes. "He had a fierce temper.") Robinson simply outplayed every white and afterward was voted the league's Most Valuable Player—this former college football star who was by no means the Negro Leagues' most valuable player, and who wasn't competing in his own best sport. Long afterward, Robinson cited spectators in Syracuse and Baltimore as that year's least welcoming. Ironically, he had played in Baltimore the year before when the touring Kansas City Monarchs, with Robinson at second base, took on the Elite Giants at Bugle Field. The spectators were sparse and orderly.

The International League Orioles had no black players, then or ever. The unwillingness of ownership and management to issue a uniform to any black player was a significant factor in the Orioles' failure to win championships (in the eight postwar years, five finishes below .500). This self-inflicted wound is bared in the story of Larry Doby. In 1947, Bill Veeck, principal owner of the Cleveland Indians, watched the National League get credit for integrating the majors, as Robinson joined the Brooklyn Dodgers; Veeck vowed at least to lead the way in the American League. He bought Doby, a heavy-hitting, 23-year-old outfielder, from the Negro Leagues' Newark Eagles. The logical process would then have been to send Doby to the Indians' AAA affiliate—Baltimore—for a few months of getting used to white baseball. Robinson, Campanella, Don Newcombe, and others profited from such an experience. Either the Orioles resisted the idea or Veeck was put off by Baltimore's racism—or both. Doby went straight to Cleveland and, in that unfamiliar atmosphere, his 1947 batting average was .156.

In their defense, the Orioles were doing what came naturally. Dur-

Why, on a Sunday afternoon in 1946, have so many people turned out for a regular-season game? to react to the sight of Montreal's second baseman, Jackie Robinson. This is Baltimore's first look at integrated pro-league baseball. *Upper left corner:* The booth houses Bill Dyer, his little red chair, and WITH radio broadcasting.

A ludicrous moment in ballpark history. The Babe Ruth sign is being taken down. It was raised some hours earlier during darkness, at the order of Rodger Pippen, sports editor and columnist of the Baltimore *News-Post*. The Board of Recreation and Parks was not amused.

majors he went. The Orioles, 65-80 and tied with Newark for sixth place, were only one game out of last place.

And last, by seven and a half games, was where they did wind up in 1948, as the fans began sniping at Tommy Thomas. The one glad note about that 59-88 season was Moss: for the fourth time, he led the IL in homers, and his .302 was Baltimore's best batting average.

For 1949, the club tried cleaning house: not only new players but, after Thomas's departure (losing self-control, he had gone into the stands after a heckler), a new manager, Jack Dunn III. (Thomas then began a third baseball career as scout for major league teams.) On the mound, Al Widmer from Ohio, tall and 24, worked up many a sweat (22-15) and was gone on up. By this time, the IL was crowning a different first-place city yearly, but it passed by seventh-place, 63-91 Baltimore.

At midcentury, the city set out to provide new and adequate physical surroundings. A municipal bond loan made it possible to tear down the earthwork stadium and its entrance building, to replace them with a reinforced-concrete, one-level, mixed-use stadium, and—that act of revolution—to reposition home plate. It would now be down by 33d Street, instead of up by 36th, and at the bottom of an evenly-proportioned U. The funding process wasn't altogether smooth; it took two elections to put through the second of two bond loans. The *Sun*, for instance, editorially urged relocating the stadium at Lake Clifton, while Rodger H. Pippen (who knew Babe Ruth from Oriole spring training in 1914, and who was by this time sports editor and columnist of the daily *News-Post*) infuriated veterans' organizations by insisting that any new stadium be named for Ruth (in World War I, Ruth and many another major leaguer had evaded military service). To do Pippen justice, his was the one newspaper voice loudly dissatisfied over the long haul with Baltimore's second-class baseball citizenship.

After the 1918 Armistice, the city had constructed a large stone auditorium facing City Hall Plaza as its memorial to Baltimoreans in service. Long before V-J Day in 1945, the nature and scope of a corresponding memorial had become a topic of civic debate. When the Board of Recreation and Parks, with City Hall behind it, decided to build Memorial Stadium, both the name and the function appealed to voters. The outbreak of war in Korea served as reminder. In 1953, their ultimate approval of this second bond loan made possible the addition of an upper deck. Fans marveled as the contractors did it all without interrupting the flow of home games on the part of its two major-sport tenants (professional football's Baltimore franchises found Memorial Stadium to their liking too; though designed primarily for baseball, the finished stadium could seat the National Football League's big crowds).

Meanwhile, a surprise: the 1950 Orioles started playing good baseball. A principal factor was the new manager, Nick Cullop, from Ohio. Inconspicuous as a big-league outfielder, Cullop became a pennant-winner once he was assigned to managing Columbus in the American Association. Approaching 50, tomato-faced, Cullop somehow brought out the best in young players. For a change, his Orioles were fielders, the IL's best: in 156 games, only 150 errors; at second and short, Bobby Young and Eddie Pellagrini had no double-play equals. And the team had grit: playing seven consecutive one-run-difference games in midsummer, it won six. Baltimore (85-68) finished a close third, eight games back—and went on to win the playoffs. First it vanquished Montreal, the big rival during this period, in seven games, and then

Player down! Clyde Kluttz, Oriole catcher, is in pain after being struck by a foul tip, during the 1950 Junior World Series against Columbus. Eddie Weidner, team trainer, ministers to him.

Rochester, the flag-winner, in six. The Junior World Series was next, ironically against Columbus, Cullop's previous team. But Baltimore, out of steam, lost in five games. A New Yorker, Karl Drews, who was between tours of major league duty, pitched the only Oriole victory.

As usual, the roster was almost all-new in 1951. The Birds (69-82) limped home sixth while Cullop was being distracted by illness and litigation. In the end, he was replaced by Don Heffner, 51, who, reared in Baltimore, had a 1930–33 learning experience at Oriole Park and then for 11 years was an AL second baseman. (From 1907 through 1928, the Orioles had one manager; in the next 25 years, they had 10.) But Heffner's 1952 Orioles (70-84) mired down in sixth place. It was their morose distinction to be the losers in a perfect game, the second in IL history—a 97-minute, 84-pitch, 2-0 misfortune in Buffalo.

By this time, the big story in baseball coverage was a weakening in Organized Baseball's mulish resolve never again to shift a major league franchise. The one force stronger than stand-pattism was of course money, and in February 1953, Boston's NL team, the unrecognizable descendant of the 1890s' proud Beaneaters, about to go broke, obtained permission to move to Milwaukee. This was a sports page earthquake. The AL, as it happened, was trying to make sense of a

The transformation of Municipal Stadium into Memorial Stadium. X marks the spot for 1954's new home plate.

parallel situation: two teams in a city, St. Louis, that was able to support only one. News of the Braves' relocation dizzied Baltimoreans, who for several March days had visions of a corresponding AL upheaval, with the St. Louis Browns franchise's being moved east to Baltimore. But a personnel matter burst the bubble. Bill Veeck had sold his Cleveland stake and taken over the lowly Browns; he had been countering pitiful attendance with innovative, audience-participation entertainment. Fellow-owners, dullards by comparison, could now hope to unseat Veeck by vetoing any move that left him in charge. The Browns played the 1953 season in St. Louis as usual, and finished in last place and lost money, as usual.

Against this imposing horizon, the minor league Orioles were widely disregarded as, in 1953, they plunged once more into the breach—and, in a flourish, won more games than they lost. (That didn't hold true the evening of August 20, when the Browns themselves, to augment their revenues, stopped off to play the Orioles as part of a nonesuch doubleheader. The Birds' victorious first-game opponent was Montreal; then St. Louis took the field, Don Larsen pitching and winning 8-2. Attendance: 10,681.) But the Orioles' 1953 finish (82-72) was good enough for the first division. Lacking individual stars, Heffner's fourth-place Birds even so almost upset first-place Rochester in a seven-game playoffs thriller.

Then it was goodbye to the likes of Ray Poat and Roy Weatherly and Ray Flanigan, Marv Rickert and Marv Rackley, Abs Tiedemann and Marty Tabachek, Johnny Wittig and Butch Woyt, Bob Kuzava and Clyde Kluttz, Ben Sankey and Beryl Richmond, Stan Lopata and Skeeter Newsome, Anse Moore and Euel Moore, Bob Miller and Russell Niller, Smoky Joe Martin and Harry Matuszak, Irv Medlinger and Joe Mellendick, Al Bool and Jim Poole, Ted Kazanski and Billy Urbanski, Dino Chiozza and Italo Cellini, Swede Hansen and Dutch Holland; the unrelated, different-decade Dixie Howells (Millard Fillmore H. and Homer Elliott H.), pitcher and catcher; Otto Freitag and Otto Greenae, Bubbles Hargrave and Charlie Hargreaves—catchers, all four; Wilson L. (Chick) Fewster from Baltimore and Bob Repass, infielders, who were Orioles on three separated occasions, as were several others; and, ever bright in memories of 1936, the out-

Sherm Lollar, the best of Baltimore's IL catchers.

fielder Henry Kauhane Oana, a Hawaiian, known accordingly as Prince. When the modern Orioles finish 51 years in the AL, with their 25-man squads, their box scores are likely to have contained some 700 names. From 1903 to 1953, inclusive, from Woody Abernathy to Edward H. (Dutch) Zwilling, the researches of Dave Howell show, the minor league Orioles gave more than 900 players a box score try. Smaller squads in those days, but simpler contracts, sterner evaluations and faster turnover.

Smaller attendance, also, though, in their way, no less lively. (For 1953, home attendance totaled 207,182.) Two fan customs carried over for a while into AL Oriole home games: the ringing of a cowbell by the fan who felt like making a noise and the waving of handkerchiefs, in derisive farewell, as a replaced opposing pitcher headed for the showers. In the 1930s and 1940s, eyewitnesses recall a section where gamblers bet with one another on the outcome or the spread in runs, even on the next at-bat or next pitch. Before Prohibition, beer and even whiskey were on sale; over at 33d Street, the landlord (the Bureau of Parks and Recreation) refused to allow beverage alcohol at IL games. (The majors tolerated no such restriction.) Among many large moments, there was the plight of Thomas D'Alesandro Jr., then a congressman, in his front-row seat on Opening Day 1947, as he leaned forward and rested head and arm on the parapet. A line-drive foul beaned him before he could duck. Happily, no damage.

The week after those 1953 IL playoffs, everything changed. At last, it all changed.

When the oligarchs of the American League of Professional Baseball Clubs assembled at the Hotel Commodore in New York City, Tuesday afternoon, September 29, 1953, their minds were on the World Series, to start the following day. Would the Yankees win for the fifth straight time, a new record; or would the Dodgers win, for Brooklyn's first time? But an agenda matter also occupied the magnates behind their closed doors: a motion authorizing the AL's first franchise transfer since 1902. Most of Baltimore held its breath, waiting for the decision.

There were reasons for gloom. The previous spring, this proposal to move the St. Louis franchise to Baltimore had drawn four yeas, four nays. Also, Baltimore lay inside the 75-mile radius that was the Washington franchise's domain. And other, larger cities were of a mind to move up from the minors; specifically, Toronto and Los Angeles.

There were grounds for optimism. Bill Veeck, unpopular with his strait-laced fellow-owners, had ended his connection with the Browns. Baltimore's power establishment, in the persons of Thomas D'Alesandro Jr. (by now the city's mayor) and Clarence W. Miles, a corporation lawyer, was finally active and visible on baseball's behalf. Third, unlike the rival contenders, Baltimore proffered a large, up-to-date arena. Finally, history, for whatever it counts—Baltimore had been, after all, present at the creation of the American League.

The motion sailed through, eight votes to none. Intensifying the new AL member's joy, a change of name was authorized: where the National League's Boston club, moving to Milwaukee, had gone on being the Braves, the name Browns was expunged: Orioles they would be, in the hallowed Baltimore tradition.

The St. Louis club, itself a 1902 transfer from Milwaukee, was now sold to a new corporation, Baltimore Baseball Club, Inc. Technically, the new owner was a holding company, Baltimore Orioles, Inc., chartered in Missouri; St. Louis interests retained 20 percent of it. But Baltimore Baseball Club had agreed to buy the other, controlling four-fifths of the stock shares. The price: $2,475,000. The International League, subsequently, was paid an indemnity of $48,749.61 (based on an attendance formula), Jack Dunn III was bought out for $350,000 plus a five-year contract for front-office employ, and Baltimore's IL franchise was transferred to Havana, Cuba.

In Baltimore, that happy day, the news of restored major league standing, of at last the end to half a century's unjust and painful subordination, came over the wires in time to catch the afternoon papers' final edition. Next morning, under an eight-column streamer in doomsday lettering—"CITY GETS THE BROWNS"—the *Sun* printed a three-cheers editorial by Hamilton Owens, the editor-in-chief. (Here and there, fusty readers questioned its placement on page one instead of the editorial page.) The people of Baltimore rejoiced at once and at length—at such length that, within some old-timers, the exaltation is still going on. A staff writer for the *New Yorker*, John McNulty, was in Baltimore; that evening, he toured downtown bars watching and listening. His account was titled "Back in the Big League." Later Ogden Nash, expressing his emotion as a resident Baltimorean, composed an overnight classic:

You Can't Kill an Oriole

Wee Willie Keeler	"Hey, Hughey Jennings!
Runs through the town,	"Hey, John McGraw!
All along Charles Street	"I got fire in my eye,
In his night gown,	"And tobacco in my jaw!
Belling like a hound dog	"Hughey, hold my halo,
Gathering the pack:	"I'm sick of being a saint;
"Hey, Wilbert Robinson!	"Got to teach the youngsters
"The Orioles are back!	"To hit 'em where they ain't!"

Analysts pondered the outcome of that session in the Hotel Commodore (now the refurbished New York Grand Hyatt), hard by Grand Central Terminal. How had Washington been placated? The club's autocrat, Clark C. Griffith, was a small man nearing age 85. Back when the AL was forming, Griffith had been the winning pitcher in 240 games; but by 1954, a Hall-of-Famer, he had mellowed. It was revealed that National Brewing Company, the Senators' scoreboard advertiser, had put money on the table; lo, Washington voted for.

Another element was the early-1950s experience of Baltimore's on-and-off pro football memberships. City Hall and Redwood Street awakened, at last, to the whole-community value of pro sports franchises, however commercial their understructure. In Tommy D'Alesandro, a genuine baseball fan, Baltimore's cause had an eloquent pleader. In Clarence Miles, other cities' owners were happy to find board-of-directors decorum and assurance. Miles, from the Eastern Shore, the Social Register, and 4105 Underwood Road in Guilford, and D'Alesandro, from City Hall and 245 Albemarle Street in Little Italy: a great battery.

In later years, one other advantage came to light: timing. During World War II, Baltimore had surged forward. What with shipping, heavy industry, and military and naval bases in or near the city, Baltimore was boomtown. Meanwhile, the unit for population comparisons was still the city, not yet the metro area; Baltimore's relatively small suburbs and hinterland did not handicap it. The 1950 census showed Baltimore sixth, nationally; its population seemed about to pass one million. The major leagues as then constituted could not dispute Baltimore's claim to importance. Had the city waited a few years longer, however, before pounding on the door, Organized Baseball in its rush to the West and the South might very well have been as deaf as during the forepart of the century.

It remained to raise $2,475,000; surely a formality? Not so. To Miles's dismay, Baltimore's leading industrialists, its prominent merchants and bankers, put up token sums at best (Miles himself, fronting as president of the new club, pledged to buy few shares). The rate-of-return specialists may have doubted an eighth-place team's profitability. The principal investments came, finally, from the owners of two rival East Baltimore breweries, Gunther's and National; by name, the Krieger, Hoffberger, and Eliasberg families. The groundwork was in place for behind-the-scenes warring in the new club's early years as to broadcasting sponsorship and advertising space on the scoreboard.

Throughout a happy winter, contracts were signed, trades made, officials appointed, and season tickets sold, all from the old IL offices at 4 East Eager Street. As manager, the AL Orioles signed James J. Dykes, a wit and an old pro. Dykes, a Pennsylvanian, had been the third baseman on Connie Mack's three-time champion Philadelphia Athletics, and then in 1953 their manager. Arthur Ehlers, also from the A's, was named general manager. Sports writers were enthusiastic about several of the former Browns, such as the outfielder and power hitter Vic Wertz and the smooth-fielding shortstop Billy Hunter, Pennsylvanians both, and two big young pitchers: Robert Lee Turley, known as Bullet Bob, from Illinois, and Don Larsen, an unpredictable Indianan. Another St. Louis team member was a genuine box office draw: Leroy R. Paige, Satchel himself. At age 47, the long-ago Baltimore Black Sox pitcher could still get batters out; used in relief, he had led the 1953 Browns in saves and his 3.53 earned run average was the staff's third lowest. Quietly, the Orioles sent him no contract.

The fans, meanwhile, had to evaluate everything unseen—except for the few able to visit Yuma, Arizona, a carryover as spring-training base.

All this while, architects (the J. L. Faisant and L. P. Kooken firms) and contractors (the DeLuca-Davis and Joseph F. Hughes Companies) buckled down to meet their April 15 deadline (and not to come in over their totaled $6.5 million budgets). As the curious rode out to the 1000 block of East 33d Street for an advance look at this newest thing nationally in stadia, many objects of interest awaited them: on the facade, a statement in large and shining letters dedicating Memorial Stadium to all who had served in World War II; at the top of nine concrete ramps, a roofless and sharply sloping upper deck, lined throughout with backless, splintery benches; a cozy midworld called the mezzanine; an immense outfield; seating for close to 50,000 spectators; two vast concrete promenades, with a great view of downtown from the upper-level one; and, underneath the stands, a warren of offices, locker and storage rooms, and empty spaces. Natural grass, in that era, a fan could still take for granted. The parking, on surrounding blacktop, looked promising; the approach and exit routes, a bit narrow and tortuous. On Opening Day, the last bricking had still to be done (fortunate, also, that the umpires for that drizzly afternoon game never bade the stadium electricians to turn on its unready lights).

But, altogether, Baltimore's new baseball grounds was turning into something Washington could not match, or Philadelphia, or New York itself; something the haughty major leagues would no doubt eventually overtake but could for the moment only admire.

And so, in the spring of 1954, finally the wait, the pain, the idle dreaming ended. The event came about: the return of Baltimore to its rightful place among the major league cities of the nation. Two away games, required by the American League schedule; then on Thursday, April 15, at Memorial Stadium in Baltimore, an umpire—that old Baltimorean, Eddie Rommel—uttered the cry that made it all real: "Play ball!"

BY THE NUMBERS

<table>
<tr><th></th><th></th><th>W</th><th>L</th><th>PCT</th><th>GB</th></tr>
<tr><td colspan="6">NATIONAL ASSOCIATION</td></tr>
<tr><td>1872</td><td>Boston (1st)</td><td>38</td><td>8</td><td>.826</td><td></td></tr>
<tr><td></td><td>Athletics (2d)</td><td>31</td><td>15</td><td>.674</td><td></td></tr>
<tr><td></td><td>Lord Baltimores (3d)</td><td>35</td><td>19</td><td>.648</td><td>7</td></tr>
<tr><td>1873</td><td>Boston (1st)</td><td>43</td><td>16</td><td>.729</td><td></td></tr>
<tr><td></td><td>Lord Baltimores (3d)</td><td>34</td><td>22</td><td>.607</td><td>7½</td></tr>
<tr><td></td><td>Marylands (9th)†</td><td>0</td><td>6</td><td>.000</td><td></td></tr>
<tr><td>1874</td><td>Boston (1st)</td><td>52</td><td>18</td><td>.743</td><td></td></tr>
<tr><td></td><td>Hartford (7th)</td><td>15</td><td>38</td><td>.283</td><td></td></tr>
<tr><td></td><td>Lord Baltimores (8th)*</td><td>9</td><td>38</td><td>.191</td><td>31½</td></tr>
<tr><td colspan="6">1875–1881: No league franchise</td></tr>
<tr><td colspan="6">AMERICAN ASSOCIATION</td></tr>
<tr><td>1882</td><td>Cincinnati (1st)</td><td>54</td><td>26</td><td>.675</td><td></td></tr>
<tr><td></td><td>St. Louis (5th)</td><td>36</td><td>43</td><td>.456</td><td></td></tr>
<tr><td></td><td>Baltimores (6th)*</td><td>19</td><td>54</td><td>.260</td><td>31½</td></tr>
<tr><td>1883</td><td>Athletics (1st)</td><td>66</td><td>32</td><td>.673</td><td></td></tr>
<tr><td></td><td>Pittsburgh (7th)</td><td>30</td><td>68</td><td>.306</td><td></td></tr>
<tr><td></td><td>Orioles (8th)*</td><td>28</td><td>68</td><td>.292</td><td>37</td></tr>
<tr><td>1884</td><td>New York (1st)</td><td>75</td><td>32</td><td>.701</td><td></td></tr>
<tr><td></td><td>Cincinnati (5th)</td><td>68</td><td>41</td><td>.624</td><td></td></tr>
<tr><td></td><td>Orioles (6th)</td><td>63</td><td>43</td><td>.594</td><td>11½</td></tr>
<tr><td colspan="6">UNION ASSOCIATION</td></tr>
<tr><td>1884</td><td>St. Louis (1st)</td><td>91</td><td>16</td><td>.850</td><td></td></tr>
<tr><td></td><td>Cincinnati (3d)</td><td>68</td><td>35</td><td>.660</td><td></td></tr>
<tr><td></td><td>Baltimore (4th)</td><td>56</td><td>48</td><td>.538</td><td>32½</td></tr>
</table>

<table>
<tr><th></th><th></th><th>W</th><th>L</th><th>PCT</th><th>GB</th></tr>
<tr><td colspan="6">EASTERN LEAGUE</td></tr>
<tr><td>1884</td><td>Wilmington (1st)</td><td>44</td><td>11</td><td>.800</td><td></td></tr>
<tr><td></td><td>Monumentals</td><td>3</td><td>10</td><td>.231</td><td></td></tr>
<tr><td colspan="6">AMERICAN ASSOCIATION</td></tr>
<tr><td>1885</td><td>St. Louis (1st)</td><td>79</td><td>33</td><td>.705</td><td></td></tr>
<tr><td></td><td>New York (7th)</td><td>44</td><td>64</td><td>.407</td><td></td></tr>
<tr><td></td><td>Orioles (8th)*</td><td>41</td><td>68</td><td>.376</td><td>36½</td></tr>
<tr><td>1886</td><td>St. Louis (1st)</td><td>93</td><td>46</td><td>.669</td><td></td></tr>
<tr><td></td><td>New York (7th)</td><td>53</td><td>82</td><td>.393</td><td></td></tr>
<tr><td></td><td>Orioles (8th)*</td><td>48</td><td>83</td><td>.366</td><td>41</td></tr>
<tr><td>1887</td><td>St. Louis (1st)</td><td>95</td><td>40</td><td>.704</td><td></td></tr>
<tr><td></td><td>Cincinnati (2d)</td><td>81</td><td>54</td><td>.600</td><td></td></tr>
<tr><td></td><td>Orioles (3d)</td><td>77</td><td>58</td><td>.570</td><td>18</td></tr>
<tr><td>1888</td><td>St. Louis (1st)</td><td>92</td><td>43</td><td>.681</td><td></td></tr>
<tr><td></td><td>Cincinnati (4th)</td><td>80</td><td>54</td><td>.597</td><td></td></tr>
<tr><td></td><td>Orioles (5th)</td><td>57</td><td>80</td><td>.416</td><td>36</td></tr>
<tr><td>1889</td><td>Brooklyn (1st)</td><td>93</td><td>44</td><td>.679</td><td></td></tr>
<tr><td></td><td>Cincinnati (4th)</td><td>76</td><td>63</td><td>.547</td><td></td></tr>
<tr><td></td><td>Orioles (5th)</td><td>70</td><td>65</td><td>.519</td><td>23</td></tr>
<tr><td colspan="6">ATLANTIC ASSOCIATION</td></tr>
<tr><td>1890</td><td>Orioles†</td><td>77</td><td>23</td><td>.770</td><td></td></tr>
<tr><td></td><td>New Haven (1st)</td><td>81</td><td>35</td><td>.698</td><td></td></tr>
</table>

	W	L	PCT	GB
AMERICAN ASSOCIATION				
1890 Louisville (1st)	88	44	.667	
Orioles (6th)	15	19	.441	
1891 Boston (1st)	93	42	.689	
Milwaukee (3d)	21	15	.583	
Orioles (4th)	71	64	.526	22
NATIONAL LEAGUE				
1892 Boston (1st)	102	48	.680	
St. Louis (11th)	56	94	.373	
Orioles (12th)*	46	101	.313	54½
1893 Boston (1st)	86	44	.662	
Cincinnati (7th)	65	63	.508	
Orioles (8th)	60	70	.462	26
1894 Orioles (1st)	89	39	.695	
New York (2d)	88	44	.667	3
Boston (3d)	83	49	.629	
1895 Orioles (1st)	87	43	.669	
Cleveland (2d)	84	46	.646	3
Philadelphia (3d)	78	53	.595	
1896 Orioles (1st)	90	39	.698	
Cleveland (2d)	80	48	.625	9½
Cincinnati (3d)	77	50	.606	
1897 Boston (1st)	93	39	.705	
Orioles (2d)	90	40	.693	2
New York (3d)	83	48	.634	
1898 Boston (1st)	102	47	.685	
Orioles (2d)	96	53	.644	6
Cincinnati (3d)	92	60	.605	
1899 Brooklyn (1st)	101	47	.682	
Philadelphia (3d)	94	58	.618	
Orioles (4th)	86	62	.581	15
1900: No league franchise				
AMERICAN LEAGUE				
1901 Chicago (1st)	83	53	.610	
Philadelphia (4th)	74	62	.544	
Orioles (5th)	68	65	.511	13½
1902 Philadelphia (1st)	83	53	.610	
Detroit (7th)	52	83	.385	
Orioles (8th)*	50	88	.362	34
EASTERN LEAGUE (INTERNATIONAL LEAGUE)				
1903 Jersey City (1st)	92	32	.746	
Orioles (4th)	71	54	.568	21½
1904 Buffalo (1st)	88	46	.657	
Orioles (2d)	77	52	.597	8½

	W	L	PCT	GB
1905 Providence (1st)	83	47	.638	
Orioles (2d)	82	47	.636	½
1906 Buffalo (1st)	85	55	.607	
Orioles (3d)	76	61	.555	7½
1907 Toronto (1st)	83	51	.619	
Orioles (6th)	68	69	.495	16½
1908 Orioles (1st)	83	57	.593	
Providence (2d)	79	57	.581	2
1909 Rochester (1st)	90	61	.596	
Orioles (7th)	66	85	.437	24
1910 Rochester (1st)	92	61	.601	
Orioles (3d)	83	70	.542	9
1911 Rochester (1st)	98	54	.645	
Orioles (2d)	95	58	.621	3½
1912 Toronto (1st)	91	62	.595	
Orioles (4th)	74	75	.497	15
1913 Newark (1st)	95	57	.625	
Orioles (3rd)	77	73	.513	17
1914 Providence (1st)	94	59	.614	
Orioles (6th)	72	79	.477	21
FEDERAL LEAGUE				
1914 Indianapolis (1st)	88	65	.575	
Chicago (2d)	87	67	.565	
Terrapins (3d)	84	69	.549	4
1915 Chicago (1st)	86	66	.566	
Brooklyn (7th)	70	82	.461	
Terrapins (8th)*	47	107	.305	40
INTERNATIONAL LEAGUE (NEW INTERNATIONAL LEAGUE)				
1916 Buffalo (1st)	82	58	.586	
Orioles (4th)	75	66	.529	7½
1917 Toronto (1st)	93	61	.604	
Orioles (3d)	88	61	.591	2½
1918 Toronto (1st)	88	39	.693	
Orioles (3d)	74	53	.582	14
1919 Orioles (1st)	100	49	.671	
Toronto (2d)	93	57	.620	7½
1920 Orioles (1st)	110	43	.719	
Toronto (2d)	108	46	.701	2½
1921 Orioles (1st)	119	47	.717	
Rochester (2d)	100	68	.595	20
1922 Orioles (1st)	115	52	.689	
Rochester (2d)	105	62	.629	10
1923 Orioles (1st)	111	53	.677	
Rochester (2d)	101	65	.608	11
1924 Orioles (1st)	117	48	.709	
Toronto (2d)	98	67	.594	19

Year	Team	W	L	PCT	GB
1925	Orioles (1st)	105	61	.633	
	Toronto (2d)	99	63	.611	4
1926	Toronto (1st)	109	57	.657	
	Orioles (2d)	101	65	.608	8
1927	Buffalo (1st)	112	56	.667	
	Orioles (5th)	85	82	.509	26½
1928	Rochester (1st)	90	74	.549	
	Orioles (6th)	82	82	.500	8
1929	Rochester (1st)	103	65	.613	
	Orioles (3d)	90	78	.536	13
1930	Rochester (1st)	105	62	.629	
	Orioles (2d)	97	70	.581	10
1931	Rochester (1st)	101	67	.601	
	Orioles (3d)	94	72	.566	6
1932	Newark (1st)	109	59	.649	
	Orioles (2d)	93	74	.557	15½
1933	Newark (1st)	102	62	.622	
	Orioles (3d)	84	80	.512	18
1934	Newark (1st)	93	60	.608	
	Orioles (8th)*	53	99	.349	39½
1935	Montreal (1st)	92	62	.597	
	Orioles (5th)	78	74	.513	13
1936	Buffalo (1st)	94	60	.610	
	Orioles (4th)	81	72	.529	12½
1937	Newark (1st)	109	43	.717	
	Orioles (4th)	76	75	.503	32½
1938	Newark (1st)	104	48	.684	
	Orioles (8th)*	52	98	.347	51
1939	Jersey City (1st)	89	64	.582	
	Orioles (6th)	68	85	.444	21
1940	Rochester (1st)	96	61	.611	
	Orioles (4th)	81	79	.506	16½
1941	Newark (1st)	100	54	.649	
	Orioles (7th)	58	94	.382	41
1942	Newark (1st)	92	61	.601	
	Orioles (5th)	75	77	.493	16½
1943	Toronto (1st)	95	57	.625	
	Orioles (6th)	73	81	.474	23
1944	Orioles (1st)	84	68	.553	
	Newark (2d)	85	69	.552	0
1945	Montreal (1st)	95	58	.621	
	Orioles (4th)	80	73	.523	15
1946	Montreal (1st)	100	54	.649	
	Orioles (3d)	81	73	.526	19
1947	Jersey City (1st)	94	60	.610	
	Orioles (6th)	65	89	.422	29
	Newark (6th)	65	89	.422	
1948	Montreal (1st)	94	59	.614	
	Orioles (8th)*	59	88	.401	32
1949	Buffalo (1st)	90	64	.584	
	Orioles (7th)	63	91	.409	27
1950	Rochester (1st)	92	59	.609	
	Orioles (3d)	85	68	.556	8
1951	Montreal (1st)	95	59	.617	
	Orioles (6th)	69	82	.457	24½
1952	Montreal (1st)	95	56	.629	
	Orioles (6th)	70	84	.455	26½
1953	Rochester (1st)	97	57	.630	
	Orioles (4th)	82	72	.532	15

KEY: W = wins; L = losses; PCT = winning percentage; GB = games behind; * = last place; † = did not finish.

SUGGESTED READING

Newspapers and Periodicals

For game-by-game accounts and the atmosphere of the times, see the newspapers *Baltimore Afro-American*, *American*, *Evening Sun*, *Morning Herald*, *News*, and *Sun*, available on microfilm. Pertinent articles appear periodically in two journals published by the American Society for Baseball Research, in Cleveland: *The National Pastime*, *A Review of Baseball History* and *The Baseball Research Journal*.

Books

Alexander, Charles C. *John McGraw*. New York: Viking, 1988.

Allen, Lee. *The Hot Stove League*. New York: A. S. Barnes, 1955.

Alvarez, Mark. *The Old Ball Game: Baseball's Beginnings*. Alexandria, Va.: Redefinition Press, 1990.

The Baltimore Orioles: A Collector's Guide. New York: Abbeville, Press, 1995.

The Baseball Encyclopedia: The Complete and Official Record of Major League Baseball. Edited by Rick Wolff. New York: Macmillan, 1997.

Baseball's First Stars: Biographies of the 19th-Century's Greatest Players, Managers, Umpires, Executives, and Writers. Edited by Frederick Ivor-Campbell, Robert L. Tiemann, and Mark Rucker. Cleveland: Society for American Baseball Research, 1996.

Bready, James H. *The Home Team*. Baltimore: Baltimore Orioles, 1985.

Chadwick, Bruce. *The Baltimore Orioles: Memories and Memorabilia*. New York: Abbeville Press, 1995.

Creamer, Robert W. *Babe*. New York: Macmillan, 1970.

———. "Inning One: The Old Orioles." In *The Ultimate Baseball Book*. Edited by Daniel Okrent and Harris Levine. Boston: Houghton Mifflin, 1979.

Early Innings: A Documentary History of Baseball, 1825–1908. Edited by Dean A. Sullivan. Lincoln: University of Nebraska Press, 1995.

The Encyclopedia of Minor League Baseball. Edited by Lloyd Johnson and Miles Wolff. Durham, N.C.: Baseball America, 1993.

Griffith, William Ridgely. *The Early History of Amateur Base Ball in the State of Maryland*. Baltimore: [Privately printed], 1897.

Guy, D. Dorsey. *Pennant Souvenir: Baltimore Base Ball Club, Season 1894*. Reprint, Frederick, Md.: Triple Play Press, 1991.

Harris, Paul F. Sr. *Babe Ruth: The Dark Side*. Glen Burnie, Md.: [Privately printed], 1995.

Holway, John. *Voices From the Great Black Baseball Leagues*. New York: Dodd, Mead, 1975.

The House of Magic: 70 Years of Thrills and Excitement on 33d Street. Edited by Robert W. Brown. Baltimore: Baltimore Orioles, 1991.

Kirsch, George B. *The Creation of American Team Sports: Baseball and Cricket, 1838–1872*. Urbana: University of Illinois Press, 1989.

Leffler, Robert V. "The History of Black Baseball in Baltimore from 1913 to 1951." Baltimore: Master's thesis, Morgan State University, 1974.

Lowry, Philip J. *Green Cathedrals: The Ultimate Celebration of All 271 Major League and Negro League Ballparks Past and Present*. Reading, Mass.: Addison-Wesley, 1992.

Miller, James Edward. *The Baseball Business: Pursuing Pennants and Profits in Baltimore*. Chapel Hill: University of North Carolina Press, 1990.

The Negro League Book. Edited by Dick Clark and Larry Lester. Cleveland: Society for American Baseball Research, 1994.

Nemec, David. *The Beer and Whiskey League: The Illustrated History of the American Association*. New York: Lyons & Burford, 1994.

Okonnen, Marc. *Baseball Memories, 1900–1909*. New York: Sterling Publishing, 1992.

Patterson, Ted. *The Baltimore Orioles: 40 Years of Magic, From 33d Street to Camden Yards*. Dallas: Taylor Publishing, 1996.

Rader, Benjamin G. *Baseball: A History of America's Game*. Urbana: University of Illinois Press, 1992.

Rampersad, Arnold. *Jackie Robinson: A Biography*. New York: Knopf, 1997.

Riley, James A. *The Biographical Encyclopedia of the Negro Baseball Leagues*. New York: Carroll & Graf, 1993.

Ritter, Lawrence S. and Mark Rucker. *The Babe: A Life in Pictures*. New York: Ticknor & Fields, 1998.

Ryczek, William J. *Blackguards and Red Stockings: A History of Baseball's National Association*. Jefferson, N.C.: McFarland & Co., 1992.

SABR Presents: The Home Run Encyclopedia, The Who, What, and Where of Every Home Run Hit Since 1876. Edited by Bob McConnell and David Vincent. New York: Macmillan, 1996.

Seymour, Harold. *Baseball: The Early Years*. New York: Oxford University Press, 1960.

———. *Baseball: The Golden Age*. New York: Oxford University Press, 1971.

The Story of Minor League Baseball, 1901–1952. Columbus, Ohio: The National Association of Professional Baseball Leagues, 1953.

Thorn, John, and Palmer, Pete, with Gershman, Michael. *Total Baseball: The Official Encyclopedia of Major League Baseball*. New York: Viking, 1997.

Wright, Marshall D. *19th-Century Baseball: Year-by-Year Statistics for the Major League Teams, 1871 through 1900*. Jefferson, N.C.: McFarland & Co., 1996.

INDEX

LIBRARY OF CONGRESS CATALOGING-IN-PUBLICATION DATA

Bready, James H.
    Baseball in Baltimore : the first hundred years / James H. Bready.
        p.   cm.
    Includes bibliographical references (p.) and index.
    ISBN 0-8018-5833-x (alk. paper)
      1. Baseball—Maryland—Baltimore—History.   I. Title.
GV863.M32B23   1998
796.357'09752'6—dc21   97-43217
                                                           CIP